P9-AFR-551

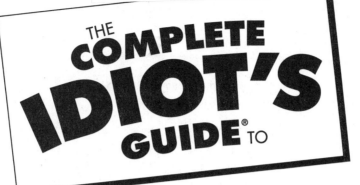

THE COMPLETE **IDIOT'S** GUIDE® TO

Microsoft®
Windows® 7

by Paul McFedries

ALPHA

A member of Penguin Group (USA) Inc.

For Karen and Gypsy, who make life fun.

ALPHA BOOKS

Published by the Penguin Group

Penguin Group (USA) Inc., 375 Hudson Street, New York, New York 10014, USA

Penguin Group (Canada), 90 Eglinton Avenue East, Suite 700, Toronto, Ontario M4P 2Y3, Canada (a division of Pearson Penguin Canada Inc.)

Penguin Books Ltd., 80 Strand, London WC2R 0RL, England

Penguin Ireland, 25 St. Stephen's Green, Dublin 2, Ireland (a division of Penguin Books Ltd.)

Penguin Group (Australia), 250 Camberwell Road, Camberwell, Victoria 3124, Australia (a division of Pearson Australia Group Pty. Ltd.)

Penguin Books India Pvt. Ltd., 11 Community Centre, Panchsheel Park, New Delhi—110 017, India

Penguin Group (NZ), 67 Apollo Drive, Rosedale, North Shore, Auckland 1311, New Zealand (a division of Pearson New Zealand Ltd.)

Penguin Books (South Africa) (Pty.) Ltd., 24 Sturdee Avenue, Rosebank, Johannesburg 2196, South Africa

Penguin Books Ltd., Registered Offices: 80 Strand, London WC2R 0RL, England

International Standard Book Number: 978-1-59257-954-9
Library of Congress Catalog Card Number: 2009924934

11   10   09   8   7   6   5   4   3   2

Interpretation of the printing code: The rightmost number of the first series of numbers is the year of the book's printing; the rightmost number of the second series of numbers is the number of the book's printing. For example, a printing code of 09-1 shows that the first printing occurred in 2009.

Printed in the United States of America

Note: This publication contains the opinions and ideas of its author. It is intended to provide helpful and informative material on the subject matter covered. It is sold with the understanding that the author and publisher are not engaged in rendering professional services in the book. If the reader requires personal assistance or advice, a competent professional should be consulted.

The author and publisher specifically disclaim any responsibility for any liability, loss, or risk, personal or otherwise, which is incurred as a consequence, directly or indirectly, of the use and application of any of the contents of this book.

Most Alpha books are available at special quantity discounts for bulk purchases for sales promotions, premiums, fund-raising, or educational use. Special books, or book excerpts, can also be created to fit specific needs.

For details, write: Special Markets, Alpha Books, 375 Hudson Street, New York, NY 10014.

Publisher: *Marie Butler-Knight*
Editorial Director: *Mike Sanders*
Senior Managing Editor: *Billy Fields*
Acquisitions Editor: *Tom Stevens*
Development Editor: *Michael Thomas*
Senior Production Editor: *Janette Lynn*
Copy Editor: *Amy Borrelli*

Cartoonist: *Steve Barr*
Cover Designer: *Kurt Owens*
Book Designer: *Trina Wurst*
Indexer: *Brad Herriman*
Layout: *Chad Dressler, Rebecca Harmon*
Proofreader: *Laura Caddell*

Contents at a Glance

Contents

Introduction

Never let a computer know you're in a hurry.

—Anonymous

The world's gardeners have told us for years that if you want to keep your plants healthy and happy, then you should talk to them in a kindly, soothing voice. The world's gardeners are, I suspect, an eccentric bunch, but who can argue with their success?

Certainly not me, so perhaps that's why I've taken to talking to my computer using the same gentle, comforting tones. "Now, my good fellow, I have a *very* important deadline tomorrow, oh yes, and I just need you to be a good boy and not crash between now and then. Okey-doke?" (This is made *much* easier by the fact that I work at home.)

I think that, subconsciously, I view my computer as though it's the electronic equivalent of some deranged lunatic who'll snap at the least provocation. Or perhaps I see it as more of a fragile, high-strung, Southern belle type, a digital Blanche DuBois who is depending on the kindness of a stranger (that is to say, me) to keep it together.

Of course, what's really happening here is that years of using various incarnations of Windows have made me certifiably paranoid. I've simply come to expect that Windows will do something weird or toss me some semicomprehensible message that will have me scratching my head for hours. So even though it has been nearly 20 years since Windows 3.0 was foisted upon an unsuspecting world, Windows remains both devilishly difficult and fiendishly fickle. Windows can, in other words, make any of us feel, temporarily, like a complete idiot.

That, in the end, is why I wrote *The Complete Idiot's Guide to Microsoft Windows 7*. My goal here is to help you and Windows 7 get along. If you aren't a computer wizard (and don't even want to be one), this book is for you; if you have a job to do—a job that includes working with Windows 7—and you just want to get it done as quickly and painlessly as possible, this book is for you; if you don't want to learn about Windows 7 using absurdly serious, put-a-crease-in-your-brow-and-we'll-begin tutorials, this book is for you.

No experience with Windows 7? No problem. In fact, this book doesn't assume you have *any* previous experience with *any* version of Windows. I begin each topic at the beginning and build your knowledge from there. So even if you've never used a computer before, this book will get you through those crucial (and scary) early stages.

No time? No problem. With *The Complete Idiot's Guide to Microsoft Windows* 7, you get just the facts you need—not everything there is to know. This means I avoid long-winded discussions of boring, technical details. Instead, you get all the information in short, easy-to-digest chunks that you can quickly skim through to find just the tidbits you need.

How This Book Is Organized

The Complete Idiot's Guide to Microsoft Windows 7 is organized into five reasonably sensible parts. To help you locate what you need fast, here's a summary of what you'll find in each part.

Part 1: "Windows 7 Everywhere: A Few Things You Need to Know." The lucky six chapters that open the book are designed to help you get your Windows 7 travels off on the right foot. New Windows users will want to start with Chapter 1, which gives you a tour of the Windows 7 screen and offers some mouse and keyboard basics. From there, you learn about controlling programs (Chapter 2), working with windows (Chapter 3), dealing with documents (Chapter 4), working with files and folders (Chapter 5), and installing and uninstalling programs and devices (Chapter 6).

Part 2: "Windows 7 at Home." Using a computer at home, we tend more toward the fun end of the computer spectrum. (Yes, there *is* a fun end.) With that in mind, I structured Part 2 to cover some of the more fun features that can be found in Windows 7. This includes working with pictures (Chapter 7); using scanners and digital cameras (Chapter 8); working with music, sounds, and other multimedia (Chapter 9); and creating and editing your own digital movies (Chapter 10). For good measure, I also show you an easy way to share your computer with other family members (Chapter 11).

Part 3: "Windows 7 at Work." This part is short but sweet (assuming that using Windows at work could be described as "sweet," that is). The three chapters in Part 3 cover workaday tasks such as using Windows 7's new Calendar program (Chapter 12), sending and receiving faxes (Chapter 13), and using Windows 7's notebook computer features (Chapter 14).

Part 4: "Windows 7 on the Internet." There are plenty of days when it seems that our computers are just one giant communications terminal. Electronic communication in all its forms is a huge part of our daily lives, and Part 4 devotes four chapters to Windows 7 Internet and communications goodies. You'll learn step by step how to get connected to the Internet (Chapter 15), how to surf the World Wide Web with Internet Explorer (Chapter 16), how to exchange Internet e-mail with Windows Mail (Chapter 17), and how to keep you and your computer safe while online (Chapter 18).

Part 5: "Windows 7 at the Shop: Customizing, Maintaining, and Troubleshooting." Like people living in row houses who paint their doors and windowpanes to stand out from the crowd, most Windows' users like to personalize their computing experience by adjusting the screen colors, changing the background, and performing other individualistic tweaks. The first two chapters in Part 5 show you how to perform these customizations in Windows 7. You'll learn how to customize the desktop (Chapter 19) and the Start menu and taskbar (Chapter 20).

The other two chapters in Part 5 can help you to prepare for problems. You'll get a step-by-step plan for maintaining your system (Chapter 21) and basic strategies for solving problems (Chapter 22).

Finally, the appendix provides you with a comprehensive list of Windows 7's all-too-numerous shortcut keys, just in case your mouse is having a bad day.

Some Things to Help Out Along the Way

I've liberally sprinkled the book with features that I hope will make it easier for you to understand what's going on. Here's a rundown:

- Stuff that you have to type will appear in a `monofaced font`, like that.

- Menus, commands, and dialog box controls that you have to select, as well as keys you have to press, appear in a **bold font.**

- Whenever I tell you to select a menu command, I separate the various menu and command names with commas. For example, instead of saying "click the **Start** button, then click **All Programs,** and then click **Windows Update,**" I just say this: "select **Start, All Programs, Windows Update.**"

- Many Windows 7 commands come with handy keyboard shortcuts, and most of them involve holding down one key while you press another key. For example, in most Windows programs, you save your work by holding down the **Ctrl** key, pressing the **S** key, and then releasing **Ctrl.** I'm *way* too lazy to write all that out each time, so I'll just plop a plus sign (+) in between the two keys, like so: **Ctrl+S.**

I've also populated each chapter with several different kinds of sidebars (some appear in the middle of the page and others appear in the margin):

Windows Wisdom

These asides give you extra information about the topic at hand, provide you with tips for making things work easier, and generally just make you a more well-rounded Windows 7 user.

def•i•ni•tion

These notes give you definitions of Windows words suitable for use at cocktail parties and other social gatherings where a well-timed bon mot can make you a crowd favorite.

See Also

Each of these elements points you to another section of the book that contains related material.

Look Out!

These notes warn you about possible Windows 7 pitfalls and tell you how to avoid them.

Hacking Windows

These juicier tidbits take you deeper into Windows 7 and show you useful tweaks that enable you to supercharge your system and take control over various aspects of Windows 7.

Acknowledgments (Kudos, Props, and Assorted Pats on the Back)

Substitute damn *every time you're inclined to write* very; *your editor will delete it and the writing will be just as it should be.*

—*Mark Twain*

I didn't follow Mark Twain's advice in this book (the word *very* appears throughout), but if my writing still appears "just as it should be," then it's because of the keen minds and sharp linguistic eyes of the editors at Alpha Books. Near the front of the book you'll find a long list of the hard-working professionals whose fingers made it into this particular paper pie. However, there are a few folks that I worked with directly, so I'd like to single them out for extra credit. A big, heaping, helping of thanks goes out to Acquisitions Editor Tom Stephens, Development Editor Mike Thomas, Production Editor Janette Lynn, Copy Editor Amy Borrelli, and Technical Editor Mark Hall.

Special Thanks to the Technical Reviewer

The Complete Idiot's Guide to Microsoft Windows 7 was reviewed by an expert who double-checked the accuracy of what you'll learn here, to help us ensure that this book gives you everything you need to know about Windows 7. Special thanks are extended to Mark Hall.

Mark Hall has been a Technology Services Consultant for the Community Colleges of Spokane for the past 22 years. He has been providing technical edits for the past 15 years and has edited over 270 books to date. He is married to his loving and supportive wife Brenda and has four children in four different colleges.

Trademarks

All terms mentioned in this book that are known to be or are suspected of being trademarks or service marks have been appropriately capitalized. Alpha Books and Penguin Group (USA) Inc. cannot attest to the accuracy of this information. Use of a term in this book should not be regarded as affecting the validity of any trademark or service mark.

Part 1

Windows 7 Everywhere: A Few Things You Need to Know

One of the great things about Windows 7 is what technoid types refer to as its "consistent interface." In plain English, this just means that a lot of the techniques you learn in one Windows program today can also be used in another Windows program tomorrow. These techniques are things you'll be using day in and day out: starting programs, using menus and toolbars, manipulating windows, opening and printing documents, and installing programs and devices. The six chapters that populate Part 1 take you through all of these techniques and quite a few more.

Windows 7: The 50¢ Tour

In This Chapter

◆ Getting Windows 7 up and at 'em

◆ Checking out the Windows 7 screen

◆ Handy mouse and keyboard techniques

◆ A cautionary tale about shutting Windows down

Thrill-seeking types enjoy diving into the deep end of any new pool they come across. The rest of us, however, prefer to check things out first by dipping a toe or two into the waters and then slipping ever so gently into the shallow end. The latter is the most sensible approach when it comes to Windows waters, which can be cold and murky to the uninitiated. You need to ease into the pool by learning a few basics about the layout of the screen and a few useful mouse and keyboard techniques. That's exactly what you'll do in this chapter.

Note, however, that this chapter assumes your Windows 7 pool has already been built and filled with water. That is, I assume that either your computer came with Windows 7 already installed or else you have (or a nearby computer guru has) upgraded your computer to Windows 7.

Starting Windows 7

After you poke your computer's power switch, Windows 7 begins pulling itself up by its own bootstraps. This *booting* process takes a few minutes on most machines, so this is an excellent time to grab a cup of coffee or tea and review your copy of *Feel the Fear and Do It Anyway.*

After your machine has churned through a few behind-the-scenes (and happily ignorable) chores, you may end up staring at the "log on" screen, which will be similar to the one shown in Figure 1.1. What's happening here is that Windows 7 wants to know who's going to be using the computer, so it's asking you to choose the name of your "account" and type your account's password. (If your Windows 7 user account doesn't have a password and you just have the one account on your system, you get a free pass to the main Windows 7 screen, so jump ahead to the next section, "A Tour of the Screen.") You'll be getting the full scoop on this user account stuff in Chapter 11, so don't sweat it too much right now.

def•i•ni•tion

The idea of Windows pulling itself up by its own bootstraps is actually a pretty good way to describe the whole process of Windows starting itself up from scratch. In fact, it's the source of the verb **boot,** which means to start a computer.

Figure 1.1

This screen usually appears while Windows 7 loads.

Here's how you take care of business in the log on screen:

1. Move the mouse pointer over your user name.

2. Click the left mouse button.

3. If you see a box with the word "Password" inside, type your password (the one you entered when you first installed Windows 7) and then press the **Enter** key on your keyboard. Note that the characters you type appear as dots for security (just in case some snoop is peering over your shoulder).

Windows 7 will now continue its seemingly endless startup chores, so be prepared to do a bit more thumb twiddling before the main screen finally puts in an appearance.

A Tour of the Screen

The screen shown in Figure 1.2 is typical of the face that Windows 7 presents to the world. (Note that your screen might have a different look, depending on how your computer manufacturer chose to set up your machine.) If you're new to Windows 7, you need to get comfortable with the lay of the Windows land. To that end, let's examine the vista you now see before you, which I divide into two sections: the desktop and the taskbar.

Recycle Bin icon

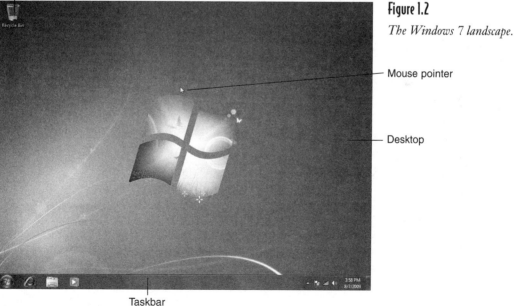

Figure 1.2

The Windows 7 landscape.

Mouse pointer

Desktop

Taskbar

The Desktop

Ivory-tower computer types enjoy inventing metaphors for the way the rest of us use a computer. The idea is that more people will put up with a computer's shenanigans if using the computer reflects the way we do things in real life.

For Windows, the metaphor of choice is the humble desktop. That is, you're supposed to think of the Windows screen as being comparable to the top of a real desk in a real office or den. Starting a program is like taking a folder full of papers out of storage and placing it on the desk. To do some work in the real world, of course, you need to pull papers out of a folder and place them on the desk. This is just like opening a file within the program (it could be a letter, a drawing, an e-mail message, or whatever). To extend the metaphor a little, most programs also come with tools, such as a ruler, a calculator, and a calendar, that are the electronic equivalents of the tools you use at your desk.

So, officially, the vast expanse that takes up the bulk of the screen real estate is the Windows 7 desktop, and it's where you'll do your work. (If looking at the same old screen all day long makes you feel a bit batty, changing to a different image, color, or psychedelic pattern is no sweat. I'll tell you how in Chapter 19.)

The Taskbar

The multicolored strip along the bottom of the Windows 7 screen is called the *taskbar*. The taskbar sports four distinct features (pointed out in Figure 1.3).

Program icons   Date and time

Figure 1.3

The features of the Windows 7 taskbar.

Start button   Notification area

- ◆ **Start button.** Believe it or not, this tiny chunk of screen real estate is one of the most important features in all of Windows 7. As its name implies, the Start button is your starting point for most of the Windows 7 features and goodies. I discuss the Start button in depth in Chapter 2.

- ◆ **Program icons.** This area contains a few icons. An *icon* is a small picture that represents something on your system, such as a program or a command. You use these icons to start programs and to control running programs, as I natter on about in Chapter 2.

◆ **Notification area.** Windows 7 uses this area to let you know when something important (or, at least, something that Windows 7 *thinks* is important) is happening with your machine. These are called *notifications*, and they'll pop up from time to time to keep you "in the know." For example, Figure 1.4 shows the notification that barges onto the desktop if Windows 7 can't find an antivirus program on your PC.

◆ **Date and time.** This area's purpose is obvious enough: it tells you the current time and the current date.

Figure 1.4

Windows 7 uses the aptly (if a bit boringly) named notification area to cough up notifications about stuff that's happening with your PC.

A Few Mouse and Keyboard Fundamentals

Windows 7 is supposed to have all kinds of fancy-schmancy features. How do I get at 'em?

Ah, that's where your mouse and keyboard come in. You use them as "input devices" to give Windows 7 its marching orders. If you're new to all the personal computer malarkey, the next few sections show you the basic mouse and keyboard techniques you need to do just that.

Basic Mouse Maneuvers

If you're unfamiliar with Windows, there's a good chance that you're also unfamiliar with the mouse, the electromechanical (and, thankfully, toothless) mammal attached to your machine. If so, this section presents a quick look at a few mouse moves, which is important because much of what you do in Windows will involve the mouse in some way.

For starters, be sure the mouse is sitting on its pad or on your desk with the cord facing away from you. (If you have one of those newfangled cordless mice, move the mouse so that the buttons are facing away from you.) Rest your hand lightly on the mouse with your index finger on (but not pressing down) the left button and your middle finger on the right button (or the rightmost button). Southpaws need to reverse the fingering.

Figure 1.2, displayed earlier, showed you the *mouse pointer*. Find the pointer on your screen and then slowly move the mouse on its pad. As you do this, notice that the pointer moves in the same direction. Take a few minutes to practice moving the pointer to and fro using slow, easy movements. (Don't be alarmed if the mouse pointer stops dead in its tracks when it reaches the edge of the screen. This is perfectly normal behavior, and you can get the pointer going again by moving the mouse in the opposite direction.)

To new users, the mouse seems an unnatural device that confounds common sense and often reduces the strongest among us to tears of frustration. The secret to mastering the mouse is twofold. First, use the same advice as was given to the person who wanted to get to Carnegie Hall: practice, practice, practice. Fortunately, with Windows 7 being so mouse dependent, you'll get plenty of chances to perfect your skills.

Second, understand all the basic mouse moves that are required of the modern-day mouse user. There are a half-dozen in all:

◆ **Point.** This means that you move the mouse pointer so that it's positioned over some specified part of the screen. For example, "point at the Start button" means that you move the mouse pointer over the taskbar's Start button.

◆ **Click.** This means that you press and immediately release the left mouse button to initiate some kind of action. Need a "fer instance"? Okay, point at the **Start** button and then click it. Instantly, a menu sprouts up in response to the click. (This is Windows 7's Start menu. I'll discuss it in detail in Chapter 2. For now, you can get rid of the menu either by clicking an empty section of the desktop or pressing the **Esc** key on your keyboard.)

◆ **Double-click.** This means that you press and release the left mouse button *twice*, one press right after the other (there should be little or no delay between each press). To give it a whirl, point at the desktop's **Recycle Bin** icon and then double-click. If all goes well, Windows 7 will toss a box titled Recycle Bin onto the desktop. To return this box from whence it came, click the **"X"** button in the upper-right corner. If nothing happens when you double-click, try to click as quickly as you can, and try not to move the mouse while you're clicking.

Windows Wisdom

Okay, so clicking initiates some kind of action, but so does double-clicking. What's the diff? The whole single-click versus double-click conundrum is one of the most confusing and criticized traits in Windows, and I'm afraid there's no easy answer. Some things require just a click to get going, whereas other things require a double-click. With experience, you'll eventually come to know which clicking technique is needed.

◆ **Right-click.** This means that you press and immediately release the *right* mouse button. In Windows 7, the right-click is used almost exclusively to display a creature called the *shortcut menu.* To see one, right-click an empty part of the desktop. Windows 7 displays a menu with a few common commands related to the desktop. To remove this menu, *left*-click the desktop.

◆ **Click and drag.** This means that you point at some object, press and *hold down* the left mouse button, move the mouse, and then release the button. You almost always use this technique to move an object from one place to another. For example, try dragging the desktop's Recycle Bin icon. (To restore apple-pie order to the desktop, right-click the desktop, click **Sort By** in the shortcut menu, and then click **Name.**)

◆ **Scroll.** This means that you turn the little wheel that's nestled in between the left and right mouse buttons. In programs that support scrolling, you use this technique to move up and down within a document. The wheel is a relatively new innovation, so your mouse might not have one. If not, never fear, as Windows provides other ways to navigate a document, as you'll see in Chapter 3.

Common Keyboard Conveniences

I mentioned earlier that getting comfy with your mouse is crucial if you want to make your Windows 7 life as easy as possible. That's not to say, however, that the keyboard never comes in handy as a timesaver. On the contrary, Windows 7 is chock-full of keyboard shortcuts that are sometimes quicker than the standard mouse techniques. I'll tell you about these shortcuts as we go along. For now, let's run through some of the standard keyboard parts and see how they fit into the Windows way of doing things.

◆ **The Ctrl and Alt keys.** If you press **Ctrl** (it's pronounced "control") or **Alt** (it's pronounced "alt" as in *alt*ernate), nothing much happens, but that's okay because nothing much is supposed to happen. You don't use these keys by themselves,

def•i•ni•tion

A **key combination** is a keyboard technique where you hold down one key and then press another key (or possibly two other keys).

but as part of *key combinations*. (The **Shift** key often gets into the act as well.) For example, hold down the **Ctrl** key with one hand, use your other hand to tap the **Esc** key, and then release **Ctrl**. Like magic, you see a menu of options sprout from the Start button. (To hide this menu again, press **Esc** by itself.)

Windows Wisdom

Windows 7 has all kinds of keyboard combo shortcuts, so they pop up regularly throughout the book. Because I'm *way* too lazy to write out something like "Hold down the **Ctrl** key with one hand, use your other hand to tap the **Esc** key, and then release **Ctrl**" each time, however, I use the following shorthand notation instead: "Press **Hold+Tap**," where **Hold** is the key you hold down and **Tap** is the key you tap. In other words, instead of the previous long-winded sentence, I say this: "Press **Ctrl+Esc**." (On rare occasions, a third key joins the parade, so you might see something like "Press **Ctrl+Alt+Delete**." In this case, you hold down the first two keys and then tap the third key.)

♦ **The Esc key.** Your keyboard's Esc (or Escape) key is your all-purpose get-me-the-heck-out-of-here key. For example, you just saw that you can get rid of the Start menu by pressing **Esc.** In many cases, if you do something in Windows 7 that you didn't want to do, you can reverse your tracks with a quick tap (or maybe two or three) on **Esc.**

♦ **The numeric keypad.** On a standard keyboard layout, the numeric keypad is the separate collection of numbered keys on the right. The numeric keypad usually serves two functions, and you toggle between these functions by pressing the **Num Lock** key. (Most keyboards have a Num Lock indicator light that tells you when Num Lock is on.) When Num Lock is on, you can use the numeric keypad to type numbers. When Num Lock is off, the other symbols on the keys become active. For example, the 8 key's upward-pointing arrow becomes active, which means you can use it to move up within a program. Some keyboards (called *extended keyboards*) have a separate keypad for the insertion point movement keys, and you can keep Num Lock on all the time.

Making It Legit: Activating Your Copy of Windows 7

Some time after you launch Windows 7 for the first time, you'll need to "activate" Windows 7 with Microsoft or else Windows will simply stop working. This is Microsoft's way of checking for illegal copies of Windows. What happens is that Windows checks the hardware configuration of your computer and ties it to the product ID of your copy of Windows 7. Don't worry: no personal information is ever sent to Microsoft and there are no fees or other hidden goings-on. You have two ways to get started on this activation business:

◆ If the next time you try to start Windows 7 you see the message "Windows license is expired," click the **Activate Windows online now** link.

◆ Click the **Start** button, click **Control Panel** in the Start menu, click **System and Security,** and then click **System.** Click the **Click here to activate Windows now** link.

If you see a dialog box named User Account Control, click **Continue** and then click **Activate Windows online now.** Windows 7 then jumps online and activates your copy. If you don't have an Internet connection, click **Show me other ways to activate,** which enables you to activate via your modem or via an automated phone system.

Shutting Down Windows for the Night

When you've stood just about all you can stand of your computer for one day, it's time to close up shop. Please tape the following to your cat's forehead so that you never forget it: *never, I repeat, never, turn off your computer's power while Windows 7 is still running.* Doing so can lead to data loss, a trashed configuration, and accelerated hair loss that those new pills don't help.

Now that I've scared the daylights out of you, let's see the proper procedure for shutting down your computer:

1. Click the **Start** button to pop up the Windows 7 Start menu.

2. Click the **Shut Down** button, shown in Figure 1.5. Windows 7 tucks itself in and turns off your PC.

Figure 1.5

*Click the Start menu's **Shut Down** button to (duh) shut down Windows 7.*

Shut Down button

Windows 7 also has a few other shut down tricks that you should know about. To check them out, click the **Start** button again, but this time click the little arrow beside the Shut Down button. Depending on your computer's configuration, you see a menu with some or all of the following options:

♦ **Sleep.** Clicking this option tells Windows 7 to shut down your computer, but it also tells Windows 7 to "remember" which windows and programs you have running. When you restart Windows 7, it restores those programs and windows automatically. Thanks!

♦ **Restart.** Choose this option if you want to start Windows 7 all over again. For example, if you find that Windows is acting strangely, restarting can often put things right.

♦ **Lock.** Choose this option to display a screen that asks you for your password. You must enter the password to get back to the Windows 7 desktop. (If you don't have a password, just press **Enter.** See Chapter 11 to learn how to protect your computer with a password.)

♦ **Log Off.** Choose this option to log off and then log back on using a different user account (see Chapter 11 to learn about user accounts).

♦ **Switch User.** Choose this option to remain logged on, but to also log on with a different user account (again, see Chapter 11 for the details).

The Least You Need to Know

◆ The Windows 7 screen is carved into two main areas: the *desktop*—the large area that covers most of your monitor—and the *taskbar*—the thin strip along the bottom of the screen.

◆ The taskbar consists of the Start button, some program icons, the notification area, and the date and time.

◆ The three most-used mouse movements are the *click* (quickly pressing and releasing the left mouse button), the *double-click* (two quick clicks), and the *drag* (holding down the left button and moving the mouse).

◆ A *key combination* involves holding down one key, pressing a second key, and then releasing the first key. I signify such a combo with the notation **Hold+Tap** (where **Hold** is the key you hold down and **Tap** is the key you tap); for example, **Ctrl+Esc.**

◆ To shut down Windows, click **Start** and then click the **Shut Down** button.

Making Something Happen: Launching and Controlling Programs

In This Chapter

- A couple of ways to get a program off the ground
- Learning about pull-down menus, toolbars, and dialog boxes
- Getting the hang of the taskbar
- Techniques for switching between programs
- Shutting down a program

If you want to get your computer to do anything even remotely nonpaperweightlike, you need to launch and work with a program or three. For example, if you want to write a memo or a letter, you need to fire up a word processing program; if you want to draw pictures, you need to crank up a graphics program. If you want to use the Windows spreadsheet program, well … there isn't one. Windows 7 comes with a passel of programs, but a spreadsheet isn't among them. If you want to crunch numbers, you need to get a third-party spreadsheet program, such as Microsoft Excel.

On the other hand, Windows 7 *does* come with a decent collection of programs that enable you to perform most run-of-the-mill computing tasks. This chapter shows you how to get at those programs as well as how to mess with them after they're up and running.

Launching a Program

If you're interested in starting a program, then you might think that the Start button in the lower-left corner of the screen would be a promising place to begin. If so, give yourself a pat on the back (or have a nearby loved one do it) because that's exactly right. Go ahead and use your mouse to point at the **Start** button and then click. As you can see in Figure 2.1, Windows 7 responds by tossing a rather large box onto the screen. This is called the *Start menu*, and you'll be visiting this particular place a lot in your Windows 7 travels.

Figure 2.1

The Start menu: your Windows 7 launch pad.

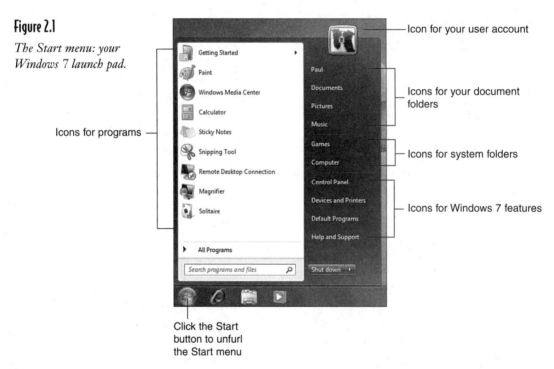

Icon for your user account

Icons for your document folders

Icons for programs

Icons for system folders

Icons for Windows 7 features

Click the Start button to unfurl the Start menu

A Look Around the Start Menu

The Start menu is populated with all kinds of icons. An icon is a picture representing something that exists on your computer. To see what I mean, let's run through the various icons that exist on the Start menu. (Again, however, I need to point out that computer manufacturers can and will customize the Start menu, so yours may be populated with a different set of icons.) As pointed out in Figure 2.1, I divide the icons into four general categories: programs, document folders, system folders, and Windows 7 features.

Windows Wisdom
Clicking the Start button is probably the most common way to get at the Start menu, but Windows 7 also offers a couple of keyboard methods that you should have in your arsenal: press **Ctrl+Esc** or press the **Windows Logo** key. (All recent keyboards sport the Windows logo key and you'll find it between the Ctrl and Alt keys.)

For the programs, the initial Start menu has a few icons for applications such as Paint (for drawing stuff on your computer), Calculator (for simple number crunching), and Windows Media Center (for playing movies and other media).

More importantly for our purposes, the standard-issue Start menu includes a program called Getting Started, which serves up a few more icons for tasks related to folks just getting acquainted with Windows 7. We'll tackle many of those tasks throughout the book, but for now I want you to puzzle over the teensy little arrow that appears to the right of the Getting Started icon. If you position the mouse pointer over that arrow, the Start menu transforms itself into the version you see in Figure 2.2. Now the right side of the menu displays a collection of smaller, cuter icons under the heading Tasks. This is called a *jump list* and it's a new feature in Windows 7. Basically, a jump list is a list of tasks associated with a particular program, and you click a task to run it. (To send the jump list back from whence it came, click an empty section of the Start menu.)

Figure 2.2

Move your mouse pointer over the little arrow to see a program's jump list (if it has one).

The document folders section of the Start menu is populated with four icons:

♦ **User name.** This icon represents the main *folder* assigned to your Windows 7 user account and it's given the same name as your user account (for example, Paul). This folder contains all of your *documents*.

♦ **Documents.** This icon represents the folder where you'll store most of the documents that you create. (You'll learn what it's all about in Chapter 4.)

♦ **Pictures.** This icon represents the folder where you'll store your picture files (which are also known as graphics files and image files; see Chapter 7 for more info).

♦ **Music.** This icon represents the folder where you'll store your music files, as described in Chapter 9.

def•i•ni•tion

A **folder** is a storage location on your computer's hard disk. What do you store in a folder? You store files, which generally come in two flavors: **documents** that you create yourself and program files that run the programs installed on your computer.

The system folders part of the Start menu is populated with two icons:

♦ **Games.** This icon represents the folder where the games on your computer are stored. Windows 7 comes with a few games, and most of the games you install will end up in this folder.

◆ **Computer.** This icon represents the folder that contains everything on your computer, including your hard disk, CD or DVD drive, floppy disk drive, and so on. (To get the details, head for Chapter 5.)

For the Windows 7 features, the Start menu is home to four icons:

◆ **Control Panel.** This icon represents the Windows 7 Control Panel feature, which you use to customize Windows 7. I talk about the Control Panel throughout this book.

◆ **Default Programs.** This icon represents a program that you can use to customize the programs that Windows 7 uses for certain actions, such as browsing the web.

◆ **Devices and Printers.** This icon opens a window that shows you all the major devices and hardware doodads that are attached to your computer.

◆ **Help and Support.** This icon represents the Windows 7 Help feature, which offers guidance and instruction on the various Windows 7 bits and pieces.

Finally, the Start menu has two other features that you need to get your head around:

◆ **All Programs.** This icon represents another menu that lists all the other programs installed on your computer. (See the next section, "Navigating the Start Menu," to learn more about this icon.)

◆ **Search programs and files.** This doohickey isn't an icon at all, but what's known in the Windows trade as a *text box*, so-called because you use it to type text. In this case, you type a word or two related to something you want to find on your computer, and Windows 7 displays icons for everything on your system that matches your typing. It all sounds quite mysterious, I know, but you'll get the full scoop in Chapter 5.

Navigating the Start Menu

Now that you've met the denizens of the Start menu, you need to know how to make them do something useful. To launch an icon, you have two possibilities:

◆ For every icon except All Programs, you need only click the icon, and Windows 7 launches the program, folder, or feature without further ado.

◆ Clicking the All Programs icon brings up another menu, as shown in Figure 2.3. As you can see, this new menu is filled with even more icons, some of which are duplicates of icons on the Start menu (for example, Windows Media Center). To launch one of these icons, click it with your mouse.

Figure 2.3

Clicking the All Programs icon displays a menu of programs.

Notice, however, that the icons at the bottom (Accessories, Games, and so on) have a folder icon to the left. When you click one of these icons, a new menu (called a *submenu*) slides out below the icon. For example, clicking the Accessories icon displays the submenu shown in Figure 2.4.

Figure 2.4

Some icons exist only to display a submenu that contains even more icons.

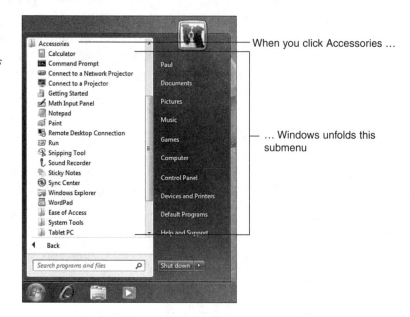

Don't be surprised if you find yourself wading through two or three of these sub-menus to get the program you want. For example, here are the steps you'd follow to fire up Disk Cleanup, the program you use to delete unneeded files from your PC (see Chapter 21):

1. Click the **Start** button to display the Start menu.

2. Click **All Programs** to open the menu.

3. Click **Accessories** to open the submenu.

4. Click **System Tools** to open yet another submenu.

5. Click **Disk Cleanup.** Windows 7 launches the Disk Cleanup program. (If you follow these steps but don't actually want to delete files right now, click the **Cancel** button in the Disk Cleanup window that appears.)

In the future, I abbreviate these long-winded Start menu procedures by using a comma (,) to separate each item you click, like so: "Select **Start, All Programs, Accessories, System Tools, Disk Cleanup.**"

Cranking Up a Program Right from the Taskbar

The Start menu makes a bit of sense in a geeky way, but it's not the only program-launching game in town. In Windows 7, you get a second way to fire up programs, and this newfangled method takes but a single mouse click. To see what I'm blathering on about, take a peek at the Windows 7 taskbar shown in Figure 2.5.

Internet   Windows
Explorer   Media Player

Windows
Explorer

Figure 2.5

In Windows 7, you can use the taskbar to launch some programs.

In particular, zero in on the three taskbar icons that I've pointed out in Figure 2.5. As you may have guessed by now, these icons represent programs:

◆ **Internet Explorer.** This icon represents the Internet Explorer program, which you use to make your way around the World Wide Web. I talk about this program in Chapter 16.

◆ **Windows Media Player.** This icon represents the Windows Media Player program, which you use to play music, watch DVD movies, create audio CDs, and perform other multimedia tricks. (Head for Chapter 9 for the full story.)

◆ **Windows Explorer.** This icon represents the Windows Explorer program, which you use to view and work with your computer's disk drives, folders, and files (see Chapter 5).

What's cool about these icons is that all it takes is a single click from you and the associated program launches without any further fuss. How easy is that?

Now What? Getting a Program to Do Something Useful

Okay, so I know how to get a program running. What's next?

Ah, now you get to go on a little personal power trip because this section shows you how to boss around your programs. Specifically, you learn how to work with pull-down menus, toolbars, and dialog boxes.

Making It Go: Selecting Commands from Pull-Down Menus

Each program you work with has a set of commands and features that define the majority of what you can do with the program. Most of these commands and features are available via the program's *pull-down menus.* Oh sure, there are easier ways to tell a program what to do (I talk about some of them later in this chapter), but pull-down menus are special because they offer a complete road map for any program. This section gets you up to speed on this crucial Windows topic.

I'm going to use the Windows Explorer program as an example for the next page or two. If you feel like following along, go ahead and launch the program by clicking the **Windows Explorer** icon on the taskbar. (If you've grown inordinately fond of the Start menu, you can also click **Start** and then click your user icon.)

The first thing you need to know is that a program's pull-down menus are housed in the *menu bar,* the horizontal strip that runs across the window, as pointed out in Figure 2.6. Note that in Windows Explorer, you need to press the **Alt** key to display the menu bar. (Most programs display the menu bar automatically.) Each word in the menu bar represents a pull-down menu.

Windows Wisdom

If I didn't know better, I'd swear that Windows 7 is a bit embarrassed to be seen with its pull-down menus. That's because many Windows 7 programs operate with the menu bar hidden away like some crazy aunt. If you open a program and you don't see hide nor hair of the menus, pressing the **Alt** key should bring the menu bar out into the light of day.

When you click View …   The menu bar

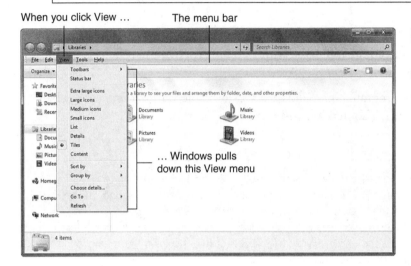

Figure 2.6

Windows Explorer's View menu.

The various items that run across the menu bar (such as File, Edit, and View in Windows Explorer) are the names of the menus. To see (that is, *pull down*) one of these menus, use either of the following techniques:

♦ Use your mouse to click the menu name. For example, click **View** to pull down the View menu.

♦ Notice in Figure 2.6 that each menu name has an underline under one letter. (If the program you're using doesn't show the underlines, press **Alt** to force them into the open.) That underline tells you that you can pull down the menu by holding down **Alt** and pressing the underlined letter on your keyboard. For example, the "V" in View gets underlined when you hold down Alt, so you can pull down this menu by pressing **Alt+V.**

The various items you see in the menu are called *commands*. From here, you use either of the following techniques to select a command:

def•i•ni•tion

> A **command** is a menu item that initiates some kind of action.

♦ Use your mouse to click the command you want.

♦ From your keyboard, use the down-arrow key (↓) or the up-arrow key (↑) to highlight the command, and then press **Enter.**

Throughout this book, I tell you to select a pull-down menu command by separating the menu name and command name with a comma (,), like this: "Select the **View, Refresh** command."

Note, too, that many program commands are also available via *shortcut menus*, which you open by right-clicking something within the program window.

def•i•ni•tion

> Many Windows programs (and Windows 7 itself) use **shortcut menus** to give you quick access to oft-used commands. The idea is that you right-click something and the program pops up a small menu of commands, each of which is somehow related to whatever it is you right-clicked. If you see the command you want, great: just click it (using the left button this time). If you don't want to select a command from the menu, either left-click an empty part of the window or press **Esc.**

What happens next depends on which command you picked. Here's a summary of the various possibilities:

♦ **The command runs without further fuss.** This is the simplest scenario, and it just means that the program carries out the command, no questions asked. For example, clicking the **View** menu's **Refresh** command updates Windows Explorer's display automatically.

♦ **Another menu appears.** As shown in Figure 2.7, when you click the **View** menu's **Sort By** command, a submenu appears on the right. You then click the command you want to execute from the new menu.

♦ **The command is toggled on or off.** Some commands operate like light switches: they toggle certain features of a program on and off. When the feature is on, a small check mark appears to the left of the command to let you know. Selecting the command turns off the feature and removes the check mark. If you select the command again, the feature turns back on and the check mark reappears. For example, click the **View** menu's **Status Bar** command, which activates the status bar at the bottom of the Windows Explorer window (see Figure 2.7).

Windows Wisdom

What if you don't want to select any commands from a menu you already opened? You can get rid of the menu by clicking any empty part of the program's window, or by pressing **Alt** by itself. Alternatively, you can choose a command from a different menu by clicking the menu's name in the menu bar, or by pressing **Alt** plus the underlined letter of the new menu.

◆ **An option is activated.** Besides having features that you can toggle on and off, some programs have flexible features that can assume three or more different states. Windows Explorer, for example, gives you eight ways to display the contents of your computer, according to your choice of one of the following **View** menu commands: **Extra Large Icons, Large Icons, Medium Icons, Small Icons, List, Details, Tiles,** and **Content** (see Chapter 5 for details). Because these states are mutually exclusive (you can select only one at a time), you need some way of knowing which of the eight commands is currently active. That's the job of the *option mark:* a small dot that appears to the left of the active command (see the Tiles command in Figure 2.7).

The check mark indicates an activated feature

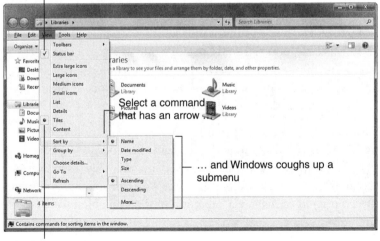

Figure 2.7

A few pull-down menu features.

The option mark
indicates the activated
command in this group

◆ **A dialog box appears.** Dialog boxes are pesky little windows that show up whenever the program needs to ask you for more information. You learn more about them in the "Dealing with Dialog Boxes" section, later in this chapter.

Your Click Is My Command: Toolbar Basics

The computer wizards who build our programs have come up with some amazing things over the years, but one of their most useful inventions has to be the *toolbar*. This is a collection of easily accessible icons designed to give you push-button access to common commands and features. No unsightly key combinations to remember; no pull-down menu forests to get lost in.

Toolbars play a big role in Windows 7, and you can reap some big dividends if you get to know how they work.

In Windows Explorer, the toolbar is the horizontal strip that sits just below the menu bar (when it's displayed, that is). This is actually a special type of toolbar called a *taskbar*, because what you see on the toolbar is really a collection of tasks you can perform for whatever item you're working on within the window. No matter: it still works like most toolbars, so it will serve us well as an example.

Most toolbar icons are buttons that represent commands you'd normally access by using the pull-down menus. All you have to do is click a button, and the program runs the command, no questions asked.

Here's a summary of a few other toolbar-related techniques you ought to know:

◆ **Button banners.** Most toolbar buttons advertise what they do using nothing more than an icon. In this case, you can find out the name of a particular button by pointing at it with your mouse. After a second or two, a banner—sometimes called a *tooltip*—with the button name pops up. Note, too, that lots of programs also display a brief description of the button in the status bar.

◆ **Hiding and showing toolbars.** In most programs, you toggle a toolbar on and off by selecting the **View, Toolbar** command (although this doesn't work in Windows Explorer). If a program offers multiple toolbars, the View menu often includes separate commands for each toolbar. In some other programs, you select the **View, Toolbars** command to display a submenu of the available toolbars, and then select the one you want.

◆ **Drop-down buttons.** You'll occasionally come across toolbar buttons that are really drop-down menu wannabes. In Windows Explorer, the Organize "button" is an example of the species. As shown in Figure 2.8, you click the downward-pointing arrow to see a list of commands or options.

Click the arrow to display the menu

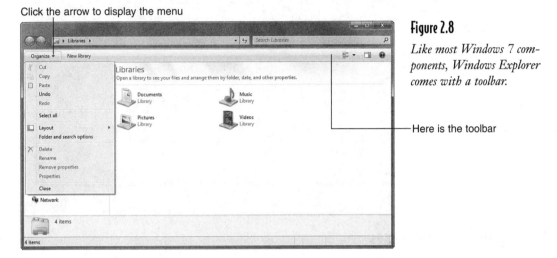

Figure 2.8

Like most Windows 7 components, Windows Explorer comes with a toolbar.

Here is the toolbar

Special Cases: WordPad and Paint

Just to confuse the issue (Windows 7 has a genius for doing that), two of the programs you may end up using fairly often have completely new (and potentially baffling) ways to run commands. These programs are WordPad (a word processor) and Paint (a graphics program). To see what I'm talking about, go ahead and get WordPad onto the desktop by selecting **Start, All Programs, Accessories, WordPad.** As you can see in Figure 2.9, WordPad is weird in two ways: there's no menu bar (and you can tap **Alt** until your finger falls off), and the toolbar is *huge*. Actually, that's not a toolbar at all, but something called a *ribbon*, which is a kind of toolbar on steroids.

The ribbon works basically the same as a regular toolbar, with the major difference being the presence of two tabs: Home and View. Click these tabs to see more buttons. Also, to get to the program's menus, you need to click the button in the upper-left corner that I point out in Figure 2.9.

Figure 2.9

In Windows 7, WordPad (as well as Paint) comes with a newfangled ribbon for faster access to program features.

Click here to see the menus   Click a tab to see more buttons

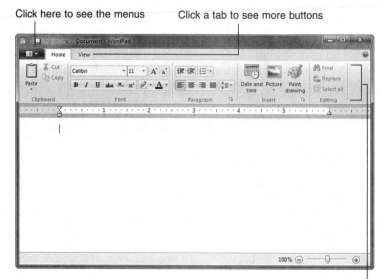

The ribbon

Dealing with Dialog Boxes

I mentioned earlier that after you select some menu commands, the program might require more info from you. For example, if you run a Print command, the program might want to know how many copies of the document you want to print.

In these situations, the program sends an emissary to parley with you. These emissaries, called *dialog boxes*, are one of the most ubiquitous features in the Windows world. This section preps you for your dialog box conversations by showing you how to work with every type of dialog box control you're likely to encounter. (They're called *controls* because you use them to manipulate the different dialog box settings.) Before starting, it's important to keep in mind that most dialog boxes like to monopolize your attention. When one is on the screen, you usually can't do anything else in the program (such as select a pull-down menu). Deal with the dialog box first, and then you can move on to other things.

> **def•i•ni•tion**
>
> A **dialog box** is a small window that a program uses to prompt you for information or to display a message. You interact with each dialog box by using one or more **controls** to input data or initiate actions.

Okay, let's get started:

- ◆ **Command buttons.** Clicking one of these buttons (see Figure 2.10) executes whatever command is written on the button. The two examples shown in the

Options dialog box are the most common. You click **OK** to close the dialog box and put the settings into effect, and you click **Cancel** to close the dialog box without doing anything.

♦ **Check boxes.** Windows uses a check box to toggle program features on and off (see Figure 2.10). Clicking the check box either adds a check mark (meaning the feature will get turned on when you click **OK**) or removes the check mark (meaning the feature will get turned off when you click **OK**).

♦ **Option buttons.** If a program feature offers three or more possibilities, the dialog box will offer an option button for each state (see Figure 2.10), and only one button can be activated (that is, have a blue dot inside its circle) at a time. You activate an option button by clicking it.

♦ **List boxes.** These controls (see Figure 2.10) display a list of items and you select an item by clicking it.

♦ **Text boxes.** You use these controls (see Figure 2.10) to type text data.

♦ **Spin boxes.** These controls (see Figure 2.10) enable you to cycle up or down through a series of numbers. The left part of the spin box is a simple text box into which you can type a number; however, the right part of the spin box has tiny up- and down-arrow buttons. You click the up arrow to increase the value, and you click the down arrow to decrease the value.

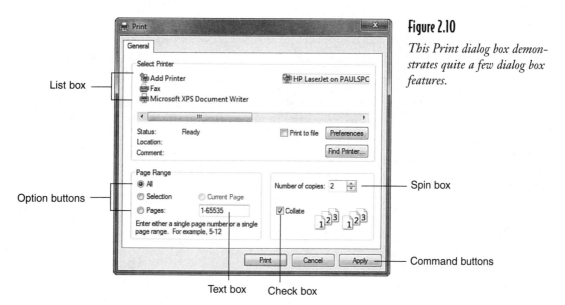

Figure 2.10

This Print dialog box demonstrates quite a few dialog box features.

◆ **Tabs.** Click any of the tabs displayed across the top of some dialog boxes (see Figure 2.11) and you see a new set of controls.

◆ **Sliders.** Click and drag the slider (see Figure 2.11) to set the value of the control.

Figure 2.11

You use tabs to navigate different sets of dialog box controls, and you click and drag a slider to set a value.

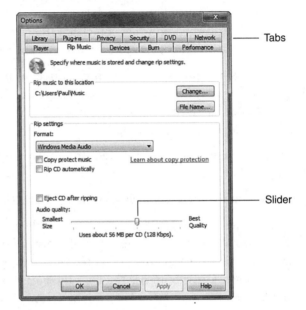

Tabs

Slider

◆ **Drop-down list boxes.** These controls represent another example of the list box genre (see Figure 2.12). In this case, at first you see only one item. However, if you click the downward-pointing arrow on the right, the full list appears and it becomes much like a regular list box.

◆ **Combo boxes.** These hybrid controls (see Figure 2.12) combine a list box and a text box. You can either select the item you want from the list or type it in the text box.

Combo boxes ──────

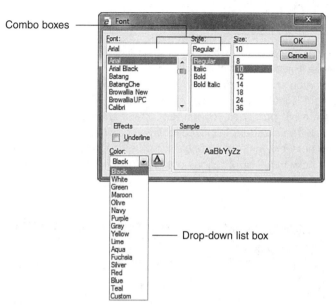

Figure 2.12

*This Font dialog box offers
several examples of both
combo boxes as well as an
example of the drop-down list
box species.*

──── Drop-down list box

Switching from One Program to Another

When you fire up a program, Windows 7 marks the occasion by adding a button to
the taskbar. If you then coax another program or two onto the screen (remember,
Windows 7 is capable of *multitasking*—running multiple programs simultaneously),
each one gets its own taskbar button.

For example, Figure 2.13 shows Windows 7 with two programs up and running:
WordPad and Paint. (To run the latter, select **Start, All Programs, Accessories,
Paint.**) It looks as though Paint has lopped off a good portion of the WordPad window, but in reality Windows 7 is just displaying Paint "on top" of WordPad. In addition, the taskbar has changed in three ways:

♦ There are now buttons for both WordPad and Paint in the taskbar.

♦ The buttons for the WordPad and Paint programs have an outline around them
  to tell you that these buttons represent running programs. This is supposed to
  help you differentiate these from the other taskbar buttons that launch programs.
  (Yes, this *does* take some getting used to.)

♦ In the taskbar, the *active* program's button (the Paint button in this figure) is
  highlighted. (The active program is the one you're currently slaving away in.)

> **Look Out!** _____
>
> Although it's true that Windows 7 is happy to deal with multiple running programs—think of it as the electronic equivalent of walking and chewing gum at the same time—that doesn't mean you can just start every program you have and leave them running all day. The problem is that because each open program usurps a chunk of the Windows resources, the more programs you run, the slower each program performs, including Windows itself. The number of applications you can fire up at any one time depends on how much horsepower your computer has. You probably need to play around a bit to see just how many applications you can launch before things get too slow.

Figure 2.13

Windows 7 with two programs on the go.

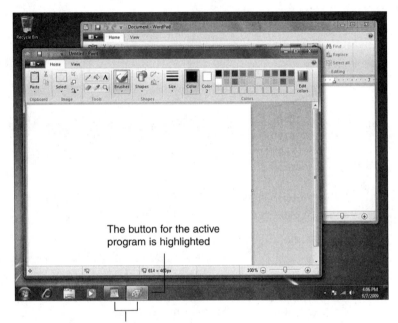

The button for the active
program is highlighted

Each running program gets its
own (outlined) taskbar button

The taskbar has another trick up its digital sleeve: you can switch from one running program to another by clicking the latter's taskbar button. For example, when I click the WordPad button, the WordPad window comes to the fore, as shown in Figure 2.14.

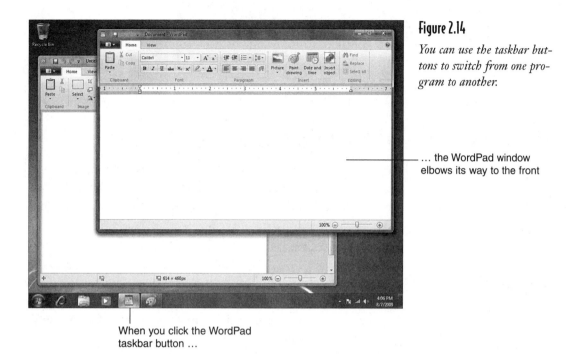

Figure 2.14

You can use the taskbar buttons to switch from one program to another.

... the WordPad window
elbows its way to the front

When you click the WordPad
taskbar button ...

Besides clicking the taskbar buttons, Windows 7 gives you three other ways to leap from one running program to another:

◆ **Click the program's window.** This is perhaps the simplest and most obvious method. All you do is point the mouse inside the program's window and then click. This method is most useful if your hand is already on the mouse and you can see at least part of the window you want to activate.

◆ **Hold down Alt and tap Tab.** When you do this, Windows 7 displays a box that boasts a miniversion of each running program, which is called a *thumbnail.* (On less powerful systems, you may only see an icon for each program, instead.) Each time you press **Tab,** the next thumbnail gets highlighted. After you highlight the thumbnail for the program you want, release the **Alt** key, and Windows 7 then switches to the program. This technique is useful if your hands are on the keyboard and you have only a few programs running.

◆ **Hold down Alt and tap Esc.** This method is similar to the **Alt+Tab** method in that Windows 7 cycles through the open programs. The difference is that with each tap of the Esc key, Windows 7 brings each program window to the fore. Use this method when you want to check out the contents of each window before you decide which program you want to work with.

◆ **Use the Flip 3D feature.** On most systems, press **Windows Logo+Tab** to display a nifty 3D "stack" of the running windows. Use your mouse's scroll wheel or the up- and down-arrow keys to cycle through the windows, and then press **Enter** when you get to the one you want.

When Enough's Enough: Quitting a Program

When you're finished with a particular program, you should close it to keep your screen uncluttered and to reduce the load on Windows' resources. The easiest way to do this is to click the **Close** button—the "X" in the upper-right corner of the program's window.

You can also use a few other methods, which you may find faster under certain circumstances:

See Also
I tell you how to handle saving documents in Chapter 4. See the section titled "The All-Important Save Command."

◆ Press **Alt+F4.**

◆ Pull down the program's **File** menu and select the **Exit** command (or, more rarely, the **Close** command).

◆ Right-click the program's taskbar button and then click **Close** in the little menu that appears.

Depending on the program you're closing and the work you were doing with it, you might be asked whether you want to "save" some files.

The Least You Need to Know

◆ To start a program, click the **Start** button to display the Start menu, and then click the command or submenus required to launch the program.

◆ To select a pull-down menu command, first display the menu by clicking its name in the menu bar, and then click the command.

◆ In a dialog box, click **OK** to put dialog box settings into effect; click **Cancel** to bail out of a dialog box without doing anything; click **Help** to view the program's Help system.

◆ To switch between running programs, click the taskbar buttons. Alternatively, click the program window if you can see a chunk of it, or else press **Alt+Tab.**

◆ To quit a program, click the **Close** (X) button. You can also usually get away with selecting the program's **File, Exit** command or pressing **Alt+F4.**

Working with Windows 7's Windows

In This Chapter

- Window gadgets and gewgaws
- Minimizing and maximizing windows
- Moving and sizing windows
- How to wield window scrollbars

Windows gets its name because, as you saw in Chapter 2, each program that you launch shows up on the screen in a box, and that box is called a *window*. Why they named them "windows" instead of, say, "boxes," I can't imagine. After all, have *you* ever seen a window on the top of a desk? I thought not.

Nincompoop nomenclature concerns aside, you're going to have to build up some window stamina because they'll come at you from the four corners of the screen. Fortunately, such stamina can be had without resorting to smelly workout clothes or Thighmasters. As you see in this chapter, all that's required is practicing a few handy mouse techniques.

Warming Up: A Window Walkabout

Your average window is a kind of mini Nautilus machine brimming with various gadgets that you push and pull. The secret to a successful window workout is to get to know where these gadgets are and what you use them for. To that end, let's take a tour of a typical window, as shown in Figure 3.1. This is a Notepad window. To get it onscreen, select **Start, All Programs, Accessories, Notepad.**

Here's a rundown of the various trinkets pointed out in Figure 3.1:

Figure 3.1

The Notepad window will be your "gym" for this chapter's exercise regimen.

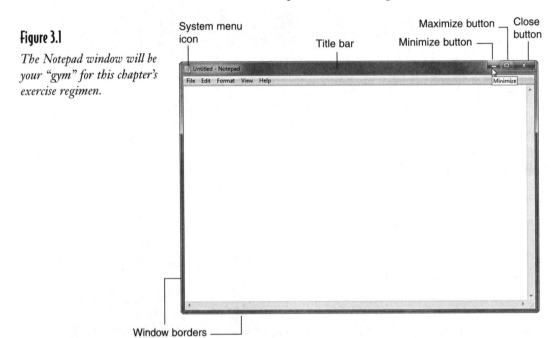

Windows Wisdom

With all those buttons crowded into the upper-right corner of a window, it's tough keeping them straight. To help us out, Windows 7 has a feature that tells you the name of each button. To check it out, move your mouse pointer over a button. A second or two later a little "tooltip" shows up with the button's name (as shown in Figure 3.1 by the word "Minimize").

- ◆ **Title bar.** This is the band that forms the top portion of the window. As its name implies, the title bar's job is to tell you the name of the currently open document. (In Figure 3.1, the document is new, so it has the temporary—and decidedly uninspiring—name "Untitled." See Figure 3.7 for a better example.) The title bar also usually shows the name of the program (with a dash in between the two names).

- ◆ **Buttons galore.** The right side of the title bar is populated with three buttons: The two blue buttons are named Minimize and Maximize, and the red button is named Close. I fill you in on what they do a bit later (see the section "Breaking a Sweat: Window Exercises").

- ◆ **Borders.** Most windows are surrounded by four borders that you can manipulate, with your mouse, to change the size of the window (I show you how to do this later in this chapter; see "Breaking a Sweat: Window Exercises").

- ◆ **System menu icon.** The system menu sports several commands that enable keyboard users to perform routine window maintenance. If you're dealing with a program window, you drop down the system menu by pressing **Alt+spacebar;** for a document window, the system menu sprouts in response to **Alt+- (hyphen).**

Now just hold on a cotton-picking second. What's the difference between a "program window" and a "document window"?

Gee, you *are* paying attention, aren't you? Here you go:

- ◆ **Program window.** This is the window in which the program as a whole appears.

- ◆ **Document window.** This is a window that appears inside the program window and it contains a single, open document. This isn't something you'll have to worry about too much if you run only the programs that come with Windows 7 because most of them are only capable of opening one document at a time. However, lots of other programs—such as those that come with Microsoft Office—are capable of working with two or more documents at once. In this case, each document appears inside its own window.

Breaking a Sweat: Window Exercises

Before getting to the specifics of the four main window techniques—minimizing, maximizing, moving, and sizing—let's see how they can solve some niggling Windows problems and help you work better:

Look Out!

You can't move or size a window if it's either maximized or minimized.

Problem #1: You have an open program that you know you won't need for a while. It's taking up desktop space, but you don't want to close it. The solution is to *minimize* the program's window, which means that it's cleared off the desktop, but it remains open and appears only as a taskbar button.

Problem #2: You want the largest possible work area for a program. The solution here is to *maximize* the program's window. This enlarges the window so that it fills the entire desktop area.

Problem #3: You have multiple programs on the go and their windows overlap each other so some data gets covered up. The way to fix this is to *move* one or more of the windows so that they don't overlap (or so that they overlap less).

Problem #4: No matter how much you move your windows, they still overlap. In this case, you need to resort to more drastic measures: *sizing* the windows. For example, you can reduce the size of less important windows and increase the size of windows in which you do the most work.

The next few sections discuss these techniques and a few more, for good measure.

Minimizing a Window

When you click a window's **Minimize** button, the window disappears from view. The window isn't closed, however, because its taskbar button remains in place, as you can see in Figure 3.2.

Maximizing a Window

Clicking a window's **Maximize** button is a whole different kettle of window fish. In this case, the window grows until it fills the entire desktop, as you can see in Figure 3.3. Note that the Maximize button has, without warning, morphed into a new entity: the Restore button. I talk about this new creature in the next section.

Windows Wisdom

The Minimize, Maximize, Restore, and Close buttons are a tad on the small side. Here are some techniques that avoid these teensy buttons: minimize the current window by clicking its taskbar button; maximize a window by double-clicking its title bar or dragging the title bar to the top of the screen; restore a maximized window by double-clicking its title bar; close a window by double-clicking its system menu icon.

Figure 3.2

When you minimize a program's window, the program remains running, but all you see is its taskbar button.

Just the window's taskbar button is visible

The Restore button

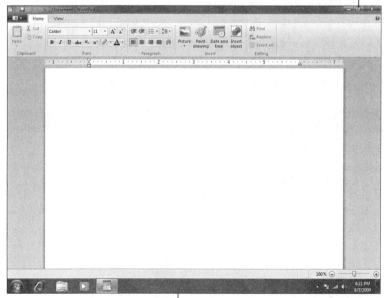

Figure 3.3

When you maximize a window, it takes over the entire desktop.

The taskbar remains conveniently visible

Restoring a Window

In Windows parlance, *restoring* a window means that you put the window back exactly the way it was before minimizing it or maximizing it. How you do this depends on what action you inflicted on the window:

◆ If you minimized the window, click its taskbar button.

◆ If you maximized the window, click the **Restore** button (pointed out in Figure 3.3).

Moving a Window

Moving a window from one part of the desktop to another takes a simple mouse maneuver. Here are the steps to follow:

1. Make sure the window isn't maximized (or that it's not, duh, minimized).

2. Position the mouse pointer inside the window's title bar (but not over the system menu icon or any of the buttons on the right).

3. Click and drag the title bar. (That is, press and hold down the left mouse button and then move the mouse.) As you drag, the window moves along with your mouse. (Although it may lag behind slightly if you have a slower system.)

4. When the window is in the position you want, release the mouse button.

Windows Wisdom

If you want to move a window so that it takes up, say, the left half of the screen, Windows 7 offers a super easy way to do this: click and drag the window title bar until the mouse pointer bumps up against the left edge of the screen. When an outline of the new window position appears, release the mouse button. You can also click and drag to the right edge to move the window so that it takes up the right half of the screen.

Sizing a Window

If you want to change the size of a window instead, you need to plow through these steps:

1. Make sure the window isn't maximized or minimized.

2. Point the mouse at the window border you want to adjust. For example, if you want to expand the window toward the bottom of the screen, point the mouse at the bottom border. When you've positioned the pointer correctly, it becomes a two-headed arrow, as shown in Figure 3.4.

3. Click and drag the border to the position you want.

4. Release the mouse button to set the new border position.

5. Repeat steps 2 through 4 for any other borders you want to size.

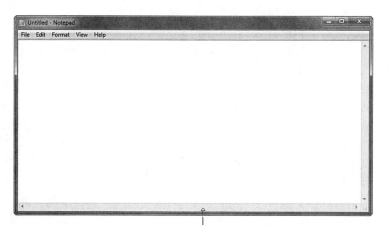

Figure 3.4

You resize a window by drag-ging the window borders hither and yon.

At a window border, the mouse pointer changes to a two-headed arrow

---

Windows Wisdom

If you want to change both the height and width of a window, you can save yourself a bit of effort by sizing two sides in one fell swoop. To do this, move the mouse pointer over a window corner. (The pointer will change to a diagonal two-sided arrow.) When you drag the mouse, Windows 7 sizes the two sides that create the corner.

Cascading and Tiling Windows

If you're pressed for time, you can take advantage of some Windows 7 features that can save you a few steps. To get at these features, right-click an empty section of the taskbar. The shortcut menu that slides into view contains (among others) the following commands:

- **Cascade windows.** This command automatically arranges all your nonmini-mized windows in a diagonal pattern that lets you see the title bar of each win-dow. Figure 3.5 shows three cascaded windows.

- **Show windows side by side.** This feature automatically arranges all your non-minimized windows into horizontal strips so that each of them gets an equal amount of desktop real estate without overlapping each other. Figure 3.6 shows the same three windows arranged horizontally.

- **Show windows stacked.** This command is similar to the Show windows side by side command, except that it arranges the windows into vertical strips.

Figure 3.5

The Cascade windows com-mand arranges your windows neatly in a diagonal pattern.

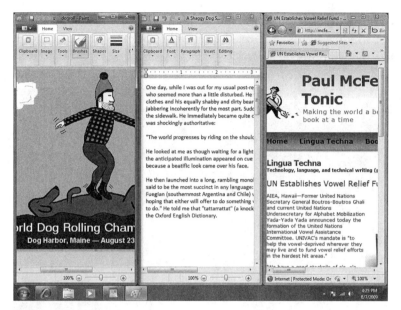

Figure 3.6

The Show windows side by side command carves out equal-size horizontal desktop chunks for your windows.

Taking a Peek at the Desktop

As your Windows 7 career progresses, you'll no doubt end up with some of your stuff on the desktop. You might create your own icons or you might give a few of Windows 7's desktop gadgets a whirl (as described in Chapter 19). Whatever your desktop ends up looking like, you'll want to take a peek at it from time to time. You'd normally do that by minimizing each of your open windows, but that might be *way* too much work if you've got a bunch of programs on the go.

To work around this problem, Windows 7 gives you two options:

- Right-click an empty stretch of the taskbar and then click **Show the desktop.** This command hides all the nonminimized windows so that you can see the full desktop. To get your windows back where they were, right-click the taskbar yet again and then click **Show open windows.**

- Move your mouse pointer over the **Show desktop** button on the far right of the taskbar. Mysteriously, the open windows fade from view, except for their ghostly

> **Windows Wisdom**
>
> If nothing happens when you hover the mouse over the Show desktop button, it means you're running Windows 7 using an older theme that doesn't support this feature. In this case, go ahead and click the **Show desktop** button to minimize the windows.

outlines, as shown in Figure 3.7. Move the mouse pointer off the **Show desktop** button to make the windows rematerialize; alternatively, click the **Show desktop** button to minimize the windows.

Figure 3.7

*Move your mouse pointer over the taskbar's **Show desktop** button to make your windows fade away.*

Show desktop

Window Weight Lifting: Using Scrollbars

Depending on the program you're using, you often find that the document you're dealing with won't fit entirely inside the window's boundaries, even when you maximize the window. When this happens, you need some way to move to the parts of the document you can't see.

def•i•ni•tion

The **scrollbar** is the narrow strip that runs along the right side of most windows. You sometimes see scrollbars along the bottom of a window, too.

From the keyboard, you can use the basic navigation keys (the arrow keys, Page Up, and Page Down). Mouse users, as usual, have all the fun. To navigate through a document, they get to learn a new skill: how to use *scrollbars*. Using the Notepad window shown in Figure 3.8, I've pointed out the major features of the average scrollbar. Here's how to use these features to get around inside a document:

Up scroll arrow

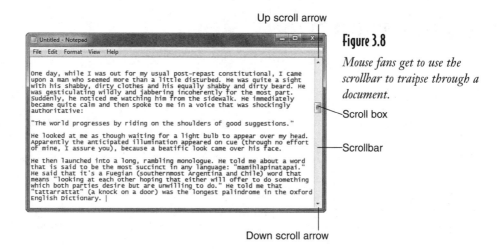

Figure 3.8

Mouse fans get to use the scrollbar to traipse through a document.

Scroll box

Scrollbar

Down scroll arrow

♦ The position of the scroll box gives you an idea of where you are in the document. For example, if the scroll box is about halfway down, you know you're somewhere near the middle of the document. Similarly, if the scroll box is near the bottom of the scrollbar, then you know you're near the end of the document.

♦ To scroll down through the document one line at a time, click the **down scroll arrow.** To scroll continuously, press and hold down the left mouse button on the **down scroll arrow.**

♦ To scroll up through the document one line at a time, click the **up scroll arrow.** To scroll continuously, press and hold down the left mouse button on the **up scroll arrow.**

♦ To leap through the document one screen at a time, click inside the scrollbar between the scroll box and the scroll arrows. For example, to move down one screen, click inside the scrollbar between the scroll box and the down scroll arrow.

♦ To move to a specific part of the document, click and drag the scroll box up or down.

Note, as well, that many of the windows you work in will also sport a second scrollbar that runs horizontally along the bottom of the window. Horizontal scrollbars work the same as their vertical cousins, except that they let you move left and right in wide documents.

Scrolling with a "Wheel" Mouse

Most modern mice feature a little wheel between the two buttons. If you have one of these rotary rodents, you can scroll up and down through a document by rotating the wheel forward or backward.

Some applications (such as Microsoft's Internet Explorer and Microsoft Office) also support a feature called *panning* that lets you scroll automatically through a document and control the speed. To enable panning, click the wheel button. The application will then display an *origin mark* (the position of this mark varies from application to application). Drag the pointer above the origin mark to scroll up; drag the pointer below the origin mark to scroll down. Note also that the farther the pointer is from the origin mark, the faster you scroll. To turn off panning, click the wheel again.

def•i•ni•tion

To **pan** means to use the mouse wheel to scroll automatically through a document.

The Least You Need to Know

 ◆ Minimizing a window means that the window disappears from the desktop, although the program continues to run. You minimize a window by clicking the **Minimize** button in the upper-right corner.

 ◆ Maximizing a window means that the window expands to fill the entire desktop. You maximize a window by clicking the **Maximize** button in the upper-right corner.

 ◆ To move a window, use your mouse to drag the title bar to and fro.

 ◆ To size a window, use your mouse to drag any of the window's borders.

 ◆ To let Windows do most of the work, right-click an empty part of the taskbar to eyeball several commands for cascading, tiling, and minimizing all windows.

Chapter 4

Saving, Opening, Printing, and Other Document Lore

In This Chapter

- ◆ Forging a fresh document
- ◆ Saving a document for posterity
- ◆ Closing a document and opening it back up again
- ◆ Getting a grip on Windows 7's newfangled libraries
- ◆ Handy document editing techniques
- ◆ Printing a document, just for the heck of it

The purpose of the chapters here in Part 1 is to help you get comfortable with Windows 7, and if you've been following along and practicing what you've learned, you and Windows should be getting along famously by now. However, there's another concept you need to familiarize yourself with before you're ready to fully explore the Windows universe: documents.

This chapter plugs that gap in your Windows education by teaching you all the basic techniques for manipulating documents. This will include creating, saving, closing, opening, editing, and printing documents, plus much more.

What on Earth Is a Document?

Most folks think a document is a word processing file. That's certainly true, as far as it goes, but I'm talking about a bigger picture in this chapter. Specifically, when I say "document," what I really mean is *any* file that you create by cajoling a program into doing something useful.

So, yes, a file created within the confines of a word processing program (such as WordPad) is a document. However, these are also documents: text notes you type into a text editor; images you draw in a graphics program; e-mail missives you compose in an e-mail program; spreadsheets you construct with a spreadsheet program; and presentations you cobble together with a presentation graphics program. In other words, if you can create it or edit it yourself, it's a document.

Manufacturing a New Document

Lots of Windows programs—including WordPad, Notepad, and Paint—are courteous enough to offer up a new, ready-to-roll document when you start the program. This means you can just dive right into your typing or drawing or whatever. Later on, however, you may need to start another new document. To do so, use one of the following techniques:

♦ Select the **File, New** command. In WordPad (select **Start, All Programs, Accessories, WordPad**), which doesn't have a menu bar, click the **WordPad** button (pointed out in Figure 4.1; a similar button appears in Paint and in the Microsoft Office programs, such as Word and Excel) to open the new style of File menu, and then click **New.**

♦ Click the **New** button in the program's toolbar.

♦ In many Windows programs, you can spit out a new document by pressing **Ctrl+N.**

In most cases, the program will then toss a fresh document on-screen. Some programs (WordPad is one) display a dialog box that asks you what kind of new document you want. (In the case of WordPad, click **Rich Text Document** if you want to format stuff, or click **Text Document** if you don't.)

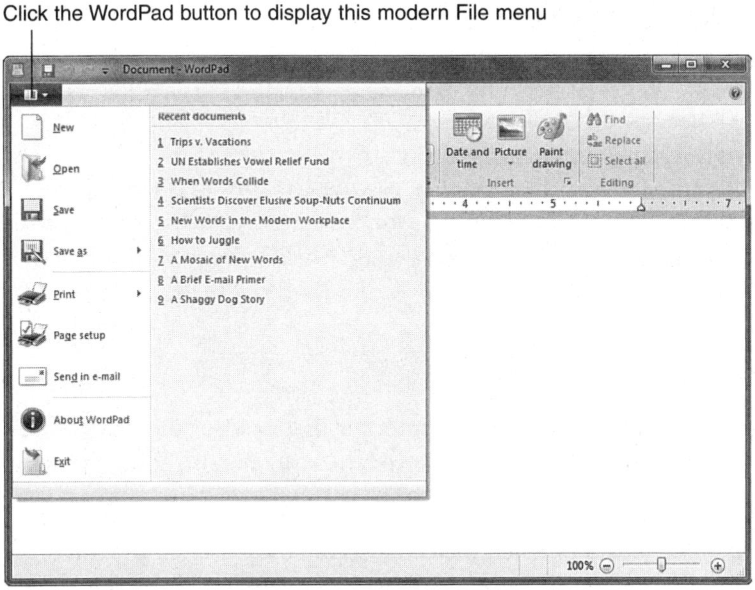

Click the WordPad button to display this modern File menu

Figure 4.1

You usually start a new document by displaying the File menu and selecting the New command.

The All-Important Save Command

Save your work as soon as you can and as often as you can.

Without even a jot of hyperbole, I'm telling you right here and now that this deceptively simple slogan is probably the single most important piece of advice that you'll stumble upon in this book.

Why all the fuss? Because when you work with a new document (or with an existing document), all the changes you make are stored temporarily in your computer's memory. The bad news is that memory is a fickle and transient medium that, despite its name, forgets all of its contents when you shut down Windows. If you haven't saved your document to your hard disk (which maintains its contents even when Windows isn't running and even if your computer is turned off), you lose all the changes you've made and it's impossible to get them back. Scary!

Look Out!

If your computer's memory doesn't go into clean slate mode until you shut down Windows, you may be wondering why you can't just wait to save until you're ready to close up shop for the night. If a power failure shuts off your system or if Windows crashes (these things happen, believe me), all your unsaved work is toast. By saving constantly, you greatly lessen the chance of that happening.

To guard against such a disaster, remember my "saving slogan" from before, and keep the following in mind:

◆ When you create a new document, save it as soon as you've entered any data that's worth keeping.

◆ After the new document is saved, keep right on saving it as often as you can. When I'm writing a book, I typically save my work every 30 to 60 seconds (I'm paranoid!), but a reasonable schedule is to save your work every 5 minutes or so.

Saving a New Document

Saving a new document takes a bit of extra work, but after that's out of the way, subsequent saves require only a mouse click or two. To save a new document, follow these steps:

1. Pull down the **File** menu and then click the **Save** command, or click the **Save** button in the program's toolbar. The program displays a Save As dialog box like the one shown in Figure 4.2.

Figure 4.2

The Save As dialog box appears when you're saving a new document.

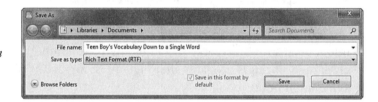

2. Use the **File name** text box to enter a name for your document. Note that the name you choose must be different from any other document in the folder. Also, Windows 7 lets you enter file names that are up to 255 characters long. Your names can include spaces, commas, and apostrophes, but not the following characters: \ | ? : * " < > .

3. Now use the **Save as type** drop-down list to choose the type of document you want to create. In the vast majority of cases you won't have to bother with this because the default type is best. Many programs can create different document types, however, and this capability often comes in handy.

4. Click the **Save** button. The program makes a permanent copy of the document on your hard disk.

Saving an Existing Document

After all that hard work saving a new document, you'll be happy to know that subsequent saves are much easier. That's because when you select the **File, Save** command, the program simply updates the existing hard disk copy of the document. This takes just a second or two (usually) and no dialog box shows up to pester you for information. Because this is so easy, there's no excuse not to save your work regularly. If you're a fan of keyboard shortcuts, here's one to memorize for the ages: press **Ctrl+S** to save your document. If you're a fan of toolbar buttons, click the **Save** toolbar button, instead.

Checking Out the Windows 7 Libraries

When you first open the Save As dialog box, the current folder is almost always one of the folders that Windows 7 refers to as a *library*. For example, in Figure 4.2's Save As dialog box, the current folder is the Documents library which, as you might figure, is a good place to store documents. Windows 7 comes with three other libraries—Music, Pictures, and Videos—and you can pretty much guess what types of files go in each library.

I highly recommend that you store all the stuff you create in one of these libraries, because they're designed to be a central storage area for all the files you create. Using libraries is a good idea for three reasons:

◆ It makes your documents easy to find because you know exactly where they are.

◆ When you want to back up your documents, you need to only select the libraries (rather than hunting around your hard disk for all your documents). (For more information about how to back up your documents, see the section in Chapter 21 titled "Step 6—Back Up Your Files.")

◆ The libraries are easy to get to: click the **Windows Explorer** icon in the taskbar to open the Libraries folder (see Figure 4.3), then double-click the icon for the library you want. (You can also select **Start** and then click an icon for a specific library: Documents, Pictures, or Music.)

Figure 4.3

Click the taskbar's **Windows Explorer** *icon to see Windows 7's library collection.*

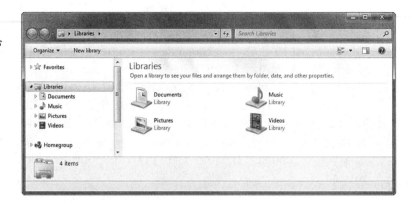

Using the Save As Command to Make a Copy of a Document

As you slave away in Windows 7, you sometimes find that you need to create a second, slightly different, copy of a document. For example, you might create a letter and then decide that you need a second copy to send to someone else. Rather than re-creating the entire letter from scratch, it's much easier to make a copy of the existing document and then change just the address and salutation.

The easiest way to go about this is to use the Save As command. This command is a lot like Save, except that it enables you to save the document with a new name or to a new location. (Think of it as the don't-reinvent-the-wheel command.) To use Save As to create a new document, follow these steps:

1. Open the original document (not a new one). (If you're not sure how to go about this, skip ahead to the section titled "Opening an Existing Document" to find out.)

2. Select the **File, Save As** command. The program displays the same Save As dialog box shown in Figure 4.2.

3. Either select a different storage location for the new document or enter a different file name (or both).

4. Click **Save.** The program closes the original document, makes a copy, and then opens the new document.

5. Make your changes to the new document (see the next section).

Getting It Right: Text Editing for Beginners

As you create your document, you have to delete text, move text chunks to different locations, and so on. To make your electronic writing life easier, it's crucial to get these basic editing chores down pat. To that end, here's a summary of some editing techniques you can use in most any program that deals with text (including Notepad, WordPad, and Windows Live Mail):

◆ **Highlighting text with the mouse.** Before you can do something to existing text, you need to *highlight* it. To highlight text with a mouse, click and drag the mouse over the characters you want. That is, you first position the mouse pointer a teensy bit to the left of the first character you want to highlight. Then you press and hold down the left mouse button and move the mouse to the right. As you do, the characters you pass over become highlighted. While you drag, you can also move the mouse down to highlight multiple lines. When you release the mouse button, the text remains highlighted.

◆ **Highlighting text with the keyboard.** To highlight text by using the keyboard, position the cursor to the left of the first character, hold down the **Shift** key, and then press the **right-arrow** key until the entire selection is highlighted. Use the **down-arrow** key (or even **Page Down** if you have a lot of ground to cover) when you need to highlight multiple lines.

> **Look Out!**
>
> If you highlight some text and then press a character on your keyboard, your entire selection will disappear and be replaced by the character you typed! (If you press the **Enter** key, the highlighted text just disappears entirely.) This is normal behavior that can cause trouble for even experienced document jockeys. To get your text back, immediately select the **Edit, Undo** command or press **Ctrl+Z**.

◆ **Copying highlighted text.** To make a copy of the highlighted text, select the **Edit, Copy** command. (Alternatively, you can also press **Ctrl+C** or click the **Copy** toolbar button). Then position the cursor where you want to place the copy, and select the **Edit, Paste** command. (Your other choices are to press **Ctrl+V** or click the **Paste** toolbar button.) A perfect copy of your selection appears instantly. Note that you can paste this text as many times as you need.

◆ **Moving highlighted text.** When you need to move something from one part of a document to another, you *could* do it by making a copy, pasting it, and then going back to delete the original. If you do this, however, your colleagues will certainly make fun of you, because there's an easier way. After you highlight what you want to move, select the **Edit, Cut** command (the shortcuts are pressing **Ctrl+X** or clicking the **Cut** toolbar button). Your selection disappears from the screen, but don't panic; Windows 7 saves it for you. Position the cursor where you want to place the text, and then select **Edit, Paste.** Your stuff miraculously reappears in the new location.

◆ **Deleting text.** Because even the best typists make occasional typos, knowing how to delete is a necessary editing skill. Put away the Wite-Out, though, because deleting a character or two is easier (and less messy) if you use either of the following techniques: position the cursor to the right of the offending character and press the **Backspace** key; or position the cursor to the left of the character and press the **Delete** key. If you have a large chunk of material you want to expunge from the document, highlight it and press the **Delete** key or the **Backspace** key.

Windows Wisdom

All this cut, copy, and paste moonshine is a bit mysterious. Where does cut text (or whatever) go? How does Windows 7 know what to paste? Does Windows 7 have some kind of digital hip pocket that it uses to store and retrieve cut or copied data? Truth be told, that's not a bad analogy. This "hip pocket" is actually a chunk of your computer's memory called the *clipboard.* Whenever you run the Cut or Copy command, Windows 7 heads to the clipboard, removes whatever currently resides there, and stores the cut or copied data. When you issue the Paste command, Windows 7 grabs whatever is on the clipboard and tosses it into your document.

◆ **To err is human, to undo divine.** What do you do if you paste text to the wrong spot or consign a vital piece of an irreplaceable document to deletion purgatory? Happily, Notepad, WordPad, and many other Windows 7 programs have an Undo feature to get you out of these jams. To reverse your most recent action, select the **Edit, Undo** command to restore everything to the way it was before you made your blunder. And, yes, there are shortcuts you can use: try either pressing **Ctrl+Z** or clicking the **Undo** toolbar button.

It's important to remember that most of the time the Undo command usually only undoes your most recent action. So if you delete something, perform some other task, and then try to undo the deletion, chances are the program won't let you do it. Therefore, always try to run **Undo** immediately after making your error. Note, however, that some programs are more flexible and will let you undo several actions. In this case, you just keep selecting the **Undo** command until your document is back the way you want it.

Closing a Document

Some weakling Windows programs (such as WordPad and Paint) allow you to open only one document at a time. In such programs, you can close the document you're currently working on by starting a new document, by opening another document, or by quitting the program altogether.

However, most full-featured Windows programs let you open as many documents as you want (subject to the usual memory limitations that govern all computer work). In this case, each open document appears inside its own window—called a *document window*, not surprisingly. These document windows have their own versions of the Minimize, Maximize, Restore, and Close buttons. Also, the name of each document appears on the program's Window menu, which you can use to switch from one document to another.

Because things can get crowded pretty fast, though, you probably want to close any documents you don't need at the moment. To do this, activate the document you want to close and select the **File, Close** command, or click the document window's **Close** button. If you made changes to the document since last saving it, a dialog box appears asking whether you want to save those changes. Click **Yes** to save, **No** to discard the changes, or **Cancel** to leave the document open. In most programs that support multiple open documents, you also can close the current document by pressing **Ctrl+F4.**

Opening an Existing Document

After you've saved a document or two, you often need to get one of them back on-screen to make changes or review your handiwork. To do that, you need to *open* the document by using any of the following techniques:

- ◆ **Use the Open dialog box.** Select the program's **File, Open** command. (Alternatively, press **Ctrl+O** or click the **Open** toolbar button.) Find the document you want to open, highlight it, and then click **Open.**

- ◆ **Use a library.** If you're using a Windows 7 library to store your stuff, you can open a document by displaying the folder (select **Start** and then click your user name), opening the appropriate library (such as Documents or Pictures), and then double-clicking the document's icon. If the appropriate application isn't running, Windows 7 will start it for you and load the document automatically.

◆ **Use the Search box.** Select **Start** and then start typing the name of the document in the Search box. When the name of the document shows up in the search results, click the document to open it.

Sending a Document to the Printer

The nice thing about printing in Windows 7 is that the basic steps you follow are more or less identical in each and every Windows program. After you learn the fundamentals, you can apply them to all your Windows applications. Here are the steps you need to follow:

1. In your program, open the document you want to print.

2. Select the **File, Print** command. You see a Print dialog box similar to the one shown in Figure 4.4 for the WordPad word processor.

   If your fingers are poised over your keyboard, you may find that in most applications pressing **Ctrl+P** is a faster way to get to the Print dialog box. If you just want a single copy of the document, click the **Print** toolbar button to bypass the Print dialog box and print the document directly.

Figure 4.4

WordPad's Print dialog box is a typical example of the species.

3. The options in the Print dialog box vary slightly from application to application, but you almost always see three things:

   ♦ A list for selecting the printer to use. In WordPad's Print dialog box, for example, use the **Select Printer** list to select the printer.

   ♦ A text box or spin box to enter the number of copies you want. In the WordPad Print dialog box, use the **Number of copies** text box.

   ♦ Some controls for selecting how much of the file to print. You normally have the option of printing the entire document or a specific range of pages. (WordPad's Print dialog box also includes a Selection option button that you can activate to print only the currently highlighted text.)

> **See Also**
>
> Before you can print, you may need to tell Windows 7 what type of printer you have. I tell you how to go about this in Chapter 6. See the section titled "Device Advice I: Installing Hardware."

4. When you've chosen your options, click the **Print** button to start printing (some Print dialog boxes have an **OK** button instead).

Keep watching the information area of the taskbar (the area to the left of the clock). After a few seconds (depending on the size of the document), a printer icon appears, as shown in Figure 4.5. This tells you that Windows 7 is hard at work farming out the document to your printer. This icon disappears after the printer is finished with its job. If you have an exceptionally speedy printer, this icon may come and go without your ever laying eyes on it. If the printer icon shows up with a red question mark icon superimposed on it, it means there's a problem with the printer.

Printer icon

Figure 4.5

The printer icon tells you that Windows 7 is printing.

The Least You Need to Know

- ◆ To forge a new document, select the **File, New** command, press **Ctrl+N,** or click the toolbar's **New** button.

- ◆ To save a document, select the **File, Save** command, press **Ctrl+S,** or click the toolbar's **Save** button. If you're saving a new document, use the Save As dialog box to pick out a location and a name for the document.

- ◆ You'll simplify your life immeasurably if you store all your files in the libraries provided by Windows 7.

- ◆ Press **Backspace** to delete the character to the left of the cursor; press **Delete** to wipe out the character to the right; press **Ctrl+Z** to undo your most recent mistake.

- ◆ To open a document, select the **File, Open** command, press **Ctrl+O,** or click the toolbar's **Open** button.

- ◆ To print a document, select the **File, Print** command, press **Ctrl+P,** or click the toolbar's **Print** button.

Chapter 5

Fiddling with Files and Folders

In This Chapter

♦ Exploring your files and folders with Windows Explorer

♦ Creating, selecting, copying, moving, renaming, deleting, and searching for files and folders

♦ Burning files to a CD

♦ Changing the file and folder view

♦ Sorting, grouping, stacking, and filtering files and folders

♦ A fistful of useful file and folder factoids

In Chapter 4, you learned that it's off-the-scale crucial to save your documents as soon and as often as you can. That way, you preserve your documents within the stable confines of your computer's hard disk. You also learned that it's best to use your user account libraries as the central storage locations for your stuff.

You learned, in other words, that your hard disk is a vital chunk of digital real estate. So, as a responsible landowner, it's important for you to tend your plot and keep your grounds well maintained. That's the purpose of this chapter, as it shows you how to use some of Windows 7's built-in tools to work with your hard disk's files, folders, and libraries. You get the scoop on creating new files, folders, and libraries; copying and moving files from one folder to another; renaming and deleting files and folders; and much more.

Navigating with Windows Explorer

The Windows 7 program you use to explore your computer and its files and folders is called, appropriately enough, Windows Explorer. There are several ways you can coax this program onto the screen, but for the purposes of this chapter we want to use Windows Explorer to navigate your personal files and folders. Therefore, start Windows Explorer by clicking the **Windows Explorer** icon in the taskbar. (If you feel like more of a workout, click **Start** to open the Start menu and then click the icon for your user name.)

You end up eyeballing a window that looks suspiciously like the one shown in Figure 5.1.

Figure 5.1

Use Windows Explorer to check out your computer's files and folders.

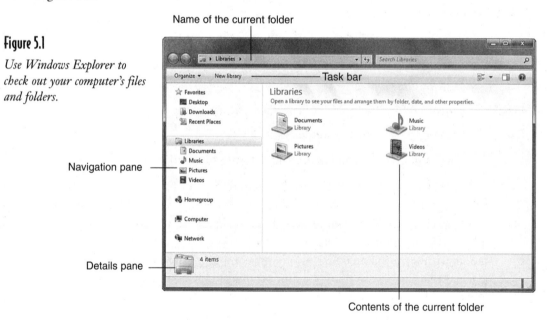

Windows Explorer's job is to display the contents of a given folder so that you can check out what's in the folder or muck about with those contents in some way (such as renaming one of your files; see the "Renaming a File or Folder" section later in this chapter). So Windows Explorer is set up to help you do just that. First, notice that the address bar shows you the name of the current folder that Windows Explorer is displaying. In this case, the name of the folder is Libraries, which displays the following icons for your user libraries:

◆ **Documents.** Use this folder to store all the documents that don't fit into more specific folders such as Music and Pictures.

◆ **Music.** Use this folder to store your music and sound files.

◆ **Pictures.** Use this folder to store your digital images and photos.

◆ **Videos.** Use this folder to store your digital videos and movies.

Navigating to a File

One of the most common chores associated with Windows Explorer is navigating through various folders and *subfolders* (folders within folders) to get to a particular file. How you go about this depends on where the file you want is housed:

◆ For any file, first open your user folder (select **Start** and then click your user name) and then double-click the folder that contains the file. For example, if the file is a video, you'd double-click the **Videos** folder.

◆ For a file in the Documents, Pictures, or Music folder, you can navigate to the folder directly by selecting **Start** and then clicking **Documents, Pictures,** or **Music.**

If the file you want resides in the folder you opened, then rest easy because your navigation chores are done. Unfortunately, you rarely get off so easy in Windows 7. That's because it's quite common to have a file squirreled away in a subfolder. For example, take a look at Figure 5.2, where I've opened the Music library on my system. As you can see, this folder consists of nothing but subfolders.

Figure 5.2

You may need to navigate several subfolders to get to the file you want.

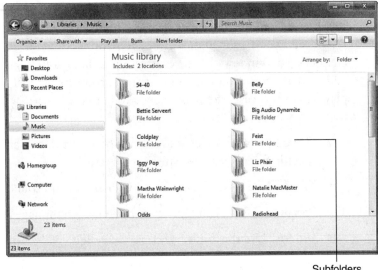

Subfolders

If the file you want is in one of the subfolders, double-click the subfolder's icon. Repeat this as often as necessary to reach the file you want. For example, Figure 5.3 shows the results on my system after I double-clicked the Be Good Tanyas folder (this is the name of a band) and then double-clicked yet another subfolder named Blue Horse (this is the name of a Be Good Tanyas album).

Figure 5.3

Opening a folder reveals the contents of that folder.

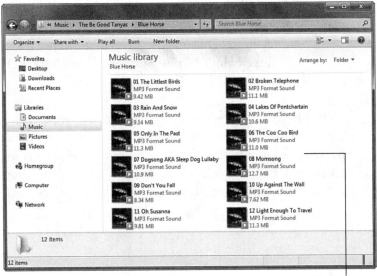

Music files

Getting Around in Windows Explorer

As you navigate from one subfolder to the next, notice that the Windows Explorer address bar changes as you do. For example, when I start out in my user folder, the address bar just shows Libraries. If I then open the Music subfolder, the address changes to Libraries > Music (see Figure 5.2). When I open the Be Good Tanyas folder and then the Blue Horse folder, the address bar looks like this (see Figure 5.3):

Libraries > Music > Be Good Tanyas > Blue Horse

In other words, each time you go down into another subfolder, Windows Explorer shows you the "path" you've taken to get there by tacking on the name of the current subfolder.

However, the address bar path isn't just to let you know where the heck you are (although that's welcome info when you're buried three or four levels deep and are up to your digital armpits in subfolders). Even better, you can use the path to navigate your way to other folders. There are two basic techniques:

◆ **To navigate back.** Click any item in the path to jump directly to that folder. For example, in the path shown in Figure 5.3, clicking Music would take me directly to the Music folder.

◆ **To navigate sideways (sort of).** Click the little arrow to the right of one of the path folders. This displays a list of all the available subfolders, as shown in Figure 5.4. Click one of those subfolders to jump directly to it.

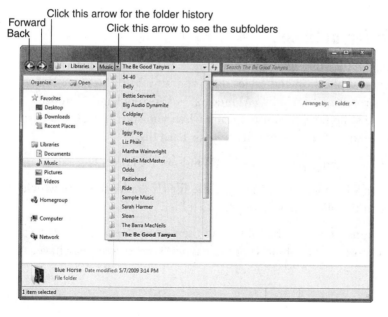

Forward
Back

Click this arrow for the folder history
Click this arrow to see the subfolders

Figure 5.4

Clicking an arrow beside a folder in the path reveals the available subfolders that you can leap to directly.

Here are a few other pointers for navigating from folder to folder in Windows Explorer:

♦ To go back to the previous folder, you can also click the **Back** button (pointed out in Figure 5.4). There are also a couple of keyboard shortcuts that you can use: **Backspace** and **Alt+Left Arrow.**

♦ After you've gone back to a previous folder, you can move forward again by clicking the **Forward** button. (The keyboard shortcut for this is **Alt+Right Arrow.**)

♦ Rather than stepping back and forward one folder at a time, you can leap over multiple folders in a single bound. To do this, click the **downward-pointing arrow** beside the **Forward** toolbar button. In the list that appears, click the folder you want to visit.

Workaday File and Folder Maintenance

Now that you and Windows Explorer are getting acquainted, it's time to put this digital domestic to good use. Specifically, the next few sections show you how to use Windows Explorer to perform no fewer than eight workaday chores for files and folders: creating, copying, moving, renaming, previewing, deleting, compressing, and burning.

Creating a New File, Folder, or Library

If you want to manufacture a shiny new file for yourself, the best way to go about it is to run the appropriate application and select that program's **File, New** command. (Note, too, that most programs—including Windows 7's WordPad and Notepad accessories—create a new file for you automatically when you start them.) You then select the **File, Save** command to save the file to your hard disk.

However, it *is* possible to create a new file within Windows Explorer. Here's how:

1. Open the folder in which you want to create the file. If you're not sure which folder to use, open the all-purpose Documents folder.

2. Right-click an empty section of the folder and then select **New.** This displays another menu with at least the following file flavors (your system may have more):

- ◆ **Folder.** This command creates a new subfolder.

- ◆ **Shortcut.** This command creates a shortcut, which acts as a pointer to a program or document. (I tell you more about shortcuts in Chapter 20.)

- ◆ **Bitmap Image.** This command creates an image file of the same type as those you create using Windows 7's Paint program. (See Chapter 7.)

- ◆ **Contact.** This command creates a new contact to whom you can send e-mail. (See Chapter 17.)

- ◆ **Journal Document.** This command creates a new Windows Journal file, which you use to jot handwritten notes if you have a digital pen and a Tablet PC.

- ◆ **Rich Text Document.** This command creates a slightly different type of WordPad file.

- ◆ **Text Document.** This command creates a plain text file that's the same as what you create using the Notepad program.

- ◆ **Compressed (zipped) Folder.** This command creates a special folder that compresses multiple files into a smaller package suitable for sending over the Internet. I talk more about this type of file later in this chapter in the section "Creating a Compressed Folder."

- ◆ **Briefcase.** This command creates a Briefcase, which is a special folder you use for transferring files between two computers.

3. Select the type of file you want. Windows 7 creates the new file and displays a generic (read: boring) name—such as "New Text Document"—in a text box.

4. Type a name that makes sense, and then press **Enter** or click some of the blank real estate inside the window.

If you misspell the file name or simply change your mind, just hold tight and I'll teach you how to change the file name later in this chapter. If Windows 7 complains about a particular character that you try to use, leave it out for now. I'll tell you about the rules for file names a bit later. (In both cases, see the "Renaming a File or Folder" section later in this chapter.)

What about creating a brand-spanking-new library if you find that the standard issue Documents, Music, Pictures, and Videos libraries don't cut the digital mustard? Sure, why not? For example, you might want a separate library for recorded TV shows, or a library for files related to some all-important project you're working on. Whatever your need, here are the steps to follow to forge a new library:

1. In any Windows Explorer window, click **Libraries** in the Navigation pane.

2. Click **New Library** in the taskbar. Windows 7 coughs up a new library and displays a generic name.

3. Type a name for the library and then press **Enter.**

Your library is sadly empty right now, but I'll show you a bit later how to fill it up (check out "Including a Folder in a Library").

Selecting Files and Folders

Before getting to the rest of the file-maintenance fun, you need to know how to select the files or folders that you want to horse around with.

Let's begin with the simplest case: selecting a single file or folder. This is a two-step procedure:

1. Open the folder that contains the file or subfolder you want to mess with.

2. In the folder contents list, click the file's icon.

So far, so good. However, there will be plenty of times when you need to deal with two or more files or folders. For example, you might want to herd several files onto a flash drive or memory card. Rather than dealing with the files one at a time, you can do the whole thing in one fell swoop by first selecting all the files and then moving (or copying, or whatever) them as a group. Windows 7 offers the following methods:

- ◆ **Selecting consecutive items.** If the files or folders you want to select are listed consecutively, say "Ooh, how convenient!" and then do this: select the first item, hold down the **Shift** key, select the last item, and then release **Shift.** Windows 7 kindly does the dirty work of selecting all the items in between.

- ◆ **Selecting nonconsecutive items.** If the files or folders you want to select are listed willy-nilly, say "Oy!" and then do this: select the first item, hold down the **Ctrl** key, click each of the other items, and then release **Ctrl.** If you click something by accident, don't sweat it: just click it again to "deselect" it.

- ◆ **Selecting all items.** If you want to select everything inside a folder, either select **Organize, Select all** or press **Ctrl+A.**

Copying and Moving a File or Folder

A copy of a file or folder is an exact replica of the original that you store on another part of your hard disk or on a removable disk (such as a flash drive or memory card). Copies are useful for making backups or if you want to transport a file or folder to another computer.

Note, too, that the location of the files and folders you create isn't set in stone. If you're not happy with the current location, there's no problem moving a file or folder somewhere else.

> **Windows Wisdom**
>
> Windows 7 has a special Send To menu that contains commonly used destinations, such as your desktop or a flash drive. To see this menu, right-click an item and then click **Send To.** Now select the destination you want, and Windows 7 copies the selected items lickety-split.

Here are the steps to follow:

1. Select the files or folders you want to transport.

2. Either select **Organize** or right-click any selected item and then click one of the following commands:

   Copy. This is the command to choose if you're copying files or folders.

   Cut. This is the command to choose if you're moving files or folders.

3. Navigate to the destination folder or disk drive.

4. Select **Organize, Paste,** or right-click an empty part of the folder and then click **Paste.**

Including a Folder in a Library

I've mentioned Windows 7's new libraries a few times now, but I haven't bothered to properly introduce them to you. Fortunately, there's not much to know: a library is a special folder that acts as a collection of folders from different parts of your system. For example, a library might include a folder from your hard drive, another folder from an external hard drive connected to your computer, and even a third folder from some other computer on your network! The library displays all the files from the various locations as a single collection, so a library is a handy way to consolidate related files from different places.

It's important to bear in mind that Windows 7 doesn't actually "consolidate" all those files in the sense that it moves them into the library. No, instead the library just "displays" the files while leaving them in their original locations. This is why the tall-forehead types at Microsoft insist on referring to libraries as *virtual* folders.

This means that when you include a folder in a library, all you're doing is telling Windows 7 to display the contents of the folder in the library; the actual folder isn't tampered with in any way.

To include a folder in a library, you've got a couple of ways to go:

- Open the library, look for the **Includes** label in the upper-right corner, and then click the *X* **library location** link (where *X* is the number of existing folders in the library). In the Library Locations dialog box that shows up, click **Add,** select the folder you want to include, and then click **Include folder.**

- Navigate to the folder you want to include in the library, click the folder icon, and then click **Include in library** in the taskbar. In the list of libraries that appears (see Figure 5.5), click the library you want to use.

Figure 5.5

*Select the folder and then click **Include in library** to add it to one of your Windows 7 libraries.*

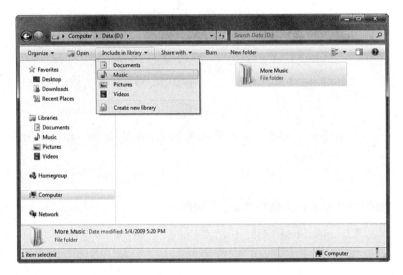

Renaming a File or Folder

Windows 7 supports file and folder names up to about 255 characters long, so you don't have to settle for boring monikers on the files and folders you create. If you don't like a name, feel free to rename it. Follow these simple steps to rename a file or folder:

1. Select the file or folder you want to rename. (You can work with only one item at a time for this.)

2. Run the **Organize, Rename** command, or press **F2**. Windows 7 creates a text box around the name.

3. Edit the name as you see fit.

4. When you're done, press **Enter.**

Bear in mind that although Windows 7 likes long file names and accepts most keyboard characters (including spaces), there are nine characters that are strictly verboten: * | \ : " < > ? / .

Previewing a File

When you want to eyeball what's in a file, you normally double-click it to load it into whatever program is associated with that type of file. That's easy enough, I suppose, but it does seem like overkill if all you want is a quick peek at what's going on inside a file.

Fortunately, Windows 7 gets this and will happily display a preview of a file in the Details pane when you select the file in Windows Explorer. Not bad, but the preview is a bit teensy. If you really want to get a proper gander at the file, don't mess around: select the file and then click the **Show the Preview pane** icon in the taskbar. Figure 5.6 shows an example of the Preview pane at work.

Show the Preview pane

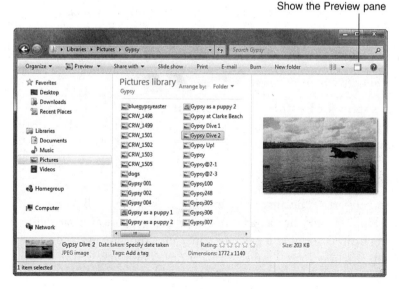

Figure 5.6

Windows Explorer with its Preview pane on the job.

Deleting a File or Folder

Although most of today's hard disks boast a mammoth amount of real estate, you could still run out of room one day if you don't delete the debris that you no longer use. Deleting unwanted files and folders is fairly easy:

1. Select the files or folders you want to blow away.

2. Run the **Organize, Delete** command, or press **Delete.** Windows 7 asks whether you're sure you want to consign these poor things to the cold, cruel *Recycle Bin.*

3. Say "But of course, my good fellow!" and click **Yes.**

def•i•ni•tion

The **Recycle Bin** is a special storage area that Windows 7 has set aside for deleted files and folders.

Windows Wisdom

Another way to delete a file or folder is to drag it from Windows Explorer and drop it on the desktop's Recycle Bin icon.

What happens if you nuke some crucial file or folder that you'd give your right arm to have back? Assuming you need your right arm, if the deletion was the last thing you did, you don't have to bother with the Recycle Bin. Just press **Ctrl+Z** to salvage the file. (Note that it will be placed back in the folder where you originally deleted it, not necessarily in the folder you are currently in.) In fact, Windows 7 is only too happy to let you reverse the last *10* actions you performed (press **Ctrl+Z** up to 10 times).

If the Undo command doesn't get the job done, then Windows 7 offers an alternative method to save your bacon: the Recycle Bin. Here's how it works:

1. Double-click the desktop's **Recycle Bin** icon. The folder that appears contains a list of all the stuff you've expunged recently.

2. Select the files or folders you want to recover.

3. Select **Restore this item** (or **Restore the selected items,** if you're rescuing multiple files or folders). Windows 7 marches the items right back to where they came from. Whew!

How the heck can the Recycle Bin restore a deleted file?

Good question. You can get part of the answer by looking at the Recycle Bin icon on your Windows 7 desktop. It looks like a garbage can, and that's sort of what the Recycle Bin is. Think about it: if you toss a piece of paper into the garbage, there's nothing to stop you from reaching in and pulling it back out. The Recycle Bin operates the same way: it's really just a special hidden folder (called Recycled) on your hard disk. When you delete a file, Windows 7 actually moves the file into the Recycled folder. So restoring a file is a simple matter of "reaching into" the folder and "pulling out" the file. The Recycle Bin handles all this for you (and even returns your file without wrinkles and coffee grounds). However, just like when you hand your trash out to the garbage man, after you empty the Recycle Bin (by right-clicking the desktop's **Recycle Bin** icon and then clicking **Empty Recycle Bin**), there is no retrieving the lost files.

Creating a Compressed Folder

When you download files from the Internet, they often arrive as Zip files. These are compressed archive files that contain one or more files that have been compressed for faster downloading. In Windows 7, a Zip file is called a *compressed folder.* Why a "folder"? Because a Zip file contains one or more files, just like a regular folder. As you'll see, this makes it easy to deal with the files within the Zip, and it enables Windows 7 to offer a few useful compression and decompression features.

To create a Zip file, there are two methods you can use:

♦ Select the items you want to store in the Zip file, right-click any of the selected items, and then click the **Send To, Compressed (zipped) Folder** command. Windows 7 creates a Zip file with the same name as the last file you selected.

♦ Create a new, empty Zip file by right-clicking an empty section of the folder and then clicking the **New, Compressed (zipped) Folder** command. Windows 7 creates a new Zip file with an active text box. Edit the name and press **Enter.** You can then drag the files you want to archive and drop them on the Zip file's icon.

To see what's inside a Zip file, double-click it. Windows 7 opens the file as a folder that shows the files within the Zip as the folder contents.

To extract all of the files, click the **Extract all files** icon to display the Select a Destination and Extract Files dialog box. Type the destination for the extracted files, or click **Browse** to select the destination using a dialog box. When you're good and ready, click **Extract.** Windows 7 extracts the files and then displays a new window showing the destination folder.

> **Windows Wisdom**
>
> What if you only want to extract one or two of the files? Not a problem. You can do this by copying the file or files in the compressed folder and then pasting them inside the destination folder. See "Copying and Moving a File or Folder," earlier in the chapter, for the details.

"Burning" Files to a CD or DVD Disc

In the world before Windows 7, burning files to a CD was an exercise in utter confusion: you had to know the difference between CD-R and CD-RW (and even CD±RW, just to be cruel), what types of discs your CD burner could take, the subtle differences between "recordable" and "rewritable," and on and on. And burning DVDs with those older versions of Windows? In your dreams!

Windows 7 changes all that by enabling you to burn files to any type of disc you want, and you can even add and remove files from any type of disc at any time. A miracle? No, it's just that now Windows 7 has figured out a way to treat a CD or DVD disc like a hard disk, flash drive, or any other file storage medium.

So if you have a CD or DVD burner attached to your computer, Windows 7 should recognize it and be ready to burn at will. To try this out, you first have to set up the disc by following these steps:

1. Insert a CD disc into your CD burner (or a CD or DVD into your DVD burner). (If the AutoPlay window shows up, click **Close** to get rid of it.)

2. In Windows Explorer, open the **Computer** branch in the Navigation pane and then click the CD or DVD drive. The first time you do this, the Burn a Disc dialog box appears.

3. Type a disc title, make sure the **Like a USB flash drive** option is selected, and then click **Next.** Windows 7 formats the disc to make it ready to receive files. This may take awhile, so groom your dog while you wait.

When all that malarkey is done (again, if you're pestered by the AutoPlay window, say "Grrr" and click **Close**), you're ready to get down to the burning thing by following these steps:

1. In Windows Explorer, select the files or folders you want to burn to the disc.

2. Click **Burn** in the taskbar and then click **Copy Here.** Windows 7 copies the files to the disc.

3. Repeat steps 1 and 2 until you've sent all the files you want to the disc.

4. Open the disc in Windows Explorer.

5. Click **Close session.** Windows 7 finalizes the disc.

6. Click **Eject.** Windows 7 spits out the disc.

Finding a File in That Mess You Call a Hard Disk

Bill Gates, Microsoft's co-founder, used to summarize his company's mission of easy access to data as "information at your fingertips." We're still a long way off from that laudable goal, but there are a few things you can do to ensure that the info you need is never far away:

◆ **Store stuff in your user profile.** The most inefficient way to store your documents is to scatter them hither and yon around your hard disk. A much better approach is to plop everything in a single place so that you always know where to look for things. The perfect place for this is the user profile (that is, your Windows 7 user account) that Windows 7 provides for you, which consists of all your libraries.

◆ **Use subfolders to organize your documents.** Stuffing stuff into your user folder is a good idea (if I do say so myself), but you shouldn't just cram all your files into that one folder. Instead, create subfolders to hold related items. As you saw earlier, Windows 7 starts you off with subfolders (actually, libraries) named Documents, Pictures, Music, and Videos. Feel free to add other subfolders for things such as letters, memos, projects, presentations, spreadsheets, tirades to the editor, bad poetry, and whatever other categories you can think of.

◆ **Give your files meaningful names.** Take advantage of Windows 7's long file names to give your documents useful names that tell you exactly what's inside each file. A document named "Letter" doesn't tell you much, but "Letter to A. Gore Re: Inventing the Internet" surely does.

◆ **Dejunk your folders.** Keep your folders clean by deleting any junk files that you'll never use again.

If you're like most people, then you'll probably end up with hundreds of documents, but if you follow these suggestions, finding the one you need shouldn't be a problem. Even so, there will be times when you don't remember exactly which document you need, or you might want to find all those documents that contain a particular word or phrase. For these situations, Windows 7 offers a Search feature that can help you track down what you need. The next few sections show you various ways to use Search.

Searching from the Start Menu

One of the nifty features in Windows 7 is the welcome capability to perform quick-and-not-even-remotely-dirty searches from the friendly confines of the Start menu. Really! Click **Start** to fire up the Start menu, and then let your gaze wander down to the lower-left corner of the menu. See the box that says "Search programs and files"? That's the ticket, right there.

What you do is use this box—it's called the Instant Search box, in case you want to impress your friends—to type in a search word or phrase. As you type, Windows 7 immediately begins scouring your system for the following:

◆ Documents, pictures, music files, or videos with names or contents that include your search text.

◆ Other files—such as e-mail messages, Internet Explorer favorites, or contacts—with names or contents that include your search text.

◆ Programs with names that include your search text.

If it finds any matches, Windows 7 replaces the list of recently used programs with a new list that displays those matches as well as the See more results links (see Figure 5.7), which you can click to see a complete list of the items that match your search text.

If you see the program or file you want, click it to open it.

Figure 5.7

Windows 7 lets you perform on-the-fly searches right from the Start menu.

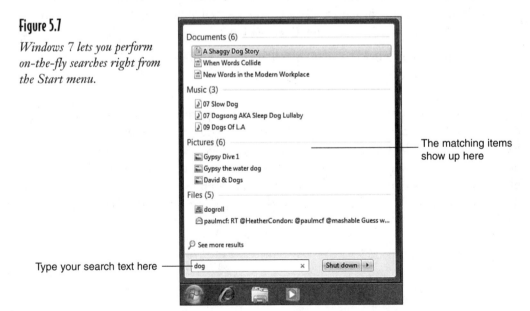

Type your search text here

The matching items show up here

As-You-Type Searching

The Start menu search scours *all* of your documents and programs. However, you may need to perform a more targeted search. For example, suppose you have thousands of music files or hundreds of digital images. How do you find a document needle in such an electronic haystack?

Windows 7's solution is to also enable you to perform as-you-type searches in any folder by using the Instant Search box that appears in the upper-right corner of every Windows Explorer window (below the Minimize, Maximize, and Close buttons). Again, you just type your search word or phrase in the box, and then Windows Explorer displays those files in the current folder with names, contents, or properties that match your search text, as shown in Figure 5.8.

See Also

To learn about document properties, check out the section "Adding Comments, Keywords, and Other Document Data," later in this chapter.

Windows Wisdom

You can also run as-you-type searches in some Windows 7 programs, including Windows Live Photo Gallery (see Chapter 7), Windows Media Player (see Chapter 9), and Windows Live Mail (see Chapter 17).

Type your search text here

Figure 5.8

You can also run as-you-type searches in any folder window.

The matching items show up here

Points of View: Changing the Windows Explorer View

In the standard Windows Explorer view, each file and folder is displayed using a smallish icon and the name of the item. However, there are also several other views you can try on for size. You access these views by pulling down the **Views** menu, which displays the slider shown in Figure 5.9. You change the view by dragging the slider up and down in the list. There are six main choices in the list:

- **Extra Large Icons.** This view displays files and folders using humongous icons arranged in rows.

- **Large Icons.** This view also displays files and folders arranged in rows, but uses a more reasonable icon size.

- **Medium Icons.** This view displays files and folders using smaller versions of the icons arranged in rows.

- **Small Icons.** This view displays files and folders using even smaller, cuter versions of the icons arranged in columns.

- **List.** This view displays a simple list of the icons arranged in columns.

- **Details.** This view displays the files and folders using a five-column list, and the columns you see depend on the folder. For example, in the Documents folder, for each file and folder you see the Name, the Date Modified (the date and time it was last changed), Type (such as WordPad Document), Authors, and Tags (for these last two, see the next section, "Adding Comments, Tags, and Other Document Data").

Hacking Windows

There are more columns available in Details view. In fact, there's actually a truckload of them, and you can see many of them by right-clicking any column header. In the list that appears, click a column name to toggle it on and off. You can also click **More** to see the complete list.

- **Tiles.** This is the default icon view that displays the files in columns and with the document name, type, and size.

- **Content.** This view displays each item in its own row with a few extra details about the item's contents.

Views slider

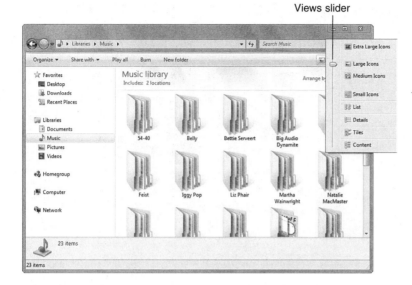

Figure 5.9

Use Windows Explorer's Views slider to change the folder view.

Adding Comments, Keywords, and Other Document Data

When you put something in the fridge at work, it's often helpful to write something like "Do not move my cheese!" on the bag. Similarly, when you drop a folder full of work on a colleague's desk, you might attach a sticky note that says "I need this yesterday." In other words, in the real world we often augment stuff with comments, labels, our name, and so on.

In the digital world, Windows 7 offers something similar by giving you easy access to various properties for any document. These properties include the author's name, the title (as opposed to the file name), comments about the document, and even a rating (from 1 to 5 stars). Since, taken together, these properties describe the document more fully, Alpha Geeks called them *metadata*—literally, data about data.

When you select a document in Windows Explorer, some of the document's properties appear in the Details pane at the bottom of the window, as shown in Figure 5.10. (To see more properties, click and drag the top edge of the Details pane up to increase the size of the pane.)

Figure 5.10

Windows Explorer's Details pane shows some of the properties for the selected document.

Some of the properties are set in stone and can't be changed. However, plenty of them are edit-friendly, including the title, tags, rating, and comments. To edit a document's metadata, click the field in the Preview pane, type the data, and then click **Save.**

Organizing Your Documents

The great thing about document properties is that they not only give you more info about each document, but they're also ridiculously useful. For example, you saw earlier that you can search for stuff using document properties. Oh, but there's more you can do with properties, lots more.

First, switch the folder into Details view as described earlier. With that done, you can now perform the following tasks:

- **Sort documents.** This changes the order that the documents appear in the folder. To sort files in ascending order (A-Z) based on the values in a property, click the property's column header (Name, Date Modified, Tags, etc.). Clicking the same header again switches the sort to descending (Z-A).

- **Arrange documents.** This organizes the files into separate stacks based on the values in a property. A stack is a kind of folder that, when you open it, displays just those files that contain that particular property value. To create the stacks for a property, pull down the **Arrange by** menu and then click a property (such as Rating or Tag).

♦ **Filter documents.** This tells Windows Explorer to display only those files that have the property value or values that you specify. When you pull down the property's menu, you see a list of the unique property values (in Figure 5.11, these are the values such as Bitmap Image, JPEG Image, and TIFF Image). Each value has a check box beside it. Activate the check box for a property value, and Windows Explorer hides all the files except those that have that property value. You're free to activate or deactivate as many of these check boxes as you need.

Click here to display the property menu

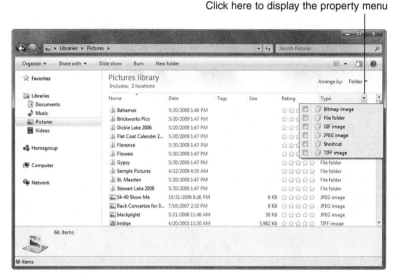

Figure 5.11

Use the menu associated with each property to sort, group, stack, and filter documents.

The Least You Need to Know

♦ You select a file or folder by clicking it. To select multiple files or folders, hold down **Ctrl** and click each item.

♦ To move stuff, select the files or folders, right-click the selection, and then click **Cut.** To copy, instead, select the files or folders, right-click the selection, and then click **Copy.** Display the destination folder, right-click it, and then click **Paste.**

♦ To burn data to a formatted CD or DVD, select the files and folders and then click the **Burn** button in the taskbar.

♦ To search for a file, type your search word or phrase in the Search box that appears either in the Start menu or in a folder window.

♦ To change the icon view, pull down the **Views** slider and then drag the slider to choose the view you prefer.

Chapter 6

Installing and Removing Programs and Devices

In This Chapter

- ◆ Installing and removing chunks of Windows 7
- ◆ Installing and removing software programs
- ◆ Step-by-step procedures for installing all kinds of devices
- ◆ Installing specific devices such as printers, modems, joysticks, and scanners
- ◆ Saying *adios* to devices you no longer need

It's one thing to understand that the PC is a versatile beast that can handle all kinds of different programs and devices, but it's quite another to actually install the stuff. This chapter will help by showing you exactly how to install Windows 7 components, software programs, and devices on your machine. For good measure, you also learn how to uninstall all those things, just in case they don't get along with your computer.

The Welcome Wagon: Installing a Program

As you work through this book, you'll see that Windows 7 comes stocked with a decent collection of programs, some of which are first-rate (such as Internet Explorer and Windows Media Player) and some of which are merely okay (such as Paint and WordPad). Also, most PC manufacturers are kind enough to stock their machines with a few extra programs.

However, it's a rare computer owner who's satisfied with just these freebies (or even wants them in the first place). Most of us want something better or faster or just plain *cooler*. If that describes you and you decide to take the plunge on a new program, this section shows you how to install it in Windows 7. To get you started, the next section shows you how to install new Windows 7 components.

Installing a Windows 7 Component

Like a hostess who refuses to put out the good china for just anybody, Windows 7 may not have installed all of its components automatically. Don't feel insulted; Windows is just trying to go easy on your hard disk. The problem, you see, is that some of the components that come with Windows 7 are software behemoths that will happily usurp acres of your precious hard-disk land. In a rare act of digital politeness, Windows bypasses these programs (as well as a few other nonessential tidbits) during a typical installation. If you want any of these knickknacks on your system, you have to tell Windows 7 to install them for you.

How you go about this depends on whether the component you want to install is a Windows 7 feature (that is, a program that comes on the Windows 7 installation disc) or a Windows Live Essentials program (that is, an extra program that you download from the web). The next two sections provide the not-so-gory details.

Installing a Windows 7 Feature

The good news about installing features is that Windows 7 makes it easy to add any of those missing pieces to your system without having to dig out the installation disc (wherever it may be) or (shudder) trudge through the entire Windows installation routine. That's because when Windows 7 was foisting itself upon your PC, it was thoughtful enough to also deposit the files necessary to install the features on your hard drive. They reside in a special folder in a compressed format so they don't take up much room. You must tell Windows 7 to decompress them, which sounds hard, but it's not. You just have to follow these steps:

1. Select **Start, Control Panel** to rustle up the Control Panel window.

2. Click **Programs.** Windows 7 displays the Programs window.

3. Click **Turn Windows features on or off.** The Windows Features dialog box appears, as shown in Figure 6.1.

Figure 6.1

The Windows Features dialog box helps you add the bits and pieces that come with Windows 7.

4. Activate the check box beside the component you want to turn on. (If a component has a plus sign (+), it means it has multiple subcomponents. Click the plus sign to see those subcomponents.)

5. Click **OK.**

Installing Windows Live Essentials Programs

Windows Live Essentials is a collection of programs that Microsoft makes available on the web for downloading to your computer. These programs include Mail (for working with e-mail; see Chapter 17), Photo Gallery (for viewing and editing digital photos; see Chapter 7), and Movie Maker (for editing digital video; see Chapter 10).

To get your mitts on these programs, you need to connect to the Internet (as explained oh-so-carefully in Chapter 15), download them, and then install them. Fortunately, Windows 7 uses an installation program to handle most of the dirty work for you automatically, so you need only follow these steps:

1. Select **Start, Getting Started, Get Windows Live Essentials.** Internet Explorer opens up and heads for the Windows Live Essentials page. (If this is the first you've seen of this Internet Explorer business, see Chapter 16 for a crash course.)

2. Click **Download.** Internet Explorer displays the File Download—Security Warning dialog box.

3. Say "Chill, dude!" and click **Run.** Now you're pestered by the User Account Control dialog box.

4. Say "When will it end?" and click **Yes.** After a minute or two, you come face-to-face with the Windows Live window shown in Figure 6.2.

> **Windows Wisdom**
>
> If you don't see the Get Windows Live Essentials command anywhere, not to worry: start Internet Explorer yourself and send it to the following address: http://download.live.com.

Figure 6.2

Use this window to decide which Windows Live Essentials programs you want to shoehorn into your PC.

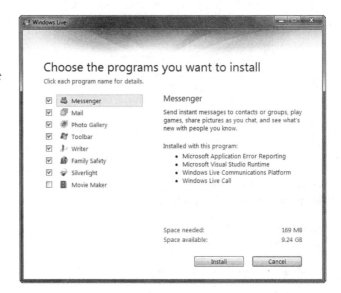

5. Activate the check box beside each program you want to install. (If you're not sure about a particular program, click it to see a description.)

6. Click **Install.** Windows 7 installs your selected programs.

Installing a New Program

The built-in Windows 7 programs (and the not-quite-built-in Windows Live Essentials programs) do the job as long as your needs aren't too lofty. However, what if your needs *are* lofty, or if you're looking to fill in a software niche that Windows 7 doesn't cover (such as a spreadsheet program, a database, or an action game)? In that case, you need to go outside the Windows box (literally!) and purchase the appropriate program. (This often means going to a computer store, but you can also purchase software over the Internet.)

After you have the program, your next chore is to install it. This means you run a "setup" routine that makes the program ready for use on your computer. Most setup procedures perform the following tasks:

♦ Create a new folder for the program.

♦ Copy any files that the program needs to run to the new folder and to other strategic folders on your hard disk.

♦ Tweak Windows 7 as needed to ensure that the program runs properly.

Windows Wisdom
I recommend that you accept the default values offered by the install program (unless you *really* know what you're doing). In particular, if the program gives you a choice of a "typical" or a "custom" installation, go the "typical" route to save yourself time and hassle. You can always go back and install additional components for the specific program later. (See "Changing a Program's Installed Components," later in this chapter.)

How you launch this setup routine depends on how the program is distributed:

♦ **If the program is on a disc:** After you insert the disc, Windows 7 automatically looks for an installation program. If it finds one, it displays the AutoPlay dialog box with an option that says something like "Run SETUP.EXE." Click that option to get the installation under way.

◆ **If you downloaded the program from the Internet:** In this case, you end up with the downloaded file on your hard disk. Be sure this file resides in an otherwise-empty folder and then double-click the file. This either launches the setup routine or it "extracts" a bunch of files into the folder. If the latter happens, look for an application file named Setup (or, more rarely, Install), and then double-click that file.

◆ **For all other cases:** If you have a disc-based program for which Windows 7 can't find an installation program, or a program distributed on some other removable medium such as a flash drive, start Windows Explorer, open the drive, and then double-click the installation program (usually called Setup or Install).

From here, follow the instructions and prompts that the setup routine sends your way. (This procedure varies from program to program.)

Hacking Windows _____

Sometimes installing a program can wreak havoc on your system. The quickest way to recover from a bad installation is to restore your system to the way it was before you ran the setup program. The only way to do that is to set a *restore point* just before you run the setup program. A restore point is a kind of digital snapshot of your computer's current configuration. If things go awry, you can tell Windows 7 to consult that snapshot and revert the system to what it was before the rogue program did its damage. To learn how to set and use restore points, see chapters 21 and 22.

Changing a Program's Installed Components

When you install most programs, the setup software puts the entire program onto your computer. However, some larger programs (such as Microsoft Office) will only install some of their components. If you find you're missing something when working with the program, follow these steps to install the component you need:

1. Select **Start, Control Panel** to crank up Control Panel.

2. Click **Programs.** Windows 7 displays the Programs window.

3. Click **Programs and Features.** Windows 7 displays a list of the programs installed on your computer.

4. Click the program you want to work with.

5. Click the **Change** button (or, in some cases, the **Uninstall/Change** button).

6. What happens from here depends on the program. For example, you may be asked to insert the program's installation disc. Eventually, you should see an option that says something like **Modify** or **Add or Remove Features.** Make sure you select that option, which means you'll eventually see a list of features that you can add to the program. Look for the feature you want and select it.

That last step is detail challenged, I know, but every program has its own way of doing things, so you'll just have to see what the program throws your way.

The Bum's Rush: Removing a Program

Most programs seem like good ideas at the time you install them. Unless you're an outright pessimist, you probably figured that a program you installed was going to help you work harder, be more efficient, or have more fun. Sadly, many programs don't live up to expectations. The good news is that you don't have to put up with a loser program after you realize it's not up to snuff. You can *uninstall* it (completely remove a program from your computer) so that it doesn't clutter up your Start menu, desktop, hard disk, or any other location where it might have inserted itself.

Uninstalling a Windows 7 Feature

You've seen how Windows 7 makes it easy to bring new Windows 7 components in from the cold. What happens, however, if you grow tired of a particular component's company? For example, if faxing just seems so twentieth century, you might want to get rid of the Fax Services component that you never use.

Happily, showing this and other Windows 7 components to the door is just as easy as installing them. And as an added bonus, lopping off some of Windows' limbs serves to free up hard disk space, giving you more room for *really* important games—uh, I mean, applications. As you might expect, removing Windows 7 components is the opposite of adding them:

1. Select **Start, Control Panel** to call up the Control Panel window.

2. Click **Programs.** Windows 7 displays the Programs window.

3. Click **Turn Windows features on or off.** The Windows Features dialog box appears.

4. Deactivate the check box beside the component you want to nuke.

5. Click **OK.**

Uninstalling a Windows Live Essentials Program

Okay, so you installed Silverlight or Family Safety from Windows Live and you *still* don't know what the heck they do. No problem! You can ditch them and any other Windows Live Essential program that's dead to you. Here's how:

1. Select **Start, Control Panel** to crank up Control Panel.

2. Click **Programs.** Windows 7 displays the Programs window.

3. Click **Programs and Features.** Windows 7 displays a list of the programs installed on your computer.

4. Click **Windows Live Essentials.**

5. Click the **Uninstall/Change** button. The Windows Live window appears after a minute or two.

6. Select the **Uninstall** option and then click **Continue.** Windows Live displays a list of the Essentials programs taking up space on your computer.

7. Activate the check box beside each program you want to throw out.

8. Click **Continue.** Windows Live sends the programs packing.

Giving a Program the Heave-Ho

If you have a Windows application that has worn out its welcome, this section shows you a couple of methods for uninstalling the darn thing so that it's out of your life forever. The good news is that Windows 7 has a feature that enables you to vaporize any application with a simple click of the mouse. The bad news is that this feature is only available for some programs.

To check whether it's available for your program, follow these steps:

1. Select **Start, Control Panel** to launch Control Panel.

2. Under **Programs,** click the **Uninstall a program** link. Windows 7 displays a list of the programs installed on your computer.

3. Click the program you want to work with.

4. Click the **Uninstall** button (or perhaps **Uninstall/Change**).

5. What happens next depends on the program. You may see a dialog box asking you to confirm the uninstall, or you may be asked whether you want to run an "Automatic" or "Custom" uninstall. For the latter, be sure to select the **Automatic** option. Whatever happens, follow the instructions on the screen until you return to the Add or Remove Programs window.

Didn't see the program in the Installed Programs list? All is not lost because there's still one more place to check: the program's home base on the Start menu. Select **Start, All Programs** and then open the program's menu (if it has one). Look for a command that includes the word "Uninstall" (or, less likely, "Remove"). If you see one, great—click it to launch the uninstall procedure.

Windows Wisdom
Don't be surprised if the uninstall routine doesn't wipe out absolutely everything for a program. If you created any documents, customized the program, or moved its Start menu items to a new location, the uninstall program leaves behind a few scraps.

Device Advice I: Installing Hardware

Software installation is usually a painless operation that often requires just a few mouse clicks on your part. Hardware, however, is another story. Not only must you attach the device to your machine (which might even require that you remove the cover to get inside the computer), but you also have to hope that Windows 7 will recognize the device and set it up correctly.

To ensure that your device and Windows 7 get along famously, check the box to see whether it says anything about being compatible with Windows 7. If you do, then you shouldn't have any problems. If the box tells you that the device was designed for Windows Vista, then you'll still probably be okay.

Understanding Hardware Types

Although thousands of devices are available, and dozens of device categories, I like to organize devices according to how you attach them to the computer. From this point of view, there are four types to worry about:

♦ **External plug-in devices.** These are devices that use some kind of cable to plug into a *port* in the back of the PC. These devices include keyboards, mice, joysticks, modems, printers, speakers, and monitors. These kinds of devices are easy to install if you remember one thing: the computer's ports each have a unique

def•i•ni•tion

A **port** is a computer receptacle into which you plug the cable for a device.

shape, and the cable's plug has a shape that matches one of those ports. So, there's usually only one possible place into which any cable can plug. The exception to this is if the back of the computer has two ports with identical configurations. That just means your machine offers two of the same port type, so you can plug your device into either one.

- ◆ **PC Card (PCMCIA) devices.** These types of devices are the easiest to install because they simply slip into any one of the computer's PC card slots (or *sockets*, as they're called). Note, however, that these slots are almost always found only on notebook computers.

- ◆ **Internal disk drives.** These are the toughest devices to install, not only because you have to get inside your computer, but also because there are many steps involved. Your best bet here is to take the machine to a computer service center or bribe a nearby computer geek into doing the job for you (a can of Red Bull often does the trick).

- ◆ **Internal circuit boards.** These are cards that plug into slots inside your computer. There are circuit boards for all kinds of things, including sound cards, graphics cards, and network cards. Again, you should get someone who knows what he or she is doing to install these kinds of devices for you.

Running the Add a Device Wizard

Your device and your computer are now shacked up, but they're not married yet. To get a full relationship going, Windows 7 has to install a tiny bit of software called a *device driver.* This miniprogram has the code that operates (drives) the device, so it acts as a kind of middleman between the device and Windows 7.

In the best of all possible worlds, after you've attached the device (and, if necessary, restarted your computer), Windows 7 recognizes the new limb and displays a message telling you that it has detected the new hardware, as shown in Figure 6.3. (This is my favorite Windows message because it means I have little if any work to do from here. An under-your-breath "Yes!" is the appropriate reaction to seeing this message.) Windows 7 then proceeds to install the device driver and any other software required to make the device go. This is automatic, for the most part, and when all is said and done (well, done, anyway; nothing much is said during this procedure), you see the message shown in Figure 6.4. However, you may occasionally be asked a few simple questions to complete the setup. In particular, you might see the Found New Hardware Wizard, which leads you through the installation of a device driver. (If this is the first time you've come across one of these wizard dudes, all you need to know is that a wizard is a series of dialog boxes designed to take you step-by-step through some task. There is, unfortunately, no magic involved.)

Figure 6.3

When you plug in and turn on your device, in an ideal world Windows 7 will recognize it right away and begin installing the necessary software bits.

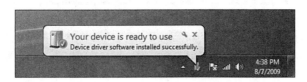

Figure 6.4

When Windows 7 has done its device duty, you see this message.

If, for some reason, Windows 7 doesn't automatically recognize your new device, all is not lost. If your device came with an installation CD, insert the disc and run the setup program.

If you don't have a disc, there's still hope for your device. That's because Windows 7 comes with a hardware helper called the Add a Device Wizard, which scours every nook and cranny of your system to look for new stuff. Here's how it works:

1. Select **Start, Devices and Printers.** The Devices and Printers window shows up with a list of the major hardware doodads connected to your computer (see Figure 6.5).

2. Click **Add a device.** The Add a Device Wizard leaps into the fray and immediately begins scouring your computer and your network for new devices. If it finds any, it displays an icon for each one (see Figure 6.6).

Figure 6.5

Windows 7's new Devices and Printers window gives you a handy list of your PC's major hardware bits and pieces.

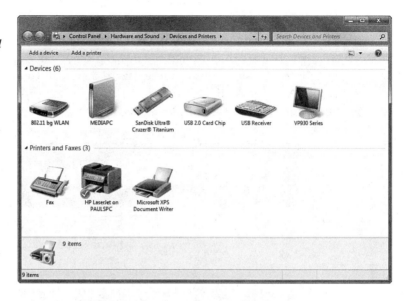

Figure 6.6

If the Add a Device Wizard locates your hardware, it displays an icon for it.

3. Click the device you want to install and then click **Next.**

What happens from here depends on the device. Ideally, Windows 7 will simply install the device, no questions asked. However, you might have to jump through a hoop or two. For example, if you're installing a wireless keyboard, you're usually given a code to type to complete the "pairing." Follow the instructions that show up on the screen.

Device Advice II: Removing Hardware

If you have a device you no longer use, or if you get a better device for your birthday, you need to remove the old device from your computer and then let Windows 7 know that it's gone. The exception to this is if the device supports Plug and Play. If it does, then Windows 7 recognizes that the device is gone and it adjusts itself accordingly. Otherwise, you need to do it by hand:

1. Select **Start, Control Panel** to open the Control Panel window.

2. Click **Hardware and Sound.**

3. Click **Device Manager.**

4. Click the plus sign (+) beside the hardware category you want to work with. For example, if the soon-to-be-toast device is a network adapter, open the **Network adapters** branch.

5. Click the device and then select the **Action, Uninstall** command. Windows 7 states the obvious and tells you that you're about to remove the device.

6. Say "Duh!" and click **OK.** Windows 7 wastes no more of your time and removes the device from the list.

7. Click **Close.**

8. If the device is an internal component, shut down your computer and then remove the device. Otherwise, just unplug the device.

The Least You Need to Know

◆ Most software discs support AutoPlay, so the installation program runs automatically after you insert the disc.

◆ Use the Windows Features dialog box (**Start, Control Panel, Programs, Turn Windows features on or off**) to help you install and remove Windows 7 components.

◆ Use Control Panel's **Installed Programs** window (**Start, Control Panel, Programs, Programs and Features**) to help you change or remove third-party programs.

◆ To ensure the easiest hardware configuration, buy only devices that are both Plug and Play—compatible and Windows 7—compatible.

◆ When installing an external device, remember that its cable can plug into only a single, complementary port on the back of the computer.

◆ If Plug and Play doesn't work, insert the disc that came with the device.

Part 2

Windows 7 at Home

This being the twenty-first century and all, computers in the home are as common as the weeds in your neighbor's yard. Just think: all that cursing and fuming you direct toward your work computer can now be continued in the privacy of your own home. But that's not the only advantage to having a home machine. Now you can perform many personal tasks that aren't appropriate at the office: making drawings, manipulating photos, playing and copying music, and making digital movies. And the best news is that Windows 7 is set up to handle all of those leisure-time activities right out of the box. The chapters in Part 2 show you how to perform these and other home-sweet-home tasks.

Chapter 7

Playing with Images

In This Chapter

- ◆ GIF, JPEG, and other image format acronyms
- ◆ Viewing image thumbnails and slide shows
- ◆ Converting an image from one format to another
- ◆ Printing images
- ◆ Taking a stroll through the Windows Live Photo Gallery

Windows has enabled us to go beyond the workaday world of letters and memos to documents that positively cry out for image enhancement: business presentations, flyers, newsletters, and web pages, to name only a few. Fortunately, Windows has various tools that let you create images from scratch, mess around with existing images, and capture digital images from an outside source (such as a scanner). None of these tools are good enough for professional artists, but they're more than adequate for amateur dabblers whose needs aren't so grandiose. This chapter gives you a bit of background about images and tells you how to work with image files.

The Alphabet Soup of Picture File Formats

There's certainly no shortage of ways that the world's computer geeks have come up with over the years to confuse users and other mere mortals. But few things get the man (or woman) on the street more thoroughly bamboozled than the bewildering array of file formats (also known as file types) that exist in the digital world. And perhaps the worst culprit is the picture file category, which boasts an unseemly large number of formats. My goal in this section is to help you get through the thicket of acronyms and minutiae that characterize picture file formats, and to show you how to simplify things so that they actually make sense.

> **Windows Wisdom**
>
> Throughout this chapter and in other parts of the book I'll use the terms *picture, image,* and *graphic* interchangeably.

Before you go any further into this file format business, you might enjoy taking a step or two in reverse to consider the bigger picture: what is a file format and why do we need so many of them? I like to look at file formats as the underlying structure of a file that's akin to a car's underlying structure. The latter is a collection of metal and plastic bits that form the frame, axles, suspension, engine, and other innards that determine how the car performs. A file format is similar in that it consists of a collection of bits and bytes that determines how the picture is viewed. As you'll see, some formats are better suited for displaying photos, while others have a better time with line drawings.

The sigh-of-relief-inducing news is that even though the computing world is on speaking terms with dozens of different image formats, Windows 7 is conversant with only five:

- **Bitmap.** This is the standard image file format used by Windows 7. It's good for color drawings, although its files tend to be on the large side. Bitmap image files use the .bmp extension, so these files are also referred to sometimes as BMP files.

- **GIF.** This is one of the standard graphics file formats used on the Internet's World Wide Web. It's only capable of storing 256 colors, so it's suitable for relatively simple line drawings or for images that use only a few colors. The resulting files are compressed, so they end up quite a bit smaller than bitmap files.

- **JPEG.** This is the other standard graphics file format that you see on the World Wide Web. This format can reproduce millions of colors, so it's suitable for photographs and other high-quality images. JPEG (it's pronounced JAY-peg) stores images in a compressed format, so it can knock high-quality images down to a manageable size while still retaining some picture fidelity. (However, the more you compress the image, the poorer the image quality becomes.)

♦ **PNG.** This is a relatively new file format that's becoming more popular on the Internet. It's a versatile format that can be used with both simple drawings and photos. For the latter, PNG supports compression to keep images relatively small. (And, unlike JPEG, the PNG compression doesn't reduce the quality of the image.)

♦ **TIF.** This format is often used with image scanners and digital cameras because it does a great job of rendering photos and other scanned images. The downside is that this format doesn't usually compress the images in any way, so it creates *huge* files. (Note that this file format sometimes goes by the name of TIFF instead of just TIF.)

Hacking Windows _____

The features available with the Pictures library (discussed in the next section) can also be applied to other folders where you store images. To do this, launch Windows Explorer and open the folder you want to work with. Select **Organize, Properties** to display the Properties dialog box. In the Customize tab, the **What kind of folder do you want?** group enables you to apply a template to the folder. This means that you can convert your folder into a special folder that uses the same features as Pictures (as well as other special folders, such as Music). In the **Optimize this folder for** list, choose the template type that best suits the content of your folder. For example, if your folder contains mostly images, choose the **Pictures** template. Note, too, that you can tell Windows 7 to use the template with all the folder's subfolders by activating the **Also apply this template to all subfolders** check box.

So which one should you use when creating your own image files? That depends:

♦ If you're creating a drawing that you'll print out or work with only on your computer, use the bitmap format.

♦ If you're creating a simple drawing that you'll be publishing to the World Wide Web, use GIF.

♦ If you're creating a more complex drawing that you'll be publishing to the web, use PNG.

♦ If you're scanning an image or downloading a photo from a digital camera for printing or for editing only on your computer, use TIF.

◆ If you're scanning an image or downloading a photo from a digital camera for e-mailing or publishing to the web, use JPEG.

A Tour of the Pictures Library

Back in Chapter 4, I told you about your main user account folder and mentioned that it's the perfect spot to store the documents you create. If you've been doing that, then you no doubt have noticed that your user folder includes a library named Pictures, and you probably guessed that this subfolder is where you ought to be hoarding your picture files. That's certainly true, but not just because of the library's name. No, Pictures is the place to squirrel away your images because it's a special library that "understands" picture files and so offers you some extra features that are designed specifically for messing around with images:

◆ It offers "thumbnail" versions of each image that show you not only the name of each file, but also give you a miniature preview of what each image looks like.

◆ It enables you to see a "preview" of any image, from which you can then rotate the image, print it, and perform a few other tasks.

◆ It enables you to view all your images one by one in a kind of "slide show."

◆ It enables you to set up a particular image as your Windows 7 desktop background.

Most of the rest of this chapter takes you through the specifics of these features. Before getting to that, however, it's probably a good idea to review just how you get to the Pictures library. Windows 7 offers two methods:

◆ Select **Start, Pictures.**

◆ If you're currently in your main user folder (Libraries), double-click the icon for the **Pictures** library.

All Thumbs: Using the Thumbnail View

When you arrive at the Pictures folder, you'll probably see the files arranged something like those shown in Figure 7.1. That is, instead of a boring (and only marginally useful) icon, each file shows a minipreview of the image contained in the file.

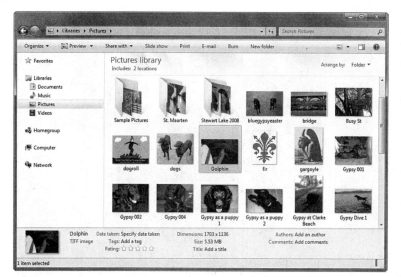

Figure 7.1

By default, Windows 7 displays a small preview of each graphics file in the Pictures folder.

In this handy way of looking at things, the little preview of each image is called a *thumbnail*, and Windows 7 displays image thumbnails no matter which view you use (even Details).

If you want to know details about an image—such as its height and width in pixels, its file type, and its size—click the file. The details then appear in the Preview pane at the bottom of the window (see Figure 7.1).

def•i•ni•tion

A **thumbnail** is a scaled-down preview of an image or other type file.

You should also note at this point that when you click an image file to select it, the folder window displays several image-related links, including **Preview** and **Slide Show.** I'll talk about these links as you work through this chapter.

A Closer Look: Previewing a Picture

If you prefer to work with one image at a time, the image preview feature might be just what you're looking for. To activate it, select the image you want to work with and then click **Preview** (an alternative method is to double-click the image). This loads the picture into the Windows Photo Viewer window, shown in Figure 7.2.

Figure 7.2

*Click **Preview** to display the selected file in the Gallery Viewer.*

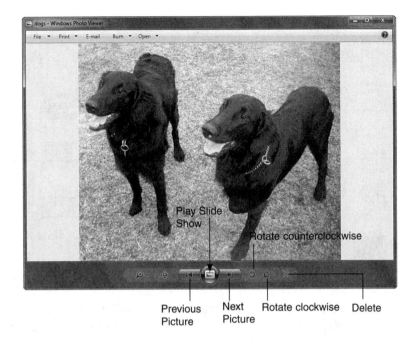

Figure 7.2

*Click **Preview** to display the selected file in the Gallery Viewer.*

This window shows you a larger version of the image and is also festooned with a few icons at the bottom:

◆ **Previous.** Click this icon to display the previous image in the Pictures folder.

◆ **Play Slide Show.** Click this icon (or press **F11**) to start a slide show of the files in the Pictures folder (more on this later in the chapter).

◆ **Next.** Click this icon to display the next image in the Pictures folder.

◆ **Rotate Clockwise.** Click this icon to rotate the image clockwise by 90 degrees. Note that this rotation doesn't apply only to the preview; Windows 7 applies it to the file itself.

◆ **Rotate Counterclockwise.** Click this icon to rotate the image counterclockwise by 90 degrees. Again, this change is applied to the file itself.

◆ **Delete.** Click this icon (or press **Delete**) to send the image to the Recycle Bin.

> **Windows Wisdom**
>
> You can also jump to the previous picture by pressing the **left-arrow key** on your keyboard. For the next picture, press the **right-arrow key.** Note, too, that you can also rotate the image counterclockwise by pressing **Ctrl+,** (comma) and you can rotate the image clockwise by pressing **Ctrl+.** (period).

Converting an Image to Another Format

One of the most common image chores is converting a file from one format to a different format. For example, I mentioned earlier that the GIF and JPEG formats are the ones most commonly used on the World Wide Web. If you've scanned an image or digital photo to the TIF format (see Chapter 8) and you want to place it on a website, then you need to convert the image to JPEG. Similarly, if you've created a drawing in Paint and saved it in the bitmap (BMP) format, then you need to convert it to GIF.

Here are the steps to trudge through to perform these and other image format conversions:

1. In the Pictures folder, select the image you want to convert.

2. Select **Preview, Paint.** (Alternatively, right-click the image and then click **Edit.**) Windows 7 hoists the image into the Paint program.

3. Select **File, Save As** to display the Save As dialog box.

4. Use the **Save as type** list to choose the new file format you want (see Figure 7.3).

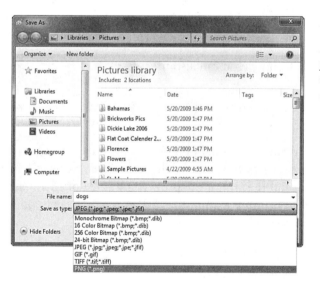

Figure 7.3

In the Save As dialog box, pick out the new image format using the options in the Save as type list.

5. (Optional) Select a new destination folder and change the **File name.**

6. Click **Save.**

Setting Up an Image Slide Show

For its next trick, the Pictures library also offers a "slide show" view. This means that Windows 7 displays a full-screen version of the first file, waits a few seconds, displays the second file, and so on. To activate the slide show, you have two choices:

◆ In the Pictures folder, click the **Slide Show** link.

◆ In the Windows Photo Viewer window, click the **Play Slide Show** icon.

Note that you can also control the slide show by hand by right-clicking the screen to display the following commands:

◆ **Play.** Restarts a paused slide show.

◆ **Pause.** Pauses the slide show.

◆ **Next.** Displays the next image (you can also press **right arrow**).

◆ **Back.** Displays the previous image (you can also press **left arrow**).

◆ **Shuffle.** Shows the pictures in random order.

◆ **Loop.** Starts over from the beginning when it has run through all the pictures.

◆ **Slide Show Speed.** These commands control the playback speed: Slow, Medium, or Fast.

◆ **Exit.** Stops the slide show (you can also press **Esc**).

Printing Pictures

Printing a picture—particularly a digital photo—is a bit different from printing a text document because in most cases you want to choose a different print layout depending on the size of the image and the size of the print you want. For that reason, Windows 7 includes a special photo printing feature that makes it easy to get your photo hard copies. Here's how it works:

1. Open the Pictures folder.

2. Select the pictures you want to print.

3. Click **Print.** Windows 7 displays the Print Pictures dialog box shown in Figure 7.4.

4. If you have more than one printer, use the **Printer** list to select the printer you want to use.

5. Use the **Paper size** list to select the size of the paper you're using.

6. Use the **Quality** list to select the printout quality, in dots per inch (the higher the number, the better the quality, but the more ink it uses).

7. Use the **Layout** list to select the print size you want. When you select a different layout, the Print preview box shows you what your printed image will look like.

8. Click **Print.** Windows 7 sends your image (or images) to the printer.

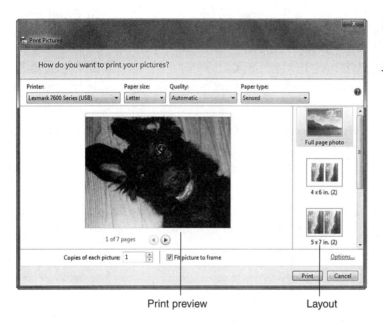

Print preview   Layout

Figure 7.4

Use this dialog box to set up your photo printing options.

Browsing Images in the Windows Live Photo Gallery

Over the past few years, digital cameras have become the photography tool of choice for everyone from novices to professionals. And it's no wonder, since digitals give photographers tremendous freedom to shoot at will without having to worry about processing costs or running out of film. If there's a downside to all this photographic freedom, it's that most of us end up with huge numbers of photos cluttering our hard drives. The result has been a thriving market for third-party programs to import, view, and manage all those digital images.

The bad news is that Windows 7 doesn't come with such a program. Boo! Ah, but wait, it *does* offer a new program called Windows Live Photo Gallery as part of the Windows Live Essentials that I droned on about back in Chapter 6. This program can import images and videos from a camera, scanner, removable media, the network, or the web. You can then view the images, add metadata such as captions and tags, rate the images, search for images, and even apply common fixes to improve the look of photos. You can also burn selected images to a DVD disc. It's actually a really good program, so head back to Chapter 6 (specifically, the "Installing Windows Live Essentials Programs" section) to learn how to get Windows Live Photo Gallery onto your system.

Once you've done that, you launch the program by selecting **Start, All Programs, Windows Live, Windows Live Photo Gallery.** Windows Live Photo Gallery immediately begins gathering the images onto your hard disk. (If you see a dialog box asking if you want to use Windows Live Photo Gallery to open certain file types, such as JPG and TIF, select **Yes.**) You can also import images by hand using the following **File** menu commands:

◆ **Import from a camera or scanner.** This command launches the Scanner and Camera Wizard, which takes you step-by-step through the process of importing images from a digital camera, a document scanner, or a removable medium (see Chapter 8 for more info).

◆ **Include a folder in the gallery.** This command displays the Include a Folder in the Gallery dialog box, which enables you to hand-pick images from a specific folder.

Grouping Images

By default, Windows Live Photo Gallery groups the images by folder, but you can change that by right-clicking any empty part of the Windows Live Photo Gallery window and then clicking the **Group By** command, which enables you to group on a number of properties, including Date Taken, File Size, Image Size, and Camera (see Figure 7.5).

Figure 7.5

*Right-click any empty spot and then click **Group By** to see all the ways you can group your images.*

Tag, You're It: Image Metadata and Tagging

You can also create your own metadata for each image. Windows Live Photo Gallery enables you to change four properties: Caption, Date Taken, Rating, and Tag. The Tag property enables you to add one or more descriptive keywords—called *tags*—to the image, similar to what you do in photo-sharing websites such as Flickr (www.flickr.com).

Follow these steps to add one or more tags to an image:

1. Click the image you want to work with.

2. Click **Info** to display the Info pane.

3. Click **Add descriptive tags.**

4. Type the tag and press **Enter.**

5. Repeat steps 3 and 4 to add other tags to the image.

Figure 7.6 shows an image with a few tags added. Notice, as well, that the tags you create also appear in the Tags list, which enables you to filter the images based on the tag you select. (You can also filter images based on the Date Taken and Ratings properties.)

Figure 7.6

You can apply descriptive tags to each of your images.

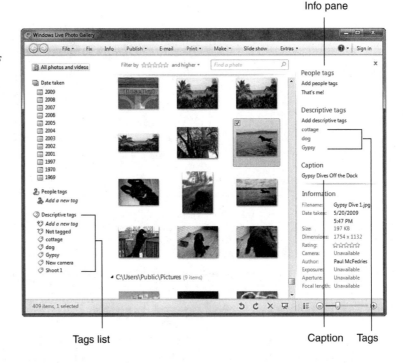

Info pane

Tags list · · · Caption · · Tags

Quick Fixes: Making Image Adjustments

Windows Live Photo Gallery also comes with a limited set of tools for altering images. Click the image you want to work with and then click **Fix** to display the image in the window shown in Figure 7.7. Here you get the following tools:

◆ **Adjust exposure.** Click this tool to expose (bad pun intended) sliders to adjust the **Brightness, Contrast, Shadows,** and **Highlights.**

◆ **Adjust color.** Click this tool to see sliders for **Color Temperature, Tint,** and **Saturation.**

◆ **Straighten photo.** Click this tool if your photo is a bit lopsided. Click and drag the slider to tilt the photo a wee bit one way or the other until your image is straight and true.

◆ **Crop photo.** Click this tool if you want to remove some extraneous material from your photo, particularly around the edges. Click and drag the corners or sides of the box that appears over your image so that the box encloses just the part of the image you want to keep, then click **Apply.**

◆ **Adjust detail.** Click this tool if you want to fine-tune a small piece of the image. Click and drag the image to bring the problematic part into view, then use the **Sharpen** slider to sharpen the area. You can also click **Analyze** and then use the **Reduce Noise** button to remove noise (extraneous bits that make the image appear grainy or not sharp) from the detail.

◆ **Fix red eye.** Click this tool to get rid of that crazed red-eye look that sometimes mars an otherwise good photo. Click and drag the mouse over the red eye and Windows Live Photo Gallery will fix it for you automatically. Thanks!

◆ **Black and white effects.** Click this tool and then click one of the half-dozen swatches to apply a black-and-white effect to the photo. (No, I have no idea why this is part of the "Fix" tool.)

If, like me, you really don't know what the heck you're doing when it comes to things like "color temperature" and contrast, you can also click **Auto adjust** to have Windows Live Photo Gallery make the adjustments for you. When you're done, click **Back to gallery** to return to Windows Live Photo Gallery.

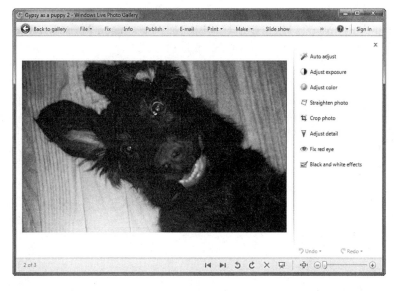

Figure 7.1

*Click **Fix** to adjust image qualities such as brightness, contrast, and tint.*

Setting a Picture as the Desktop Background

The Windows 7 desktop usually comes with a fairly spiffy background image. However, you may find that you get bored with it after awhile or that you have a picture of your own that you'd prefer to use. Either way, it's no problem to change the desktop background to any picture on your system. In fact, it takes just two measly steps:

1. In the Windows Live Photo Gallery, right-click the file that contains the image you want to use.

2. Select **Set as Desktop Wallpaper.**

Capturing a Picture of the Screen

In Chapter 8 you'll learn how to get images into your computer by using a scanner or digital camera. Another way to get an image without having to draw anything is to "capture" what's on your screen. You have two ways to go about this:

◆ To capture the entire screen, lock, stock, and taskbar, press your keyboard's **Print Screen** key. (Depending on your keyboard, this key may be labeled **Print Scrn, PrtScn, PrtSc,** or some other variation on this theme.)

◆ If you want to capture only whatever is in the active window, press **Alt+Print Screen.**

Either way, you can then toss the captured image onto your hard disk by launching Paint (select **Start, All Programs, Accessories, Paint**) and selecting **Edit, Paste.** If Paint complains that the image you're pasting is too large, click **Yes** to enlarge your drawing to fit the image.

The Least You Need to Know

◆ If you're working only on your computer, the best formats to use are bitmap for drawings and TIF for photos. If you're going to e-mail pictures or publish them on the web, use GIF for drawing and JPEG for photos.

◆ In the Pictures folder, click **Preview** to load the selected image into the Gallery Viewer.

- To convert the selected image, select **Preview, Paint** to load it into Paint, select **File, Save As,** and then use the **Save as type** list to choose the new format.

- Select **Start, All Programs, Windows Live Photo Gallery** to run the Windows Live Photo Gallery program.

- To grab a screen shot, press **Print Screen** to capture an image of the full screen, or **Alt+Print Screen** to capture an image of just the active window.

Chapter 8

Getting Images from Scanners and Digital Cameras

In This Chapter

◆ Telling Windows 7 about your scanner or digital camera

◆ Making sure your scanner or camera works properly

◆ Getting images from the scanner or camera to your computer

◆ Working directly with the photos stored in a digital camera

It used to be that the only way to get an image onto your computer was either to create it yourself or to grab a prefab pic from a clip-art collection or photo library. If you lacked artistic flair, or if you couldn't find a suitable image, you were out of luck.

Now, however, getting images into digital form is easier than ever, thanks to two graphics gadgets that have become more affordable. A *document scanner* acts much like a photocopier in that it creates an image of a flat surface, such as a photograph or a sheet of paper. The difference is that the scanner saves the image to a graphics file on your hard disk instead of on paper. A *digital camera* acts much like a regular camera in that it captures and stores an image of the outside world. The difference is that the digital camera stores the image internally in its memory instead of on exposed film. It's then possible to connect the digital camera to your computer and save the image as a graphics file on your hard disk.

The big news is that Windows 7 understands both types of doohickeys and often identifies them by a single generic name: *imaging devices* (since both produce image files). Windows 7 comes with support for a variety of scanners and cameras, so getting your digital images from out here to in there has never been easier, as you see in this chapter.

Installing a Scanner or Digital Camera

Windows 7 offers a number of options for installing scanners and digital cameras. Make sure the device is turned on and connected to your computer, and then try the following:

◆ **Rely on Plug and Play.** Most of today's crop of scanners and cameras are Plug and Play compatible. This means that as soon as you turn on and connect the device to your computer, Windows 7 should recognize it and set it up for you automatically. Do you have one or more USB ports on your computer? If so, then if you're looking to buy a new scanner or digital camera, you'll save yourself a lot of grief if you make sure that the device supports USB. (Fortunately, it's a rare camera that doesn't support USB these days.) The advantages to this are two-fold: first, it means that Windows 7 will almost certainly recognize and install the device as soon as you plug it in to the computer; second, it will take far less time to transfer images from the device to your computer.

◆ **Use the Scanners and Cameras window.** If Windows 7 doesn't recognize your scanner or camera, it may just need a bit of convincing. To do that, select **Start**, type "scanners" in the Search box, and then click **View cameras and scanners** in the search results. When the Scanners and Cameras window shows up, click **Add Device** (you need to enter your Windows 7 administrator credentials at this point; see Chapter 11) to get the Scanner and Camera Installation Wizard on the job. Click **Next** to see a list of scanner and digital camera manufacturers and models. Find your camera or scanner in this list, click **Next,** and follow the instructions on the screen.

◆ **Install the device software.** Any scanner or digital camera worth its salt will come with software for setting up the device. If the first two options don't work, try installing the software.

When your scanner or camera is installed, you'll probably see an icon for it not only in the Scanners and Cameras window, but also in the Devices and Printers window (select **Start, Devices and Printers**), as shown in Figure 8.1. Note, however, that if you turn off or disconnect the device, then it no longer appears in either window.

Windows Wisdom

Bear in mind that, despite its name, the Scanners and Cameras window doesn't show some digital cameras, for some reason. So don't panic if your camera doesn't show up there.

Figure 8.1

The Devices and Printers window contains icons for each imaging device installed on your system.

You should also know that Windows 7 considers a digital camera to be a type of file storage device. This makes sense because a digital camera uses some kind of memory module or disk to store the digital photos you've taken. The kicker is that because the camera stores files, Windows 7 treats it as a folder attached to your computer, so it appears in the Computer folder (select **Start, Computer**), as shown in Figure 8.2. Later in this chapter I'll show you how to use the Computer folder to get at the images stored in your camera.

Figure 8.2

Windows 7 considers a digital camera just another folder, so the camera shows up in the Computer folder.

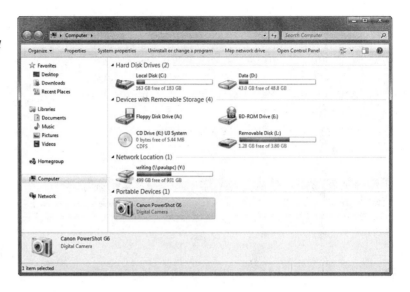

Getting Images from Your Scanner or Camera

The whole point of a scanner or digital camera is to transfer an image of something from the device to your computer hard drive. From there you can edit the image, e-mail it to a friend or colleague, publish it to the World Wide Web, or simply store it for safekeeping. This section shows you how to make a hard (disk) copy of an image.

Importing Pictures from a Digital Camera

Although it's occasionally fun to browse photos on your digital camera, the images are too tiny to be satisfying. If you want to take a good peek at your handiwork, you need to get those pics onto your computer. Fortunately, Windows 7 gives you not one but *two* ways to go about this: you can use Windows 7 itself, or you can use Windows Live Photo Gallery.

Windows Wisdom
If you've just connected your camera and you're eyeballing the AutoPlay window, you can bypass step 1 by clicking **Import Pictures and Videos Using Windows.**

To use Windows 7, follow these easier-done-than-said steps:

1. Select **Start, Computer** to open the Computer window.

2. Right-click the camera and then click **Import Pictures and Videos.** Windows 7 offers up the Importing Pictures and Videos dialog box, shown in Figure 8.3.

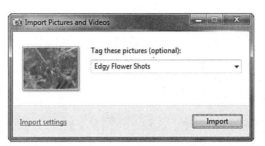

Figure 8.3

Use this dialog box to get your Windows 7 digital camera import underway.

3. Use the **Tag these pictures** text box to type a word or short phrase that describes the pictures. This is called a *tag*, and Windows 7 uses the tag as follows:

   ◆ It creates a subfolder in the My Pictures folder, and the name of the new subfolder is today's date followed by your tag. For example, if today is August 23, 2009, and your tag is Lampshade on My Head, then the new subfolder will have the following name:

   2009-08-23 Lampshade on My Head

   ◆ It gives the file the same name as the tag, with the number 001 after it, like so:

   Lampshade on My Head 001.jpg

   If you're importing a bunch of images from your digital camera, then the number gets bumped up for each image: 002, 003, and so on.

4. Click **Import.** Windows 7 starts lugging the photos from the camera to your PC. If you want Windows 7 to delete the photos from the camera when it's done, activate the **Erase after importing** check box. When the import is complete, Windows 7 drops you off in the Imported Pictures and Videos folder.

If you've downloaded Windows Live Photo Gallery from the Windows Live Essentials website (as I yammered on about back in Chapter 6), you can use that program to handle your importing chores. Here's how it works:

1. Select **Start, All Programs, Windows Live, Windows Live Photo Gallery** to get the program up and running.

> ### Windows Wisdom
>
> If you've just connected your camera and you've got the AutoPlay window on-screen, you can bypass steps 1 and 2 by clicking **Import Pictures and Videos Using Windows Live Photo Gallery.**

2. **Select File, Import from a scanner or camera.** The Import Pictures and Videos dialog box appears.

3. Click the camera you want to use and then click **Import.** The Import Photos and Videos dialog box shown in Figure 8.4 appears.

Figure 8.4

Use this dialog box to perform your Windows Live Photo Gallery importing duties.

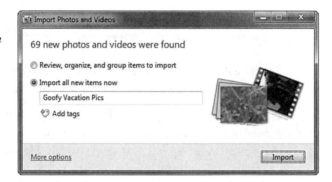

4. Click the **Import all new items now** option.

5. Type a name for the import in the text box. (This will be the name of the folder that Windows Live Photo Gallery creates to store the imported photos.)

6. Click **Import.** Windows Live Photo Gallery starts importing the photos from the camera to your computer. If you want Windows Live Photo Gallery to delete the photos from the camera when the dust clears, activate the **Erase after importing check box.** When the import is complete, Windows 7 drops you off in the Imported Pictures and Videos folder.

Scanning an Image

Windows 7 comes with its own Scanner and Camera Wizard to give you a step-by-step method for capturing images. Let's see how it works. First, place the picture or document or whatever on the scanner glass. Then launch the Scanner and Camera Wizard using one of the following methods:

♦ If your device is a scanner and it has some kind of "scan" button, press that button.

♦ Select **Start, Devices and Printers,** click your scanner, and then click **Start scan.**

♦ Select **Start, All Programs, Windows Fax and Scan.** In the Windows Fax and Scan window, select **File, New, Scan,** click your scanner, and then click **OK.**

◆ In Windows Live Photo Gallery (select **Start, All Programs, Windows Live, Windows Live Photo Gallery**), select **Import, Import from Scanner or Camera.** In the Import Pictures and Videos dialog box, click your scanner and then click **Import.**

Whichever method you choose, you see the New Scan dialog box. Feel free to click the **Preview** button to see what your image will look like before fiddling with any of the options or committing yourself to the scan. A preview of your scan appears as shown in Figure 8.5.

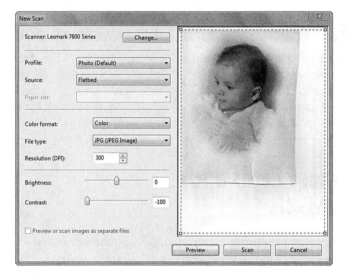

Figure 8.5

You use the New Scan dialog box to grab an image from a scanner.

If the dotted rectangle in the preview area isn't the same size as the image, click and drag the bottom-right corner of the rectangle to make it the same size.

Before getting to the scan, you might want to make a few adjustments. For example, the **Color Format** list offers three options:

◆ **Color.** Choose this option if the document you're scanning is a color photograph or drawing.

◆ **Grayscale.** Choose this option if your document is a picture that renders colors using different shades of gray.

◆ **Black and white.** Choose this option if your document uses only black and white (for example, if it's a page of text).

def•i•ni•tion

The **resolution** determines the overall quality of the scanned image. The higher the resolution, the higher the quality and (on the downside) the bigger the resulting file. Resolution is measured in dots per inch (DPI).

You can also use the File type list to select the image format you prefer: JPEG, Bitmap, PNG, or TIFF. Finally, you can also mess about with the Resolution spin box to set your preferred resolution, which determines the quality of the scan.

When you're ready, click **Scan** to get the scanning show on the road. After Windows 7 scans the image, the Importing Pictures and Videos dialog box shows up. Type a tag for the image and then click **Import.**

Windows Wisdom

Windows 7 gives you another way to scan pictures: in Paint, select the **File, From Scanner or Camera** command. If the Select Device dialog box shows up, select the imaging device you want to use and then click **OK**. Note that any decent graphics program also comes with support for scanning stuff. So if you have a better program than Paint, check to see if you can use it to scan pictures.

Dealing with Memory Cards and Other Removable Media

Many digital cameras store images using a special kind of doohickey called a memory card. These miniature memory modules come in many different shapes and sizes, including CompactFlash cards, MultiMedia cards, Memory Sticks, SecureDigital cards, and more. They're handy little devils because after you transfer your images to your computer, you can wipe out the card and start all over again. Although you usually get at the card's images by connecting the camera directly to your computer as described in the previous section, there are special devices called memory card readers into which you can insert one or more memory cards and then connect the unit to the computer.

Windows 7 treats each slot in a memory card reader as a disk drive, and they show up in the Computer folder as Removable Disk drives. You're then free to insert a memory card and browse its images directly, as described in the next section. In some cases, however, inserting the memory card prompts Windows 7 into displaying the dialog box shown in Figure 8.6.

Figure 8.6

When you insert a memory card, Windows 7 may toss this dialog box your way.

Windows wants to know just what the heck you'd like to do with the images on the card, so click the action you prefer. If you want to make this the default action, activate the **Always do this for pictures** check box.

In particular, if you want to copy the card's images to your hard disk, follow these steps:

1. Click the **Import Pictures and Videos using Windows** command. The Importing Pictures and Videos dialog box appears.

2. To apply a tag to all the images, type the tag in the **Tag these pictures** text box.

3. Click **Import.** Windows 7 begins importing the images.

4. If you also want Windows 7 to remove the images from the memory card when the import is complete, activate the **Erase after importing** check box.

Browsing Digital Camera Images

One of Windows 7's nicer features is the capability to parley directly with a digital camera using Windows Explorer. This is possible because, as I mentioned earlier, Windows 7 treats whatever the camera uses to store the digital photos as an honest-to-goodness folder. This means you can open the folder and get your hands dirty by working with the images yourself.

To do this, select **Start, Computer** and then double-click the camera icon (see Figure 8.2 earlier in this chapter). Windows 7 connects to the camera and displays the folders the camera uses for storage:

◆ **Removable storage.** Open this folder if your pictures are stored on a memory card that you plug into the camera.

◆ **Fixed storage.** Open this folder if your pictures are stored on some memory chip or other internal storage doodad.

Open the folders to get to your pictures (you may have to wade through a few levels of subfolders). Windows 7 then displays the images thumbnail-style, as shown in Figure 8.7. To copy an image from the camera to your hard disk, click and drag the image and drop it onto the **Pictures** library.

Figure 8.7

Windows 7 is happy to show your camera's digital photos in a folder window.

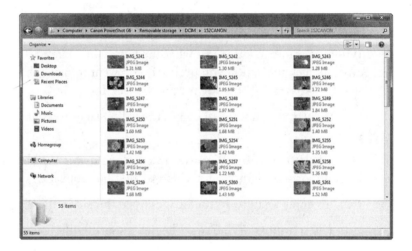

Note, too, that you can also clear out the camera's photos by selecting all the images (press **Ctrl+A**) and then pressing **Delete**.

The Least You Need to Know

◆ For the easiest installation, go with a scanner or camera that supports Plug and Play, particularly one that connects via a USB cable (provided your computer has a free USB port).

◆ To see your installed imaging devices, select **Start, Devices and Printers.**

◆ To get pictures from a camera, select **Start, Computer** to open the Computer window, right-click the camera, and then click **Import Pictures and Videos.**

◆ To scan an image, either press the device's "scan" button or select **Start, Devices and Printers,** click your scanner, and then click **Start scan.**

◆ To import pictures using Windows Live Photo Gallery, select **File, Import Pictures and Videos.**

◆ To access your digital camera's stored images via Windows Explorer, open the Computer folder (select **Start, Computer**) and double-click the camera's icon.

9

Sights and Sounds: Windows 7's Digital Media Tools

In This Chapter

- ◆ Playing multimedia files
- ◆ Listening to audio CDs and watching DVD movies
- ◆ Ripping music tracks from an audio CD
- ◆ Burning music tracks to a CD or DVD
- ◆ Synchronizing your computer with a digital audio device
- ◆ Connecting your PC and a TV or set-top box for use with Media Center

The graphics you gawked at in the last two chapters represent only a selection of Windows 7's visual treats. There are actually quite a few more goodies that fall into the "sights for sore eyes" category, and even a few that could be called "sounds for sore ears." In this chapter, you see that Windows 7 turns your lowly computer into a multimedia powerhouse capable of showing videos, playing audio CDs, making realistic burping noises, watching slick DVD movies, and even creating your own sound recordings.

Making Multimedia Whoopee with Media Player

Windows supports all kinds of multimedia formats, including sound files, digital video files, audio CDs, DVD movies, and more. The good news is that to play all of these formats, you need to wrestle with only a single program: Windows Media Player. This clever chunk of software is a true one-stop multimedia shop that's capable of playing sound files, music files, audio CDs, animations, movie files, and even DVDs. It can also copy audio CD tracks to your computer, burn music files to a CD, tune in to Internet radio stations, and more.

To try Media Player, you have a bunch of ways to proceed:

♦ Click the **Windows Media Player** icon in the Windows 7 taskbar. If that's just too easy, you can also convince Media Player to come out to play by selecting **Start, All Programs, Windows Media Player.**

Windows Wisdom
The first time you start Windows Media Player, you'll probably see the Welcome to Windows Media Player dialog box. This is a one-time-only wizard that will get Media Player set up and ready to rock (or whatever). I heartily encourage you to use the default setup, so select the **Recommended settings** option and then click **Finish** to move on with your life.

♦ Insert an audio CD in your CD drive, or insert a DVD disc in your DVD drive. (Note that most DVD drives are also happy to play audio CDs for you.) If Windows displays a dialog box asking you what you want it to do with the CD, click **Play audio CD using Windows Media Player,** activate the **Always do the selected action** check box, and then click **OK.**

♦ If you have a memory card reader, insert a memory card with music files. If Windows 7 asks what you want to do with this disk, highlight **Play using Windows Media Player.** If you don't want to be pestered with this dialog box each time, activate the **Always do the selected action** check box. Click **OK** to proceed.

♦ Use Windows Explorer to find a media file and then double-click the file. Remember that your user profile folder has a library named Music, which is the default folder that Windows 7 uses when you save music files.

◆ Download media from the Internet. In most cases, Media Player will launch right away and start playing the sound or movie or whatever. (This is called *streaming* the media.) Sometimes, however, you may have to wait for the entire file to download before Media Player will spring into action.

Figure 9.1 shows what the Media Player window looks like when you launch the program without also starting some media. Your window will look a bit different unless you have precisely the same musical tastes as I do, in which case there are probably some larger issues we need to discuss.

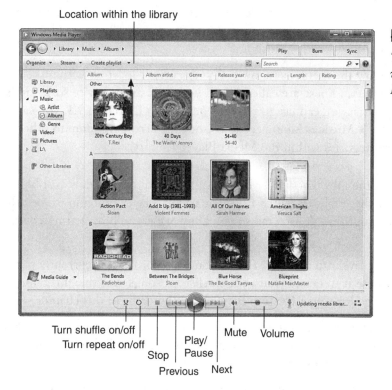

Figure 9.1

This is the window you see when you launch Media Player.

The first thing we should do here is ward off a potential area of confusion. In Chapter 5, you learned that Windows 7 organizes your user profile stuff into various libraries: Documents, Pictures, Music, and Video. No big whoop, except that Media Player *also* uses the library metaphor, but just to keep folks scratching their heads, it's not in any way related to libraries in your Windows 7 user profile. Thanks a lot, Microsoft!

So just to try and keep things straight here, I'll use the phrase *Media Player Library* to refer to the various media knickknacks that Media Player makes available to you.

To get around in the Media Player Library, there are two things you need to know:

> **Windows Wisdom**
>
> If you don't see the navigation pane, you can resurrect it by pressing **Alt** and selecting **View, Library,** or by pressing **Ctrl+1**.

- ◆ The navigation pane on the left side of the window shows the contents of the Media Player Library, and you see five categories: Playlists, Music, Video, Pictures, and Recorded TV. Double-click a category to open it, then click a subcategory (such as Artist, Album, or Genre for Music).

- ◆ The links just below the menu bar show you your current location within the Media Player Library. (These are called *breadcrumb links* since they're sorta kinda like breadcrumbs that you can use to retrace your steps.) In Figure 9.1, you can see I'm in the Library > Music > Album section. Click the arrows to jump to other sections and other categories within the Media Player Library.

I should also point out the tabs that appear on the right side of the window, just below the menu bar. You use these tabs to switch from one Media Player function to the other. Let's take a second to run through each tab so you know what you'll be getting yourself into:

- ◆ **Play.** This tab displays info about whatever album and/or track is currently playing, and you can use it to create your own playlists of songs. See the "Becoming a Program Director: Creating a Custom Playlist" section later in this chapter.

- ◆ **Burn.** This section enables you to copy music from your computer to a recordable CD, a process known as *burning*. The scoop on this is in the "Rollin' Your Own Music: Burning Tracks to a CD" section.

- ◆ **Sync.** This section enables you to synchronize media files on a portable media device or a memory card. See the section "In Sync: Synchronizing Media on a Device."

Giving Media Player Some Media to Play

I mentioned earlier that Media Player will launch and start playing automatically if you double-click or download a media file or insert an audio CD or DVD disc. If you opened Media Player directly or if you want to get it to play something else, then you need to learn how to load media from within the program.

To open a media file, you have two possibilities:

♦ **Open a file on your computer.** Press **Alt** and select the **File, Open** command (or press **Ctrl+O**), use the Open dialog box to highlight the file, and then click **Open.**

♦ **Open a file from the Internet.** Press **Alt** and select **File, Open URL** (or press **Ctrl+U**), use the Open text box to enter the Internet address of the file, and then click **OK.**

Let's Make Some Noise: Playing Media

To control the playback of your media, the Media Player program offers the following buttons (see Figure 9.1):

♦ **Play/Pause.** Starts the media file; pauses the file while it's playing. Alternatives: select **Play, Play/Pause** or press **Ctrl+P.**

♦ **Stop.** Stops the media file and returns to the beginning of the file (or to the beginning of the current audio CD track). Alternatives: select **Play, Stop** or press **Ctrl+S.**

♦ **Previous.** Plays the previous file or track. Alternatives: select **Play, Previous** or press **Ctrl+B.**

Windows Wisdom

If you want to fast-forward through a video, press and hold down the left mouse button over **Next.** (If the mood strikes, you can also press **Alt** and select **Play, Fast Forward** or press **Ctrl+Shift+F.**) To rewind, instead, press and hold down the left mouse button over **Back.** (Alternatives? You bet: Press **Alt** and select **Play, Rewind** or press **Ctrl+Shift+B.**)

♦ **Next.** Plays the next file or track. Alternatives: press **Alt** and select **Play, Next** or press **Ctrl+F.**

♦ **Mute.** Turns off the sound playback. Alternatives: press **Alt** and select **Play, Volume, Mute** or press **F7.**

♦ **Volume.** Controls the playback volume. Drag the slider to the left to reduce the volume, or to the right to increase the volume. Alternatives: press **Alt** and select **Play, Volume, Up** or press **F9** to increase the volume; press **Alt** and select **Play, Volume, Down** or press **F8** to decrease the volume.

♦ **Turn shuffle on/off.** Toggles shuffle mode on and off. Shuffle mode means that your library files or an audio CD's tracks play in random order. Alternatives: press **Alt** and select **Play, Shuffle** or press **Ctrl+H.**

♦ **Turn repeat on/off.** Toggles repeat mode on and off. When repeat mode is on, Media Player plays a media file over and over until you can't take it anymore. Alternatives: press **Alt** and select **Play, Repeat** command or press **Ctrl+T.**

And here are a few juicy tidbits you might want to keep in mind:

♦ To get a DVD, Video CD (VCD), or audio CD up and running, press **Alt,** select **Play,** and then choose the **DVD, VCD,** or **CD Audio** menu option. (If you have multiple drives in your system, select the drive that contains the disc from the menu that appears.)

Windows Wisdom

Some audio CDs do double-duty as data CDs and come with programs you can run. In some cases, the program will run automatically when you insert the CD. So be fore-warned that after you insert an audio CD, you may see something other than (or in addition to) Media Player on the screen.

♦ If you started a video a-playing, but you don't see it on-screen, press **Alt** and select **View, Now Playing,** or press **Ctrl+3.**

♦ You can eject a DVD, VCD, or audio CD right from Media Player, so you can avoid having to fumble around for the drive's often-hard-to-find eject button. To do this, press **Alt** and select **Play, Eject,** or press **Ctrl+J.** (If you have multiple drives in your system, use the menu that appears to select the drive that contains the disc.)

Messing with Media Player's Audio CD Features

If you like to listen to music while you use your computer, it's possible to convince Media Player to crank up an audio CD. No joke. Audio CDs use the same dimensions as CD-ROM discs, so any audio CD will fit snugly inside your CD drive (or your DVD drive, if you have one). From there, you use Media Player to play the CD's tracks.

Let's run through a few notes to bear in mind when playing audio CDs in Media Player. First, Media Player can access information about a CD over the Internet:

◆ If your computer is connected to the Internet when you insert the disc, Media Player will automatically reach out and grab various bits of data about the CD: its title, the name of the performer or group, the name and length of each track, and more.

◆ If you connect to the Internet after the disc is already playing, you can get the disc info by right-clicking the album or any track and then clicking **Find Album Info.**

> **Windows Wisdom**
>
> As an added and slightly surprising bonus, the list of tracks is customizable. If Media Player can't get the name of a track, or if you want to change the existing name, right-click the track and then click **Edit.** Type in the new name and then press **Enter.**

Hard Disk Rock: Ripping Tracks from a CD

Media Player's audio CD playback is flexible, for sure, but playing audio CDs suffers from two important drawbacks:

◆ Shuffling discs in and out of the drive can be a hassle.

◆ There isn't any way to mix tunes from two or more CDs into a single playlist, even if your system has multiple CD and/or DVD drives.

To solve these dilemmas, Media Player enables you to copy—or *rip*, as the kids say— individual tracks from one or more CDs and store them on your computer's hard disk. From there, you can create a custom playlist that combines the tracks in any order you like.

Before I show you how you go about ripping tracks from an audio CD, let's take a second to set a few options related to track copying. In the Media Player window, select the **Organize, Options** command to display the Options dialog box and then select the **Rip Music** tab.

There are two main things you can do in this tab:

◆ **Change the file format.** Use the **Format** list to select the audio file format that you want to use for the ripped tracks:

Windows Media Audio. This is Media Player's default audio file format. WMA compresses digital audio by removing extraneous sounds that are not normally detected by the human ear. This results in high-quality audio files that are a fraction of the size of uncompressed audio.

Windows Media Audio Pro. This version of WMA can create music files that are smaller than regular WMA and so are easier to play on mobile devices that don't have much room.

Windows Media Audio (Variable Bit Rate). This version of WMA is a bit "smarter" in that it changes the amount of compression depending on the audio data: if the data is more complex, it uses less compression to keep the sound quality high; if the data is less complex, it cranks up the compression.

Windows Media Audio Lossless. This version of WMA doesn't compress the audio tracks at all. This gives you the highest possible audio quality, but it takes up much more space (up to about 400 MB per CD).

MP3. This is a popular format on the Internet. Like WMA, MP3 compresses the audio files to make them smaller without sacrificing quality. MP3 files are generally about twice the size of WMA files, but more digital audio players support MP3 (although not many more, these days).

WAV. This is an uncompressed audio file format that is compatible with all versions of Windows, even going back to Windows 3.0.

◆ **Change the audio quality.** The quality of the copied files is proportional to the acreage they consume on your hard disk. That is, the higher the quality, the fatter the file. Use the **Audio quality** slider to choose which quality level you want. Each level is measured in kilobits per second (Kbps), where there are 8 bits in a byte and 1,024 bytes in a kilobyte (KB). To help you decide, next is a summary of each quality level for the WMA format (other formats offer different choices) and how much disk space it will usurp in kilobytes per minute and megabytes (MB; 1,025 kilobytes) per hour:

Kbps	KB/Minute	MB/Hour
32	240	14
48	360	21
64	480	28
96	720	42
128	960	56
160	1,200	70
192	1,440	84

Click **OK** when you've made your choices.

To do the actual ripping, you have a couple of ways to go. The no-muss-no-fuss method is to insert the audio CD you want to rip, wait until you see Media Player's Now Playing window, move your mouse over the window to display the controls, and then click **Rip CD.**

If you want more control over the ripping process, then you need to put up with a bit of muss and fuss (but just a bit). In this case, you need to follow these steps:

> **Windows Wisdom**
>
> To save a bit of time, Media Player offers a faster way to choose the format and audio quality. In the navigation pane, click the audio CD, then click **Rip Settings** in Media Player's taskbar to display a menu. Select either **Format** (to select an audio file format) or **Bit Rate** (to select an audio quality).

1. Insert the audio CD you want to rip. If you see the Media Player's Now Playing window, press **Ctrl+1** to switch to the Media Player Library.

2. You should see the contents of the CD. If not, click the audio CD in Media Player's navigation pane.

3. For each track that you don't want to rip, deactivate the check box to the left of the track number. (They're all activated at first.)

4. Click **Rip CD.**

5. The first time you rip a CD, Media Player displays the Rip Options dialog box, which asks if you want to change rip options such as the format and file location. You've done this already, so select **Keep my current format settings** and then click **OK.**

Media Player starts the copy process, which you can monitor by watching the **Rip Status** column (see Figure 9.2).

Figure 9.2

You can use Media Player to rip audio CD tracks to your hard disk.

Becoming a Program Director: Creating a Custom Playlist

Once you've copied a mess of CD tracks to your hard disk, you're free to combine these tracks and play them in any order. If you just want to play an individual track, here's the easiest way to go about it:

> **Windows Wisdom**
>
> The techniques in this section apply equally to MP3 files and other music files that you download from the Internet.

1. Display the **Library, Music** section.

2. In the **Music** branch, select one of the sub-branches: Album, Artist, or Genre.

3. Double-click the album, artist, genre, or whatever that contains the track you want.

4. Double-click the track.

Rather than playing single tracks using this method, you might prefer to combine multiple tracks into a playlist. You can then select the playlist and Media Player will play all the tunes for you automatically.

The first thing you need to do is create a new playlist:

1. Click **Create Playlist.** Media Player adds a new playlist to the Playlists section of the Library and creates a text box around the playlist name.

2. Type a descriptive name in the text box and press **Enter.**

3. Display the track or tracks you want to add to the playlist.

4. Click and drag the track or tracks and drop the selection on the playlist name in the Playlists section. (If your click-and-drag skills aren't what they used to be, you can also right-click the track or tracks, click **Add to,** and then click the name of your playlist in the menu that appears.)

5. Repeat steps 3 and 4 to add all the tracks you want in your playlist.

6. Click the playlist to review your handiwork (see Figure 9.3).

Figure 9.3

Click and drag tracks from the Library and drop them on the playlist to create a custom playlist.

With that done, use the following techniques to work with the playlist:

♦ **Removing a song from the playlist.** Open the **Playlists** branch and select the playlist. Right-click the song and then click **Remove from List.**

♦ **Changing the playlist order.** Open the **Playlists** branch and select the playlist. Then use your mouse to drag the songs up or down in the list.

♦ **Playing a playlist.** Open the **Playlists** branch, select the playlist, and then click the **Play** button.

♦ **Renaming a playlist.** Open the **Playlists** branch, right-click the playlist, and then click **Rename.** Type in the new name and then press **Enter.**

♦ **Deleting a playlist.** Open the **Playlists** branch, right-click the playlist, and then click **Delete.**

Rollin' Your Own Music: Burning Tracks to a CD or Device

Listening to music while working on your computer is loads of fun, but I certainly hope you don't spend every waking minute in front of your PC. When it's time to get away, why not take some of your digital music with you? Sure you can. Media Player can perform the neat trick of copying—say *burning* when you're on the street—music files from your computer to a recordable CD or DVD. Here's how it works:

1. Select the **Burn** tab.

2. Display the track or tracks you want to burn.

3. Click and drag the track or tracks and drop the selection inside the Burn List. (Alternatively, right-click the selected tracks and then click **Add to, Burn list.**)

4. Repeat steps 2 and 3 to add all the tracks you want to burn.

5. Click **Start burn.** Media Player begins burning the tracks to the disc.

Look Out!

Remember that once Media Player finishes writing to a CD-R or DVD-R disc, it "closes" the disc, which means that you can never write anything else to the disc. Therefore, make sure you have enough music available to fill up the CD-R (about 70 minutes) or DVD-R (about 500 minutes) so as not to waste space on the disc.

In Sync: Synchronizing Media on a Device

If you have a portable digital audio player that connects directly to your computer, or that uses a memory card that you can attach to your computer using a memory card reader, you can use Media Player to synchronize music on the device. This means that you maintain in Media Player a Sync List for the device. The Sync List is a list of tracks that Media Player will copy to the device. If you later add, reorder, or remove items in the Sync List, the next time you attach the device you can get Media Player to write all of these changes to the device, so that Media Player and the device are always in sync with each other. Here's how this works:

Look Out!

Media Player can work with many newer digital audio players, but it doesn't recognize all of them. So don't be surprised (frustrated, yes, but not surprised) if Media Player completely ignores your music player after you plug it in to your computer.

1. Connect your digital audio player or its memory card to your computer.

2. Select the **Sync** tab.

3. Display the track or tracks you want to sync.

4. Click and drag the track or tracks and drop the selection inside the Sync List. (Alternatively, right-click the selected tracks and then click **Add to, Sync list.**)

5. Repeat steps 3 and 4 to add all the tracks you want to sync.

6. Click **Start sync.** Media Player adds the tracks to the device.

Generously Sharing Your Media Library

It can take quite awhile to set up and customize your Media Player Library just the way you like it. Once you do, however, Media Player is a real pleasure to use. So much so that you'll probably be tempted to duplicate your efforts on other computers in your home. Fortunately, Media Player gives an easy way to do that: turn on *media streaming*, which is just a fancy-schmancy name for sharing your media library.

Here's what you do:

1. Select **Stream, Turn on media streaming.** The Media streaming options window appears.

2. Click **Turn on media streaming.** Media Player enables media streaming and then displays the streaming options.

3. Type a name for your media library. (This is the name that other network folks see in their versions of Media Player.)

4. For each item in the list of media devices and computers, click the device and then click either **Allowed** (if you want that computer or device to have access to your library) or **Blocked** (to prevent access to your library).

5. Click **OK.**

Movies, Tunes, and More: Running Media Center

Proving that digital media is a big deal these days, some versions of Windows 7 come with yet another digital media tool called Media Center. As its name implies, Media Center is meant to act as a kind of hub for your home entertainment center.

In a basic setup, you connect your computer to your TV and you can then use Media Center to play DVDs or downloaded movies, listen to music, watch picture slide shows, view TV listings, and even record TV programs.

A more space-age approach is to set up a wireless network and add an *extender* such as an Xbox 360 game console that enables you to "stream" movies, music, tunes, and TV to other devices on the network, even if they reside in another room or another floor of your house.

def•i•ni•tion

A Media Center **extender** is a device that enables you to watch or listen to your computer's media using other devices on your network.

As you can imagine, all of this is a bit complex and would require a book in itself to learn how to connect everything, configure it, and then use it. So this section just provides you with a bit of an overview so you can at least get some idea of what Media Center is all about.

Making the Connection

There are many ways to configure a Media Center PC as an entertainment hub, but the simplest and most common is to connect the PC to a TV, which enables you to "watch" what's on the PC using the TV instead of a regular computer monitor. In particular, it means that whatever you do with the Media Center program—watch a DVD, run an image slide show, and so on—appears on the TV.

How you connect your computer to the TV depends on the configuration of both, but there are two basic concepts you need to know:

◆ You attach one end of a cable to a port on your computer's video card and the other end to an input port in back of your TV.

◆ The video card port and the TV port must be of the same type.

For example, many people use a cable with RCA connectors, which are the red, white, and yellow jacks that are commonly used with audiovisual equipment. Another common choice is an S-Video cable.

Looking at things the other way around, you might want to use Media Center to watch TV and record programs. In this case, you also need to connect your TV set-top box to your computer:

◆ You attach one end of a coaxial cable to the output port (usually labeled "Cable Out" or "Out to TV") in back of your set-top box, and the other end to a port on your computer.

◆ The computer connection must be a coaxial cable port on either your computer's video card or on a separate TV tuner device.

Firing Up Media Center

Once you've gone through all that rigmarole, get Media Center on the job by selecting **Start, All Programs, Media Center.** The first time you launch Media Center, the program leads you by the hand through a series of configuration screens, some of which are optional. By judiciously skipping the unimportant parts of the process, you can get through it in just a few minutes. (If you're the impatient type, just click **Cancel** to get on with the whole thing. You can also do the configuration chores later.)

Taking a Look Around

Figure 9.4 shows the initial Media Center screen that appears after you've trudged through the program's setup chores.

Figure 9.4

The initial Media Center screen.

Media Center starts off by displaying a list of the main tasks you can perform, which include the following:

◆ **Pictures + Videos.** Use this task to access your picture and video libraries. Second-level tasks here are Picture Library, Play Favorites, and Video Library. (I'm not sure why Microsoft chose to combine these rather different media into a single task, but it does take some getting used to.)

◆ **Music.** Use this task to work with music and radio. Second-level tasks are Music Library (a list of the music files on your system), Play Favorites, Radio (listen to radio either through a tuner or via the Internet), and Search (search your system for music).

◆ **Movies.** Use this task to work with DVD movies. Second-level tasks are Movie Library (a list of the DVD movies you've watched) and Play DVD.

◆ **TV.** Use this task to work with your TV tuner. Second-level tasks are Recorded TV (a list of TV shows you've recorded to your hard disk), Guide (what's on and when), and Live TV Setup (configuring TV options).

◆ **Sports.** Use this to look up sports stats. Secondary tasks are Scores (recent results from various leagues), Players (enables you to add players so that you can track your favorites or anybody you've got in a pool or fantasy league), and Leagues (configuring options for each sports league).

◆ **Spotlight.** Use this task to access media online and run other Media Center programs installed on your computer. Second-level tasks are Online Spotlight and More Programs.

◆ **Tools.** Use this task to access Media Center tools. Second-level tasks are Help and Settings.

◆ **Tasks.** Use this task to run other Media Center features. Second-level tasks are Shutdown (close Media Center), Settings (configure Media Center), Learn More (get help with Media Center), Burn CD/DVD, Sync (synchronize content with an external device), Add Extender (add networked devices such as an Xbox 360 to view your content on those devices), and Media Only (locks Media Center in full screen mode).

The Least You Need to Know

◆ The Media Player program can handle almost any kind of multimedia file. To use it, click the taskbar's **Windows Media Player** icon or double-click a media file.

◆ In most cases, you'll see the AutoPlay dialog box automatically after you insert an audio CD or DVD movie disc. The dialog box usually gives you a choice between playing the disc in Media Player and playing it in Media Center.

◆ Before ripping audio CD tracks to your computer, your first task should be to choose the quality setting you want. To do this, select **Tools, Options,** and then use the **Rip Music** tab's **Audio quality** slider.

◆ Before using Media Center, make sure your PC is connected to your TV via an RCA or S-Video cable. If you want to record and watch TV on your computer, connect your PC's TV tuner and the set-top box with a coaxial cable.

Making Movies with Windows 7

In This Chapter

◆ Movie Maker's hardware hurdles

◆ How to capture video from a camcorder, VCR, or other device

◆ Getting comfortable with video clips

◆ Inserting clips into a movie

◆ Editing a movie by trimming clips, adding transitions, and more

In the magical multimedia tour of the past three chapters, you've seen how Windows 7 handles images and sounds. In this chapter you'll take all of that to its logical conclusion by learning how to string together multiple images and sounds. You'll learn, in other words, how to record and edit videos on your computer. The tool that will turn you into a veritable videographer is Windows Live Movie Maker—a scaled-down, but still quite functional, video recording and editing program.

Introducing Windows Live Movie Maker

Windows Live Movie Maker can capture video from a camcorder, VCR, desktop camera, or even a TV, and save it on your computer. From there, you can cut out the bits you don't want, rearrange the footage, add narration and between-scenes transitions, and perform other Spielbergian tasks. You can then save your creation to a recordable CD or DVD, plop it onto your website, or e-mail it to an unsuspecting friend or coworker (or even to a suspecting one, for that matter).

As you might have surmised by now, the "Live" portion of Windows Live Movie Maker means you must download and install this program from the Windows Live Essentials website, as I described back in Chapter 6. I'll wait here while you go ahead and do that.

Done? Good. This section tells you what equipment you need for Movie Maker to do its thing, how to record footage, how to edit it into a crowd-pleasing shape, and how to distribute the final product.

What Hardware Do You Need to Use Movie Maker?

Before I answer the question that forms the title of this section, let me first say that you don't necessarily need *any* extra hardware to use Movie Maker. That's because the program is perfectly happy to work with existing digital video files. As you'll see a bit later, it's possible to import video files into Movie Maker and then play with them as you see fit. In fact, Movie Maker can deal with video files in all of the following formats (and a few more obscure formats, too):

- Advanced Streaming Format (also known as ASF)
- Motion Picture Experts Group (MPEG or MPG)
- Video for Windows (AVI)
- Windows Movie File (WMF)
- Windows Media Video (WMV; this is the format that Movie Maker uses when it saves your movies)

Besides all that, Movie Maker can also import many image and audio file formats. However, if it's your own video footage you're after, then you need to attach a video device to your computer. How you do this depends on what type of device you have and what type of attachment (port or jacks) your computer has:

◆ **If you have an analog camcorder, VCR, or TV and your computer has a video capture card:** Analog camcorders, VCRs, and TVs usually output *composite* video and audio using three RCA-style jacks, which are almost always colorcoded: yellow for the video and red and white for the audio. If your computer has a separate video capture card or a graphics card that's capable of capturing video, then you'll see the corresponding yellow, red, and white jacks on the back of your computer. (Some cards have a separate cable that has the RCA jacks on it.) In this case, you need to use the appropriate cable (usually supplied with the card) to attach the camcorder or VCR to your computer. Many camcorders, VCRs, and TVs have an S-Video jack that outputs both audio and video, but you need a corresponding S-Video input jack on your computer's video card.

◆ **If you have an analog camcorder or VCR and your computer has a USB port:** There are products—known affectionately as *video dongles* in the trade—available that have the yellow, red, and white RCA jacks on one end and a USB connector on the other. In this case, you run an RCA cable from the camcorder or VCR to the dongle and then attach the dongle to your computer's USB port.

◆ **If you have a digital camcorder or desktop video camera (also called a web camera or webcam) and your computer has a USB port:** If your camcorder or camera supports USB, it should come with a USB cable that you attach directly to the computer's USB port.

◆ **If you have a digital camcorder or desktop video camera and your computer has an IEEE 1394 (FireWire) port:** IEEE 1394 is still a relatively uncommon method for getting digital video (and other kinds of data) into a computer. IEEE 1394 is one of those names that only a geek could love; fortunately, there's a more fun synonym that the likes of us can use: *FireWire*. A few new computers are now shipping with FireWire ports, and there are also FireWire boards and PC cards that you can install. If your digital camera supports FireWire, it should come with a FireWire cable that you attach directly to the computer's FireWire port.

A Tour of the Movie Maker Screen

With all that out of the way, it's time to start making some digital movies. To get Movie Maker rolling, select **Start, All Programs, Windows Live, Windows Live Movie**

Maker. Windows 7 releases the Windows Live Movie Maker window onto the screen. Figure 10.1 shows the Movie Maker window with a movie project already on the go to help you understand the various parts of the program.

Figure 10.1

The Movie Maker window with a movie project in progress.

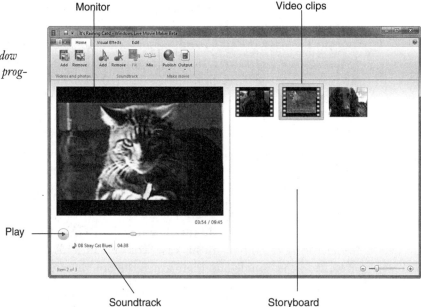

Let's run through the various Movie Maker actors and the roles they play:

- **Storyboard.** This is the area that holds the clips for your current movie project and it's where you edit the movie.

- **Video clips.** These thumbnails represent the video clips that you've added to your project. Each clip shows the first *frame* of the video segment.

- **Monitor.** You use this area to play a clip or play your movie.

- **Play.** Click this button to play the current clip.

- **Soundtrack.** If you add a music soundtrack to your project, it appears here.

def•i•ni•tion

A **frame** is a single image from a movie. All movies simulate motion by playing a rapid sequence of still images. The more images displayed per second, the better the quality of the movie. This measure is called the frame rate and it's measured in frames per second (fps). Low quality is about 8 fps and high quality is 30 fps.

Importing Footage from a Video Camera

In previous versions of Movie Maker you could use the program to import video from a camera. This chore is now handled by Windows 7 itself, so I'll handle it here separately, too. As the next two sections show, you can import either existing footage or a live feed.

Importing Existing Footage from a Video Camera

When you record from a camera, you can either import existing footage or a live feed. Here I'll talk about importing existing footage, and hold off on live recordings until the next section.

Assuming you now have your camcorder, VCR, or desktop camera ready to go, you can get right to the action by following these steps:

1. Turn on your video camera, switch it into playback (sometimes called VCR) mode, and then attach the camera to your computer. The first time you do this Windows 7 rummages around in its files and installs support for the camera. Once that's done, the Import Video dialog box appears. This is a wizard that will take you through the import process.

Windows Wisdom

If you don't see the Import Video dialog box, select **Start, Windows Live, Windows Live Photo Gallery,** then select **File, Import from a scanner or camera.** Click your camera, and then click **Import** to get the video importing show on the road.

---

2. Type a name for the imported video.

3. If your device uses digital tape, the wizard asks how you want to import the footage. Choose one of the following options (there's also a third option to **Burn the entire video to DVD** that I'm going to studiously ignore here) and then click **Next.**

   ◆ **Import the entire video**—Select this option if you want the entire contents of the tape imported to your PC. Skip to step 8 when the import is done.

   ◆ **Choose parts of the video to import**—Select this option if you want to pick and choose what parts of the tape you import. Continue with step 4.

4. The wizard displays controls such as Play and Rewind. Use those controls to cue the tape to the position where you want to start importing (watch the little monitor to know when to stop), and then click **Pause,** as shown in Figure 10.2.

Figure 10.2

Use this dialog box to cue your tape and then start importing it.

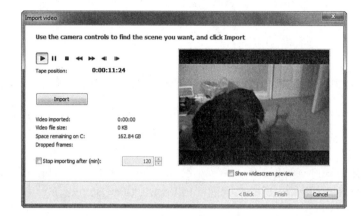

5. Click **Import.** Movie Maker starts importing the footage.

6. If you get to a spot on the tape that you don't want to record, click **Stop.**

7. Repeat steps 4 to 6 to import all the parts of the movie you want to play with.

8. When the import is complete, click **Finish.**

Importing Live Footage from a Video Camera

If you want to import a live feed, follow these steps:

1. Turn on your video camera, switch it into record mode, and then attach the camera to your computer. The Import Video dialog box appears.

2. Type a name for the imported video.

3. Click **Import.** Movie Maker starts importing the live feed.

4. If you want to pause the import for a bit, click **Stop.**

5. Repeat steps 3 and 4 to import all the live footage you can stand.

6. When the import is complete, click **Finish.**

Starting a Fresh Movie Maker Project

In Movie Maker, the "files" you work with are called *projects*, and they consist of video clips, still images, music and sound effects, scene transitions, and titles.

Movie Maker starts a new movie project for you automatically when you crank it up. However, you can start a fresh project at any time by selecting the **File, New** command (or by pressing **Ctrl+N**).

From Projector to Project: Creating Your Movie Project

Your footage is safely ensconced on your hard disk and you've got a piping hot project ready to go. Now what? Now it's nitty-gritty time as you start constructing your movie piece by piece.

Creating a movie in Movie Maker roughly involves the following steps:

1. Add a video clip to the storyboard.

2. Use the storyboard to move the video clip into the section of the movie where you want it to be seen.

3. Cut out unwanted sections of the video clip.

4. Add a transition effect between the previous clip and the new clip.

5. Apply a video effect to the clip.

6. Repeat steps 1 through 5 until you're done.

7. Insert a soundtrack.

The rest of this section takes you through each of these steps.

Adding a Video Clip to the Project

Your first step in any Movie Maker project is to get some video "in the can" (as they say in the movie biz). That is, you need to add a collection of clips to the project to use as your editing raw materials. Here's how it works:

1. Click the **Home** tab.

2. In the **Videos and photos** section, click **Add.** Predictably, the Add Videos and Photos dialog box appears.

3. Select the media file you want to add. You can select either a video file or a photo. If you go with the latter, note that Movie Maker sets up the photo as a "clip" that displays as is for three seconds.

4. Click **Open.** Movie Maker adds the media to the storyboard.

Using the Storyboard to Juggle Clips

When you insert your clips into the project, you don't need to worry too much about the order the clips appear because the order is easy to change by using any of the following techniques:

> **Windows Wisdom**
>
> You can work with multiple clips in the storyboard, if that suits your fancy. To select multiple clips in a row, click the first clip, hold down **Shift,** and click the last clip. To select clips willy-nilly, hold down **Ctrl** and click each clip.

◆ To move a clip, use your mouse to drag the clip to a new position within the storyboard. A black vertical bar tells you where the clip will appear when you drop it.

◆ To copy a clip, hold down the **Ctrl** key, drag the clip to the position where you want the copy to appear (again, the black vertical bar lets you know where the clip will end up), and then drop the clip.

◆ To delete a clip, click it and then press **Delete.**

Trimming a Clip

When you add a video clip to the storyboard, Movie Maker adds the entire clip, including those first few seconds when the camera was pointing at your feet. Nobody wants to see your feet (although you know your audience best), so how do you get rid of that unwanted footage? The secret is to trim the bad footage from the clip's beginning or end (or both). Here's how:

1. In the storyboard, click the clip you want to trim.

2. Display the **Edit** tab.

3. Click **Trim.** Movie Maker displays the Trim tab and the trim controls, as shown in Figure 10.3.

Figure 10.3

Use Movie Maker's trim controls to lop off unsightly video clip footage.

Trim the beginning of the video   Trim the end of the video

4. Drag the **Trim the beginning of the video** bar to the right to set the starting point of the good footage. As you drag the bar, the current clip position appears in the monitor, so you can see exactly where you are within the clip.

5. Drag the **Trim the end of the video** bar to the left to set the ending point of the good footage.

6. Click **Save and close.**

> **Windows Wisdom**
>
> I mentioned earlier that Movie Maker sets up a photo as an honorary member of the clip club by setting it up to display for 3 seconds. To change that, click the photo in the storyboard, click the **Edit** tab, then use the **Duration** control to set the time, in seconds, that you want the photo to stay on-screen.

Adding a Transition Between Two Clips

In video editing, a *transition* is an effect that accompanies the change from one scene to another. In Movie Maker, the default transition from one clip to another is a *jump cut:* an immediate scene change from the first clip to the next. However, you don't have to settle for something so plain. Movie Maker has three other transitions you can use to make people sit up and take notice. Here are the steps to follow to add transitions between scenes:

1. Select the **Visual Effects** tab.

2. Select the second of the two clips that you want involved in the transition.

3. In the **Transitions** group, click the transition you want to use. Movie Maker adds the transition between the selected clip and the one before it.

4. Repeat steps 2 and 3 to add other transitions to your project.

Adding Video Effects

A *video effect* is a visual treatment applied to a clip. For example, the Sepia Tone effect makes a clip look as though it is quite old. Movie Maker comes with a half dozen effects that you can apply. Here are the steps to follow to apply an effect to a clip:

1. Select the **Visual Effects** tab.

2. Select the clip that you want to work with.

3. In the **Effects** group, click the visual effect you want to use. Movie Maker applies the effect.

4. Repeat steps 2 and 3 to add other effects to your project.

Adding a Soundtrack

If you choose to record both video and audio when capturing your footage, your clips will come with a video track that represents the audio portion of the video. You can supplement this track with a separate audio track that can play narration, background music, sound effects, or whatever other auditory marvels your project needs.

You don't need a separate program to record narration, because Movie Maker is happy to handle that chore for you. Here's how it works:

1. Display the **Home** tab.

2. In the **Soundtrack** tab, click **Add.** The Add Music dialog box shows up.

3. Click the music file you want to use as a soundtrack.

4. Click **Open.** Movie Maker adds the track to the movie.

5. To control the relative volume between the clip audio and the soundtrack audio, click **Mix** and then drag the slider (see Figure 10.4) either left (to bring up the clip audio) or to the right (to bring up the soundtrack audio).

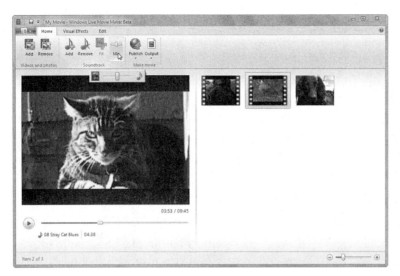

Figure 10.4

*Click **Mix** and then drag the slider to bring up either the clip audio (left) or the soundtrack audio (right).*

Outputting Your Project to a Movie File

If you want to watch your movie in Movie Maker itself, just click the **Play** button. If you want to watch your movie elsewhere, then you need to output the project to a movie file. Movie Maker gives you just two choices here:

♦ **Windows Media DVD quality.** This option saves your movie as a high-quality file suitable for burning to a DVD.

♦ **Windows Media portable device.** This option uses a lower quality and a smaller video size, making it suitable for viewing on portable devices that can play Windows Media video files.

Follow these steps to output your project to a file:

1. Display the **Home** tab.

2. Click the arrow beside the **Output command.**

3. Click the output format you want to use. Movie Maker displays the Output Movie dialog box.

4. Type a name for your movie and select a location.

5. Click **Save.** Movie Maker lives up to its name by making the movie. (This may take awhile, depending on the length of your movie and the number of transitions and effects you added.)

6. When the movie is at long last complete, you can either click **Open** to give it a whirl, or click **Close** to move on to other pursuits.

The Least You Need to Know

◆ If you have an analog camcorder, VCR, or TV, you need a video capture card (or a graphics card that supports video capture) and you need the proper composite or S-Video cable to make the attachment. If your device supports USB, attach it to one of your computer's USB ports.

◆ For a digital camcorder or camera, attach the device to either a USB port or to an IEEE 1394 (FireWire) port.

◆ To record video footage in Windows 7, put your camera in playback mode (if you want to import existing footage) or record mode (to capture a live feed), turn it on, and then attach the camera to your PC.

◆ To add clips to the storyboard, display the **Home** tab and click **Add** in the **Videos and photos** group.

◆ To add a soundtrack to your project, display the **Home** tab and click **Add** in the **Soundtrack** group.

◆ To turn your project into an honest-to-goodness digital movie file, display the **Home** tab, click **Output,** and then click the movie format you prefer.

Sharing Your Computer with Others

In This Chapter

◆ Creating accounts for each person who uses your computer

◆ Understanding the differences between administrators and limited accounts

◆ Setting up accounts with passwords and custom pictures

◆ Sharing and hiding your documents

◆ Keeping an eye on the kids (sort of) with parental controls

Do you share your computer with other people, either at work or at home? Then you've probably run smack dab into one undeniable fact: people are individuals with minds of their own! One person prefers Windows in a black-and-purple color scheme; another person just loves changing the desktop background, the wackier the better; yet another person prefers to have a zillion shortcuts on the Windows desktop; and, of course, *everybody* uses a different mix of applications and creates their own documents. How can you possibly satisfy all these diverse tastes and prevent people from coming to blows?

Well, it's a lot easier than you might think. Windows 7 enables you to set up a different *user account* for each person who uses the computer. These accounts keep your stuff separate from everyone else's stuff, which includes not only documents and programs, but also the desktop and Start menu configuration, Internet Explorer favorites, and more. This means that everyone can customize Windows 7 to their heart's content without foisting their tastes on anyone else. This chapter shows you how to set up, maintain, and use Windows 7's user accounts.

def•i•ni•tion

A **user account** is a kind of storage area where Windows 7 keeps track of one person's documents, e-mail, programs, and customizations.

Understanding These User Account Doodads

In a sense, a user account gives everyone their own version of Windows 7 that they can muck around with as they see fit. This includes the following:

♦ All the customization stuff covered in Part 5 of the book. This means that each user can set up his or her own colors, desktop background, screen saver, toolbar customizations, and Start menu icons.

♦ Favorite websites defined in Internet Explorer.

♦ E-mail and newsgroup accounts set up in Windows Live Mail.

Not only that, but Windows 7 also supports a doohickey called *fast user switching*. What this means is that different users can switch in and out of Windows while leaving their programs running. For example, suppose little Alphonse is blowing away some aliens and Dad needs to check his e-mail. In the old days, Alphonse would have to shut down his game so that Dad could log on and run his e-mail program. In Windows 7, Alphonse can leave his game running while Dad switches to his account and does his e-mail duties. Alphonse can then switch back right away and resume doing nasty things to strange creatures.

The last thing you need to know before getting started is that Windows 7 offers two different user account types:

♦ **Administrator.** This type of account has wide (but not complete) access to the computer. An administrator can install any type of program or device, make changes that affect the entire system, and add, change, and delete user accounts. Note, however that administrators cannot examine the private documents of any other user.

◆ **Standard user.** This type of account has access to only some of the computer's features. It can view its own files, view those files that have been set up to be shared with other users, perform its own customizations, and change its password.

The idea here is that you set up only the most trusted or competent users (such as yourself, of course, and maybe, just *maybe*, your spouse) as administrators and you set up everyone else (such as the kids) as standard users.

Creating a New Account

When you or some suitably savvy geek set up Windows 7 on your computer, the installation program asked for the name of a user. Windows 7 then set up an administrator account for that person. If you're the administrator, then you're free to add more accounts as you see fit.

Here are the steps to follow:

1. Select **Start, Control Panel** to open the Control Panel window.

2. Under **User Accounts and Family Safety,** click **Add or remove user Accounts.**

3. Click **Create a new account.** This launches the Create New Account window.

4. Use the **New account name** text box to enter a name for the user.

5. Choose an account type: **Standard user** or **Administrator.**

6. Click **Create Account.** Windows 7 forges the new account and returns you to the Manage Accounts window, where you see an icon for the new user.

Changing an Existing Account

If you need to make changes to a user account, what you can do depends on your account type:

◆ **If you're an administrator:** You can change anything about any account, including the user's name, password, picture, and account type. You can also delete any account.

◆ **If you're a standard user:** You can only change your own account and there are only two tasks you can perform: creating or changing your password, and changing the picture associated with your account.

In either case, you get started by following these steps:

1. Select **Start, Control Panel** to open the Control Panel window.

2. Click **User Accounts and Family Safety.**

3. Click **User Accounts** to open the User Accounts window.

4. Use the **User Accounts** window to make changes to your own account. If you're an administrator and you want to make changes to another user's account, click **Manage another account** and then click the icon for the user you want to work with to open the Manage Accounts window.

The next few sections run through the instructions for all the available tasks. Note that in each case I assume you're already in the User Accounts window (if you're tweaking your own account) or the Manage Accounts window (if you're messing with someone else's account).

Changing the User's Name

If a user doesn't like the name you supplied, or if he's changed his name or joined a cult, it's not a problem to supply him with a new name that's more to his liking. If you're one of the pooh-bah administrators, here's what you do to change the user's name:

1. If you've got the User Accounts window on-screen, click **Change your account name.** (If you're in the Manage Accounts window, instead, double-click the user you want to work with and then click **Change the account name.**)

2. In the **New account name** text box, enter the new name for the user.

3. Click **Change Name.** Windows 7 changes the user name, just like that.

Creating an Account Password

After you go to all this trouble to set up separate user accounts, you'll likely be shocked and appalled to discover a dismaying fact: any other user can log on to your account just by selecting it in the log-on screen! Doh! To get around this, and to beef up the overall security of your computer, you can protect your things with a password.

Here are the steps to cruise through to set a password for an account:

1. If you've got the User Accounts window on-screen, click **Create a password for your account.** (If you're in the Manage Accounts window, instead, double-click the user you want to work with and then click **Create a password.**)

2. Use the **New password** text box to type the password for the user. (Note that you see a bunch of asterisks instead of the actual characters you type. This is a security feature to prevent someone from spying the password.)

Look Out!

If you store sensitive data on your computer (or just don't want someone to snoop), then you should think carefully about the password you choose. That is, don't use an obvious word (such as your name), use words that are at least eight characters long (the longer the better), mix uppercase and lowercase letters, and toss in a number or two.

3. Use the **Confirm new password** text box to type the password once again.

4. Use the **Type a password hint** text box to enter a password hint. This word or phrase is accessible in the log-on screen and is visible to all and sundry. Therefore, make the hint as vague as possible while still being useful to you if you forget your password.

5. Click **Create password.**

Once you've created a password, the list of tasks for the user account sprouts two new choices:

♦ **Change the password.** Click this link to change the password. Note that you need to enter the old password before Windows 7 lets you set the new one.

♦ **Remove the password.** Click this link to stop using a password. (Again, you need to enter the existing password first.)

Changing the Account Picture

The user account isn't the most exciting topic in the computing world, so it's a welcome relief that Windows 7 includes a feature that lets you have a bit of fun: you can assign a picture to each user. This picture is visible in the log-on screen and on the top of the Start menu when the user is logged on. Windows 7 supplies a random picture when you create an account, but here's how you change it to something else:

1. If you've got the User Accounts window on-screen, click **Change your picture.** (If you're in the Manage Accounts window, instead, double-click the user you want to work with and then click **Change the picture.**) Windows 7 displays a selection of pictures, as shown in Figure 11.1.

2. Click the picture you want to use. If you have your own picture, click **Browse for more pictures,** use the Open dialog box to find the image you want, and then click **Open.**

3. Click **Change Picture.**

Figure 11.1

Use this window to select a picture for the user's account.

Changing the Account Type

If you want to promote a trusted user to administrator status, or if you want to demote some miscreant to standard status, it's not hard:

1. If you've got the User Accounts window on-screen, click **Change your account type.** (If you're in the Manage Accounts window, instead, double-click the user you want to work with and then click **Change the account type.**)

2. Activate either **Standard user** or **Administrator.**

3. Click **Change Account Type.**

Deleting an Account

If you no longer need an account, you may as well delete it to reduce clutter in the Manage Accounts window. Here's how:

1. In the Manage Accounts window, double-click the user you want to get rid of.

2. Click **Delete the account.** Windows 7 asks if you want to keep the contents of the account's folders and desktop.

3. If you want to save these things, click **Keep Files** to store them in a new folder named after the user. Otherwise, click **Delete Files.**

4. Click **Delete Account.**

Logging On to an Account

Once you have two or more user accounts on the go (excluding the Guest account, that is), then each time you crank up Windows 7 you see the Welcome screen, as shown in Chapter 1 in Figure 1.1. Click your user icon to log on to Windows. If the account is protected by a password, a text box will appear. In that case, enter the password and press **Enter.** (If you need to see your password hint, click the question mark button.)

Once you're logged on to an account, you can return to the log-on screen by following these steps:

1. Select **Start** to open the Start menu.

2. Click the arrow beside the **Shut Down** button. Windows 7 displays the menu shown in Figure 11.2.

3. Select one of the following commands:

   ◆ **Switch User.** Click this command if you want to leave the current user's windows and programs open and running. (This is the *fast user switching* feature that I mentioned earlier in the chapter.) At the log-on screen, Windows 7 displays "Logged on" under the user's name.

   ◆ **Log Off.** Click this command if you prefer to shut down all of the current user's windows and programs. Windows 7 drops you off at the log-on screen.

◆ **Lock.** Click this command to leave all your programs running and display a version of the log-on screen that just includes your user name. This is a good choice when you'll be leaving your desk for a bit and you don't want some snoop seeing what's on your screen.

Figure 11.2

*Click the **Shut Down** button's arrow to see various commands for returning to the log-on screen.*

Click the arrow

What's with All the Dialog Boxes? (User Account Control)

You may have noticed while traipsing around the Windows 7 landscape that from time to time the system asks for permission to perform some task. This happens only once in awhile if you're an administrator, but standard users get pestered with these dialog boxes fairly regularly. Why the persnicketiness? It's all about security.

I mentioned earlier that administrator accounts have lots of power over the system. That's not a bad thing on its own, but the social misfits who create viruses and other malicious programs found out ways to take advantage of the situation. Specifically, if you were logged on as an administrator and a virus leeched into your system, that virus could also act as an administrator behind the scenes. With complete access to the system, the virus could do what it wanted, and that almost always spelled disaster.

So the famously big brains at Microsoft figured out a way to thwart viruses and their ilk. It's called *user account control* (UAC), and in a nutshell it means that administrators no longer have complete run of the system. Sure, they can still do all of the things they used to, but now they have to provide credentials to Windows 7 to, in a sense, prove that they're not a virus.

In Windows Vista, UAC was annoyingly pervasive, but Microsoft has thankfully toned things down a notch or three in Windows 7, although there are still lots of situations where you'll need to provide credentials to complete some task. How you provide those credentials depends on the type of user account you're logged on with:

◆ If you're an administrator, you see the User Account Control dialog box shown in Figure 11.3. In this case, all you have to do is click **Yes** to proceed with whatever you wanted to do.

Figure 11.3

If you're an administrator, Windows 7 displays this dialog box when it needs your permission to perform some action.

◆ If you're a standard user, you see the User Account Control dialog box shown in Figure 11.4, instead. Windows 7 shows the name of the original computer administrator (you may see other administrator accounts, if your computer has them) and prompts you for that user's password. After you type the administrator's password, click **Yes** to continue on your way.

Figure 11.4

If you're a standard user, Windows 7 displays this dialog box when it needs your permission to perform some action.

Sharing Documents with (and Hiding Them from) Other Users

Although you'll want to keep most of your documents to yourself, it's conceivable that you'll want other users to be able to see and work with some files. For example, you might scan in some family photos that you want everyone to see or you might store some music that you want other folks to hear.

In Windows 7 no user can access another user's documents directly. However, it's possible to change this behavior and allow other users to access some or all of your folders or files, as well as to control what they can do with those folders or files. To see how, follow these steps:

1. Select **Start** and then click your user name to open your main user account folder.

2. Open the folder you want to share. If you want to share a file, instead, open its folder and then click the file.

3. Click **Share with** and then click **Specific people.** Windows 7 asks you to choose the user accounts you want to share the item with.

4. Type the user name and click **Add.**

5. Repeat step 4 as necessary to share the folder or file with other users.

6. For each user you added, assign a Permission Level by clicking the downward-pointing arrow and selecting one of the following (see Figure 11.5).

   ◆ **Read.** This is the default level and it means the user can only view the shared file or folder; he or she can't change anything.

   ◆ **Read/Write.** This level means that the user can view the shared file or folder, as well as create new items, and make changes to or delete any item.

Figure 11.5

After you add a user, be sure to set the permission level.

7. Click **Share.** Windows 7 takes a few moments to share the item.

8. If you want to send an e-mail to the users to let them know the folder or file is shared, click **e-mail;** otherwise, click **Done.**

If you no longer want to share a folder or file, you can change the sharing using either of the following methods:

◆ **To remove a user from the sharing.** Follow steps 1 to 3 in this section to display the list of shared users. Click the permission level for the user you want to work with, and then click **Remove.**

◆ **To stop sharing the folder or file entirely.** Follow steps 1 and 2 in this section, click **Share with,** and then click **Nobody.**

Protecting Your Kids with Parental Controls

If you have children who share your computer (how brave of you!), or if you're setting up a computer for the kids' use, it's wise to take precautions regarding the content and programs that they can access. Locally, this might take the form of blocking access to certain programs (such as your financial software), using ratings to control which games they can play, and setting time limits on when the computer is used.

All of this sounds daunting, but never fear: Windows 7's Parental Controls make it relatively easy to set all of the aforementioned options and lots more.

Before you begin, be sure to create a standard user account for each child who will use the computer. Once that's done, you set up the Parental Controls by following these steps:

1. Select **Start, Control Panel.**

2. Under the **User Accounts and Family Safety** icon, click the **Set up parental controls for any user** link.

3. Click the user you want to work with to get to the User Controls page.

4. Activate the **On, enforce current settings** option. This enables the Time Limits, Games, and Allow and Block Specific Programs links in the Settings area, as shown in Figure 11.6.

Figure 11.6

*Activate the **On, enforce current settings** option to turn on parental controls.*

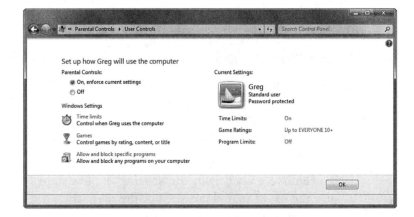

5. Use the following links in the Settings area to set up the specific controls for this user:

   ◆ **Time limits.** Click this link to display the Time Restrictions page, which shows a grid where each square represents an hour during the day for each day of the week. Click the squares to block computer usage during the selected times.

   ◆ **Games.** Click this link to display the Game Controls page. Here you can allow or disallow all games, restrict games based on ratings and contents, and block or allow specific games.

◆ **Allow and block specific programs.** Click this link to display the Application Restrictions page, which displays a list of the programs on your computer. Click the check boxes for the programs you want to allow the person to use.

6. Click **OK.** Windows 7 activates and configures parental controls for the user.

Sharing Stuff with a Windows 7 Homegroup

If you got a home network on the go, and the other computers on your network are running Windows 7, too, then you can take advantage of a new Windows 7 innovation: the *homegroup*. A homegroup is a relatively informal link between two or more Windows 7 PCs on a home network. By using a single password for every user and every PC, the homegroup lets you easily share libraries and printers with your network neighbors.

> **Windows Wisdom**
>
> To make sure your PC is part of a home network, select **Start, Control Panel,** click **View network status and tasks,** and then examine the icon for your network. If you see a **Work network** (or **Public network**) link, click the link and then click **Home network.**

Creating a Homegroup

Windows 7 doesn't create a homegroup automatically, so you must cobble one together yourself by hand. Here's how:

1. Select **Start, Control Panel** to open the Control Panel window.

2. Under **Network and Internet,** click the **Choose homegroup and sharing options.** The Homegroup window appears.

3. Click **Create a homegroup.** Windows 7 coughs up the Create a Homegroup dialog box, shown in Figure 11.7.

4. Activate the check box beside each item you want to share, and then click **Next.** Windows 7 generates a password for your homegroup and displays it.

5. Make a note of the password and then click **Finish.**

Figure 11.7

Use this dialog box to specify which libraries and devices you want to share with the folks in your homegroup.

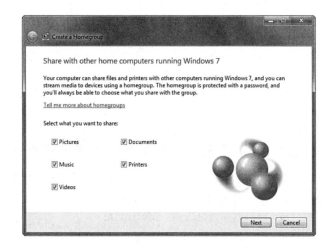

Joining a Homegroup

Once you've got a homegroup hanging around on your network, other Windows 7 PCs can join in the fun by following these steps:

1. Select **Start, Control Panel** to open the Control Panel window.

2. Under **Network and Internet,** click the **Choose homegroup and sharing options.** The Homegroup window appears.

3. Click **Join now.** Windows 7 displays the Join a Homegroup dialog box and prompts you for the homegroup password.

4. Type the password and then click **Next.** Windows 7 joins your computer to the homegroup.

5. Click **Finish.** Windows 7 drops you off back at the Homegroup window.

6. Click the **Choose what you want to share, and view the homegroup password** link. The Homegroup dialog box shows up.

7. Activate the check box beside each item you want to share, and then click **Next.**

8. Click **Finish.**

Windows Wisdom
To change the homegroup password, use the computer that you used to create the homegroup to select **Start, Control Panel, Choose homegroup and sharing options.** In the Homegroup window, click **Change the password** to open the Change Your Homegroup Password dialog box, click **Change the password,** and then either use the password that Windows 7 generates or type your own.

The Least You Need to Know

◆ Windows 7 supports two types of user: *administrators* who can pretty much do what they want, including install programs and devices, change system settings, and work with user accounts; and *standard users* who can only view their own files, view shared files, and perform their own Windows customizations.

◆ The Manage Accounts window is where everything happens; you get there by selecting **Start, Control Panel, Add or remove user accounts.**

◆ To create a new user account, click **Create a new account** in the Manage Accounts window.

◆ To change a user's account doodads, open the Manage Accounts window and then click the **user's icon.**

◆ To switch to a different user, select **Start,** click the **Shut Down** arrow, click **Switch User,** and then click the user's icon.

◆ To work with parental controls, select **Start, Control Panel, Set up parental controls for any user.**

◆ To create or join a homegroup, select **Start, Control Panel, Choose home-group and sharing options.**

Part 3

Windows 7 at Work

Playing around with images and videos and music can be a heckuva lot of fun, but one of these days you've gotta get some work done. (Insert groan of disappointment here.) When the time comes for your nose and the grindstone to get reacquainted, Windows 7 will be there for you with some competent business tools. The chapters in Part 3 look at the most commonly used of these tools. Chapter 12 covers the new Windows Calendar program; Chapter 13 covers faxing; and Chapter 14 covers the Windows 7 notebook features. Don't work too hard!

Places to Go, People to See: Using Windows Live Mail's Calendar

In This Chapter

- ◆ Taking a tour of the Calendar window
- ◆ Setting up an appointment
- ◆ Creating an appointment that occurs at a regular interval
- ◆ Setting up an all-day event
- ◆ Getting Calendar to remind you when appointments or tasks are looming large
- ◆ Using Calendar to keep on top of your things-to-do-places-to-go-have-your-people-call-my-people life

It seems almost redundant to describe modern life as "busy." Everyone is working harder, cramming more appointments and meetings into already-packed schedules, and somehow finding the time to get their regular work done between crises. As many a management consultant has advised over the years (charging exorbitant fees to do so), the key to surviving this helter-skelter, pell-mell pace is *time management.* And although there are as many theories about time management as there are consultants, one of the keys is that you should always try to make the best use of the time available. Although that often comes down to self-discipline and prioritizing your tasks, an efficient scheduling system can sure help.

That's where Windows Live Mail's Calendar feature comes in. It's a sort of electronic secretary that, while it won't get coffee for you, will at least help you keep your affairs in order. Calendar is a simple electronic day-planner you can use to keep track of appointments, meetings, tasks, and other commitments. So, whether you have a date and you can't be late, or you have a rendezvous you need to remember, Calendar can handle it.

> **Windows Wisdom**
>
> Since Calendar is part of Windows Live Mail, it goes without saying (but, apparently, I'm going to say it anyway) that you need to download and install Windows Live Mail before you traipse through the rest of this chapter. See Chapter 6.

Navigating the Calendar Window

To open Calendar, first start Windows Live Mail by selecting the **Start** menu, **All Programs, Windows Live, Windows Live Mail.** You then either click **Calendar** in the lower-left corner of the window, or take the long road and press **Alt** and select **Go, Calendar** (pressing the shortcut key combo **Ctrl+Shift+X** will also get you where you want to go). You see a window similar to the one shown in Figure 12.1 on the following page.

As you can see, Calendar is laid out more or less like a day planner or desk calendar. Here's a quick tour of the three main sections:

- **Date Navigator.** This area shows one month at a time (usually the current month). You use the Date Navigator to change the date displayed in the Events area. Note that today's date always has a blue circle around it.

- **Events.** This part of the Calendar window at first shows one day at a time, divided into half-hour intervals. The appointments and meetings you schedule will appear in this area.

- **Calendars.** This area displays a list of your calendars. Most people use just a single calendar, but you might want separate calendars for, say, business use and personal use.

Previous Next   Currently displayed date
Month   Month

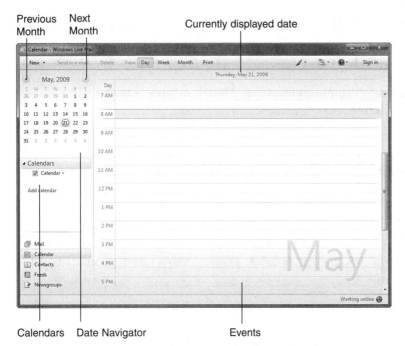

Figure 12.1

Use Calendar to keep track of appointments, all-day events, and tasks.

Calendars   Date Navigator   Events

Time Traveling: Changing the Date

Calendar usually opens with today's date displayed. However, if you want to work with a different day, the Date Navigator makes it easy. All you have to do is click a date, and Calendar will display it in the Events area. If the month you need isn't displayed in the Date Navigator, use either of the following techniques to pick a different month:

- Click the **Previous Month** arrow beside the month to move backward one month at a time. Similarly, click the **Next Month** arrow to move forward one month at a time.

- Move the mouse pointer over the month name and then click to display a list of the months in the current year. Click the month you want to jump to.

Changing the Calendar View

By default, Calendar uses the Day view in the Events area, which shows a single day's worth of appointments and meetings. However, Calendar is quite flexible and has several other views you can use. Here's the complete list:

- **Day.** Click **Day** or press **Alt** and select **View, Day** (or press **Ctrl+Alt+1**).

- **Week.** Displays Sunday through Saturday for the current week. Click **Week** or press **Alt** and select **View, Week** (or press **Ctrl+Alt+2**).

- **Month.** Displays the current month. Click **Month** or press **Alt** and select **View, Month** (or press **Ctrl+Alt+3**).

Setting Your Social Schedule: Entering Events

Got a party to plan, a meeting to make, or a lunch to linger over? The gadabouts, hobnobbers, and other social butterflies in the crowd will like how easy Calendar makes it to schedule these and other get-togethers.

Before getting down to brass Calendar tacks, you should know that Calendar lets you create two kinds of items:

- **Appointment.** An appointment is the most general Calendar item. It refers to any activity for which you set aside a block of time. Typical appointments include a lunch date, a trip to the dentist or doctor, or a back waxing. You can also create *recurring* appointments that are scheduled at regular intervals (such as weekly or monthly).

- **All-day event.** An all-day event is any activity that consumes one or more entire days. Examples include conferences, trade shows, vacations, and "mental health" days. In Calendar, events don't occupy blocks of time. Instead, they appear as banners above the affected days. You can also schedule recurring events.

The next few sections show you how to create appointments and all-day events.

Look Out! _____

Calendar insists on using the term *event* to apply to both appointments and all-day events. Nothing wrong with that, I guess, but I'll keep using the terms *appointment* and *all-day event* throughout the rest of this chapter so you always know exactly what kind of Calendar item I'm yammering on about.

Adding an Appointment

Here are the steps you need to trudge through to set up an appointment:

1. Navigate to the date on which the appointment occurs.

2. Make sure you're in the Day view by clicking **Day.**

3. Select the time you want to set aside for the appointment:

   ◆ If the appointment is a half hour long, double-click the half-hour block in the Events area.

   ◆ For all other appointments, click and drag your mouse in the Events area to select the appointment time you want to use. (Don't worry too much if you don't get the time exactly right; you'll get a chance to fix it in a sec.)

4. Right-click the selected time block and then click **New event.** Calendar opens the New Event window.

5. Use the **Subject** text box to type a title that describes your appointment. Note that Calendar changes the name of the window from New Event to your Subject text.

6. Use the **Location** text box to specify the location (such as a room number or address) for the appointment.

7. If necessary, use the two **Start** controls to set the date and time that the appointment starts. Use the left control to change the date, and use the right control to change the time.

8. If necessary, use the two **End** controls to set the date and time that the appointment ends. Use the left control to change the date, and use the right control to change the time.

9. If you happen to have multiple calendars going, click the **Select a calendar** list and then click the calendar you want to use for this appointment.

10. Use the large text box at the bottom of the window (see Figure 12.2) to type anything else you can think regarding the appointment: a longer description, talking points, a few good jokes, and so on.

> **Windows Wisdom**
>
> To create another calendar, either click the **Add calendar** link in the **Calendars** area, or select **Action, New calendar** (slamming **Ctrl+Shift+D** also does the job). Type a name for the calendar, pick out a suitable color, and then click **Save.**

11. Click **Save & close** (or press **Ctrl+S**). Calendar adds your appointment to the Events area, as shown in Figure 12.3.

Windows Wisdom

If your appointment's start and end times change, you can use your mouse to make the adjustments right in the Events area. To change the start time, click and drag the top edge of the appointment in the Events area; to change the end time, click and drag the bottom edge of the appointment.

Figure 12.2

Use this window to specify the details of your new appointment.

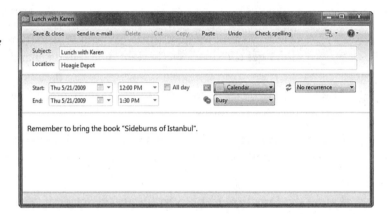

Figure 12.3

An example of an appointment added to Calendar's Events area.

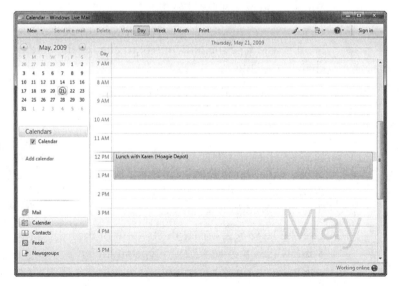

Creating a Recurring Appointment

If you have an appointment that occurs at a regular interval (say, weekly or monthly), Calendar lets you schedule a *recurring* appointment. For example, if you create a weekly appointment, Calendar will fill in that appointment automatically on the same day of the week at the same time for the duration you specify. Thanks!

To schedule a recurring appointment, follow the steps from the previous section. In the event window, use the **Set recurrence** list to select one of the recurrence patterns, including **Daily, Weekly, Monthly,** or **Yearly.** You can also select **Custom** to pop up the Event Recurrence dialog box and use it to set the recurrence pattern to a specific number of days, weeks, months, or years.

Scheduling an All-Day Event

As I mentioned earlier, an all-day event is an activity that consumes one or more days (or, at least, the working part of those days; you do have a life outside of work, right?). Some activities are obvious all-day events: trade shows, sales meetings, corporate retreats, and so on. But what about, say, a training session that lasts from 9 A.M. to 4 P.M.? Is that an all-day event or just a (really) long appointment?

From Calendar's point of view, the main difference between an appointment and an all-day event is that an appointment is entered as a time block in the Events area, but an all-day event is displayed as a banner at the top of the Events area. This means that you can also schedule appointments on days that you have all-day events.

A good example that illustrates these differences is a trade show. Suppose the show lasts an entire day and you're a sales rep who will be attending the show. You could schedule the show as a day-long appointment. However, what if you also want to visit with customers who are attending the show? It's possible to schedule conflicting appointments, but having that day-long appointment in there just clutters the Events area. In this case, it makes more sense to schedule the show as an all-day event. This leaves the Events area open for you to schedule appointments with your customers.

Scheduling an all-day event is exactly the same as setting up an appointment. In fact, there's just two differences in the Details area (see Figure 12.4):

- You need to activate the **All day** check box.

- You can only specify dates for the Start and End of the event.

Figure 12.4

All-day events appear at the top of the Events area.

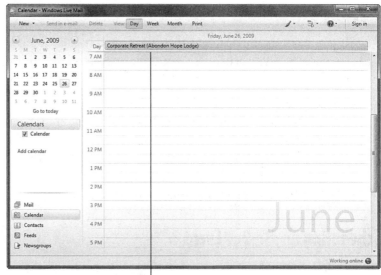

All-day event

The Least You Need to Know

◆ To use Calendar, you need to download and install Windows Live Mail, as described in Chapter 6.

◆ To open Calendar, select **Start, All Programs, Windows Live, Windows Live Mail,** and then click **Calendar** (or press **Alt** and select **Go, Calendar** or press **Ctrl+Shift+X**).

◆ To change dates, use the **Date Navigator** to click the date you want; use the arrows to the left and right of the month to move back or forward one month at a time.

◆ To create an appointment, navigate to the date, click and drag to select the block or time, right-click the block, and then click **New event.**

◆ To create a recurring appointment, start a new event and use the **Set recurrence** list to select a recurrence pattern.

◆ To create an all-day event, either right-click the date and then click **New all day event,** or start a new appointment and activate **All day.**

Fax-It-Yourself: Using Windows 7's Faxing Features

In This Chapter

- ◆ Getting Windows 7 ready for faxing
- ◆ Sending a fax message
- ◆ Creating custom fax cover pages
- ◆ Receiving incoming faxes

If you're of a certain age, you can probably remember when faxing was one of the wonders of the modern world. Imagine being able to send a "facsimile" of a document anywhere in the world over a phone line! Nowadays, faxing is a humdrum, even faintly anachronistic, part of the workaday world, and that miracle machine of the 1980s—the fax machine—is practically obsolete.

Now hang on a sec, Jack. How can I fax without a fax machine!?

I'm glad you asked. The secret is a little device inside your computer called a *fax/modem*—a modem that has the capability to send and receive faxes in addition to its regular communications duties. Not only does this make faxing affordable for small businesses and individuals, but it also adds a new level of convenience to the whole fax experience.

For one thing, you can send faxes right from your computer without having to print the document. And if you have hard copy anyway? Not a problem, because Windows 7 can send a fax right from a document scanner. For another, because faxes sent via computer are high resolution (as opposed to a fax machine's decidedly low resolution), the document that the recipient gets is sharper and easier to read. Finally, you can use your printer to get a hard copy of a fax on regular paper, thus avoiding the fax machine's slimy fax paper.

See Also

Before you can send or receive faxes, you must connect your computer's fax/modem to a phone line. For the details, see the section "Doing It with Dial-Up" in Chapter 15.

If you want to enjoy the fax fast lane from the comfort of your computer, look no further than the Windows Fax and Scan program that comes with Windows 7. This chapter introduces you to Fax and Scan and shows you how to use it to send and receive faxes.

Running Windows Fax and Scan

To get the faxing show on the road, select **Start, All Programs, Windows Fax and Scan.** Windows 7 displays the Windows Fax and Scan window, as shown in Figure 13.1. Fax and Scan is where you'll do your fax work in Windows 7. It includes five "folders" that store fax-related things:

♦ **Incoming.** This folder displays information about the fax that is currently being received. For example, during fax reception the **Status** column displays **In progress** and the **Extended Status** column displays **Answered** and then **Receiving.**

♦ **Inbox.** This folder stores the incoming faxes that were received successfully. Note that the *TSID* column shows the name or phone number of the sender.

def•i•ni•tion

Each fax device has its own name, which is known in the trade as the **TSID—Transmitting Subscriber Identification** (or sometimes Transmitting Station Identifier).

♦ **Drafts.** This folder stores copies of saved faxes that you're composing but haven't sent yet.

♦ **Outbox.** This folder stores data about the fax that's currently being sent. For example, during the send the **Status** column displays **In progress,** and the **Extended Status** column displays **Transmitting.**

♦ **Sent Items.** This folder stores a copy of the faxes that were sent successfully.

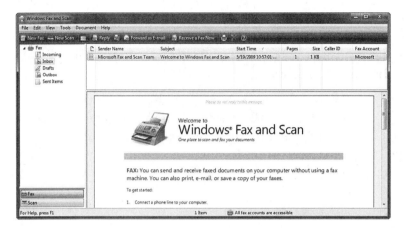

Figure 13.1
Windows Fax and Scan is your home base for Windows 7 faxing.

After you first start Windows Fax and Scan, there are two chores you need to perform before going on to more useful pursuits: create a fax account and tell the program a bit about yourself. The next two sections take you through these mundane but necessary tasks.

Creating a Fax Account

Before you can do anything useful with Windows Fax and Scan, you have to create a fax account, which the program uses to store your incoming and outgoing faxes. Here's what you have to do to create an account:

1. Select **Tools, Fax Accounts** to get the Fax Accounts dialog box in your face.

2. Click **Add** to launch the wizard that will help you get through this.

3. Select **Connect to a fax modem** to move on to the next wizard dialog box.

4. Use the **Name** text box to type a name for your account, and then click **Next.** The Choose How to Receive Faxes dialog box shows up.

5. Click one of the following options:

    ◆ **Answer automatically.** Click this option to have Windows Fax and Scan automatically answer the line after five rings. This is the way to go if you have separate voice and fax lines.

    ◆ **Notify me.** Click this option to answer incoming calls manually. This is the route to take if you have a single phone line that you use for both voice and fax calls.

◆ **I'll choose later; I want to create a fax now.** Click this option if you can't make up your mind and would rather just move on with your life. Fortunately, you can configure this stuff later; see "Setting Up Fax Receiving," later in this chapter.

6. If at this point you see a Windows Security Alert dialog box, try to stay calm. Take a deep breath and then click the **Allow access** button, which tells Windows Firewall that Windows Fax and Scan can talk to the Internet, just in case. The wizard returns you to the Fax Accounts dialog box, where you'll see your freshly minted account in the list.

7. Click **Close.**

Entering Some Personal Data

When you send a fax with a cover page, Windows Fax and Scan includes fields for your name, fax number, business phone number, and home phone number. (You can customize these fields; see the "Covering Your Fax: Creating a Fax Cover Page" section later in this chapter.) If you don't want your recipients to see blanks in these fields, follow these steps to add this personal data to your fax account:

1. Select **Tools, Sender Information** to see the Sender Information dialog box.

2. Type your full name.

3. Type your fax number.

4. Type your home phone.

5. Type your work phone.

6. Fill in the other fields if you feel like it.

7. Click **OK.**

With your account up and running and your personal data safely stored, you're ready to start faxing stuff left and right.

Using "Fax" as a Verb: Sending a Fax

To fax something to a friend or colleague (or, heck, even a total stranger), Windows Fax and Scan gives you three ways to proceed:

◆ You can fax a simple note by sending just a cover page.

◆ You can fax a more complex document by sending it to Windows 7's fax "printer."

◆ You can fax a document right from your scanner.

The next three sections take you through the specifics of each method.

Faxing a Simple Note

Let's start with the simple cover page route, which requires the following steps:

1. Select **File, New, Fax** (or click the **New Fax** button). The New Fax window shows up (see Figure 13.2).

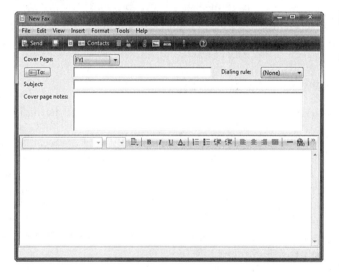

Figure 13.2

Use the New Fax window to send a simple cover page fax.

2. The top part of the New Fax window defines your cover page. Fill in the following fields:

◆ **Cover page.** Select the cover page you want to use. (See the "Covering Your Fax: Creating a Fax Cover Page" section later in this chapter to find out about these predefined cover pages.)

◆ **To.** Enter the recipient's fax number. If you need to add details such as the recipient's company name, address, and phone number, click **To**, click **New Contact,** and then use the tabs in the Properties dialog box to fill in all the information about the recipient. (Be sure to fill in the **Fax** field in either the Work tab or the Home tab.) Click **OK** when you're done. When you return to the Select Recipients dialog box, make sure the new contact name is highlighted, click **To,** and then click **OK.**

♦ **Subject.** Enter the subject of the fax.

♦ **Cover page notes.** Enter your message.

3. Select **File, Send Message.** (You can also press **Alt+S** or click the **Send** toolbar button.) Windows Fax and Scan dials the number and sends the fax. The Fax Monitor window shows up to enable you to follow the progress of the send.

Faxing a Document

Simple notes on a cover page are fine, but if you want to go beyond this, you have to take a different tack. Specifically, you have to use WordPad or some other program to create a document, and you then fax that document to the recipient. Here's how it works:

1. Create the document that you want to ship.

2. Select the program's **File, Print** command to get to the Print dialog box.

3. Select the **Fax** printer and then click **Print.** Your old friend, the New Fax window, reappears. Notice that your document has been converted to an attachment.

4. Follow the steps in the previous section to set the fax options and send the fax. (Note that with this method you don't have to bother with a cover page. If you add a cover page note, you don't need to print it out. Instead, Fax and Scan sends it electronically with the document.)

Faxing a Hard Copy from a Scanner

If you already have a document hard copy that you want to fax, that's no problem for Windows Fax and Scan because the program is happy to grab a copy from your document scanner and then fax the copy. It'll even grab multiple-page scans if your scanner supports that kind of thing. Here's how it works:

1. Place the document (or documents) on your scanner.

2. Select **File, New, Fax From Scanner.** Windows 7 scans the document and the New Fax window appears with the scanned document converted to an attachment.

3. Follow the previously outlined steps to set the fax options and send the fax. (Again, note that with this method you don't have to bother with a cover page. If you go ahead and enter a cover page note, don't bother printing it out because Fax and Scan sends it electronically with the scanned document.)

Covering Your Fax: Creating a Fax Cover Page

You learned earlier that the New Fax window offers predefined cover pages. Here are the four prefab pages you can use:

◆ **Confidential.** This cover page includes the word "confidential" on it, so it's useful for faxes that you want only the recipient to see.

◆ **FYI.** This cover page includes the phrase "for your information" on it, so use it for faxes that don't require a response.

◆ **Generic.** This cover page has no extra text on it, so use it for basic faxes.

◆ **Urgent.** This cover page includes the word "urgent" on it, so it's good for faxes that you want someone to read and respond to as soon as possible.

If you're not exactly thrilled with these default pages, you can create your own pages from scratch.

To edit and create fax cover pages, Windows 7 offers the Fax Cover Page Editor. To launch this program, select **Tools, Cover Pages** to open the Fax Cover Pages dialog box. You now have two choices:

◆ To create a cover page from scratch, click **New.**

◆ To use one of Windows 7's prefab cover pages as a starting point, click **Copy,** click the cover page file, and then click **Open.** This adds the cover page to the Fax Cover Pages dialog box. Click the cover page and then click **Open.**

Figure 13.3 shows the Fax Cover Page Editor with a cover page already on the go (this is a copy of the generic cover page).

Figure 13.3

Use the Fax Cover Page Editor to create cover pages to use with your faxes.

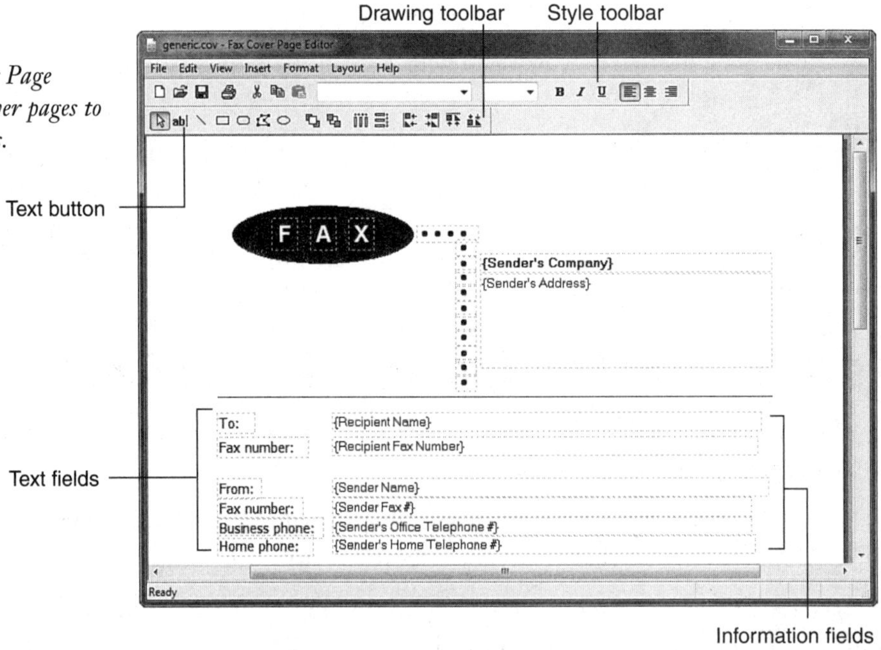

Drawing toolbar   Style toolbar

Text button

Text fields

Information fields

You work with the Fax Cover Page Editor by inserting information, text, and graphics fields. *Information fields* hold data. For example, the **{Sender's Company}** field (these fields always show up surrounded by braces) tells Windows 7 to insert the name of the sender's company each time you use this cover page when you send a fax. With the Fax Cover Page Editor, you can insert fields for recipient, sender, and message data:

- **Recipient fields.** These are fields related to the recipient of the fax. Select **Insert, Recipient** and then select either **Name** or **Fax Number.**

- **Sender fields.** These are the fields you fill in during the Send Fax Wizard (particularly if you use the Address Book method). Select **Insert, Sender** to get a submenu with a boatload of choices, including Name, Fax Number, and Company.

- **Message fields.** These are fields related to the fax message. Select **Insert, Message,** and then select one of the following: **Note, Subject, Date/Time Sent,** or **Number of Pages.**

> **Windows Wisdom**
>
> To select a field, give it a click. If you need to select multiple fields, hold down **Ctrl** and click each field.

When you select a field command, the editor plops the field onto the cover page. You then use your mouse to drag the field to the position on the page that you want. You also can format a field by using the buttons on the Style toolbar or by selecting the **Format, Font** or **Format, Align Text** commands.

Text fields are basically just text boxes. They're used to provide captions for the information fields or to jazz up the cover page with titles, subtitles, and headings. Here are some techniques you can use with text fields:

◆ **To insert a text field:** Click the **Text** button on the Drawing toolbar. Now drag the mouse inside the cover page to create a box for the field and then type in your text.

◆ **To change the text in an existing field:** Double-click the field and then edit the text.

◆ **To format a text field:** Use the Style toolbar or the **Format** menu commands.

Graphics fields hold images that you can use for logos, separators, or just to add some style to the cover page. The Cover Page Editor's Drawing toolbar sports several buttons for drawing objects. All these tools work the same way as the corresponding tools in Paint.

The Cover Page Editor also contains quite a few options for mucking around with the layout of the fields. Here's a rundown of the buttons and commands that are available.

Click This	To Do This
🔲	Move the selected field in front of any fields that overlap it. You also can select **Layout, Bring to Front,** or press **Ctrl+F.**
🔲	Move the selected field behind any fields that overlap it. Alternatively, select **Layout, Send to Back,** or tap **Ctrl+B.**
🔲	Space the selected fields evenly across the page. The other way to go about it is to select **Layout, Space Evenly, Across.**
🔲	Space the selected fields evenly down the page. For some variety, select **Layout, Space Evenly, Down.**
🔲	Align the selected fields along their left edges. The other way to go is to select **Layout, Align Objects, Left.**
🔲	Align the selected fields along their right edges. You also can choose the **Layout, Align Objects, Right** command.

continues

(continued)

Click This	To Do This
🔲	Align the selected fields along their top edges. Selecting **Layout, Align Objects, Top** also works.
🔲	Align the selected fields along their bottom edges. As you've probably guessed by now, you can also select **Layout, Align Objects, Bottom.**

When you're finished with a cover page, save it in the **Personal Cover Pages** folder. Select **File, Save As** and, in the Save As dialog box, open **My Documents,** then **Fax,** then **Personal Cover Pages.**

"Incoming!" Receiving a Fax

The ability to broadcast a fax to the far corners of the planet right from your computer is handy, to say the least. However, my favorite part of computer-based faxing is the opposite chore: receiving incoming faxes. Why? Let me count the ways:

- **No more slimy, curly, fax paper.** When you receive a fax on your computer, it's stored as a file which you can keep electronically or later print on *real* paper.

- **No more wasted paper.** If a junk fax comes in, you can delete it from existence without having to ever print it.

- **Easier storage.** Because received faxes are digital files, you don't need to print them and then file them. Instead, you can use Fax and Scan's folders to store them for safekeeping.

Setting Up Fax Receiving

You probably need to configure Windows Fax and Scan to answer incoming faxes. Here are the steps to follow:

1. Select **Tools, Fax Settings.** The Fax Properties dialog box appears.

2. In the **General** tab, activate the **Allow the device to receive fax calls** check box.

3. Select one of the following options:

    - **Manual answer.** Activate this option to answer incoming calls manually. This is the best option if you have a single phone line that you use for both voice and fax calls.

◆ **Automatically answer after *X* rings.** Activate this option and set the number of rings you want the program to wait before answering. This is the best option if you have a second phone line that you only use for data (faxing, Internet, and so on).

4. Click **OK.**

Handling Incoming Calls

When a fax call comes in, what happens next depends on whether you set up Windows Fax and Scan to answer calls automatically or manually. If it's the latter, you hear a ringing tone and the taskbar's notification area pops up a message that says *FaxID* **is calling** (where *FaxID* is the fax identification or phone number of the faxer).

Click that message to receive the fax. (If you happen to have the Fax Monitor open already, click the **Answer now** button.)

When the fax service answers the call, the Fax Monitor dialog box elbows its way to the fore and shows you the progress of receiving the fax (see Figure 13.4). When it's done, you see a **New fax received** message in the notification area. Click that message to open the Fax and Scan window, where you'll see the new fax in the Inbox folder.

> ### Windows Wisdom
>
> If you find the fax service's sounds (such as the ringing associated with an incoming call) annoying, you can disable them. Select **Tools, Fax Settings** and then display the **Tracking** tab. Click **Sound Options** and then deactivate the check boxes for each sound you want to silence.

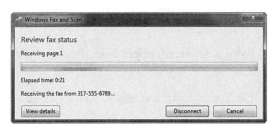

Figure 13.4

The Fax Monitor appears when the fax service answers the incoming call.

Getting the fax service to answer incoming calls is great if you have a dedicated fax line, but what if you share voice and fax calls on the same line? In this case, the first thing you need to do is make sure that the fax service is set up so that you can handle incoming calls manually. Then, the next time the phone rings, pick up the telephone handset. If you hear a series of tones, then you know it's a fax, so click the taskbar's

FaxID **is calling** message and then hang up the handset. (Don't replace the handset before clicking the message or you'll disconnect the call.)

From the Fax and Scan window, you can perform the following chores:

◆ **Read the fax.** Double-click the fax in the Inbox folder (or highlight the fax and select **File, Open**).

◆ **Print the fax.** Highlight the fax and then select **File, Print**.

◆ **Save the fax as an image of a file.** Highlight the fax and then select **File, Save As.** Use the Save As dialog box to choose a name and location for the file and then click **Save.** Note that the fax is saved as a TIF image.

<table>
<tr><td>

See Also

See Chapter 17 for the Windows 7 e-mail details.

</td><td>

◆ **E-mail the fax as an attachment.** Highlight the fax and then select **Document, Forward as E-mail** (or click the **Forward as E-mail** button). Use the New Message window to set up the e-mail message and then click **Send.**

</td></tr>
</table>

◆ **Delete the fax.** Highlight the fax and then select **Edit, Delete** (or just press the **Delete** key).

The Least You Need to Know

◆ Start Windows Fax and Send by selecting **Start, All Programs, Windows Fax and Send.**

◆ To fax a simple note on a cover page, select Fax and Send's **File, New, Fax** command.

◆ To fax a document from a program, select **File, Print,** choose the **Fax** "printer," and then click **Print.**

◆ To fax a document hard copy from a scanner, select Fax and Send's **File, New, Fax from Scanner** command.

◆ To answer a call manually and then have the computer intercept the fax, click the taskbar's *FaxID* **is calling** message.

◆ To view a received fax, click the taskbar's **New fax received** message and then double-click the fax in Fax and Scan's Inbox folder.

Chapter 14

Windows 7 and Your Notebook Computer

In This Chapter

◆ Becoming friends with the Mobility Center

◆ Keeping an eye peeled on your battery status

◆ Using power management to extend the life of your notebook's battery

◆ Setting up your notebook for making presentations

◆ Checking out Windows 7's notebook niceties

If you have a notebook computer, then you know full well that these machines are fundamentally different from their desktop cousins, and that the difference goes well beyond mere luggability. There are batteries to monitor, presentations to set up, and on and on.

The Windows 7 programmers must have had to wrestle with notebooks a time or two themselves, because they've put together a passel of portable perks. Windows 7 offers power management for sensitive notebook batteries, an easy way to configure your notebook to make a presentation, and powerful tools for bringing it all together. I discuss all of these capabilities in this chapter.

Your One-Stop Notebook Shop: The Mobility Center

Windows 7 is chock-full of notebook knickknacks, most of which seem to have been designed with a single purpose in mind: to give us notebook toters easier access to those notebook-related features that we use most. Thanks!

This makes sense (oh, such a rare phrase when talking about computers) because when you're using a notebook on the go, you may have only a limited amount of juice in your battery, and you don't want to waste precious power trying to locate some configuration option. And, sadly, it's still the case that most notebook keyboards and pointing devices are harder to use than their full-size desktop cousins, so the fewer keystrokes and mouse clicks required to perform Windows tasks the better.

Your first indication that Windows 7 wants to make your mobile computing life easier is the Windows Mobility Center, shown in Figure 14.1. Fire it up yourself by selecting **Start, Control Panel** and then clicking the **Adjust commonly used mobility settings** (it's under the Hardware and Sound heading).

The idea behind the Mobility Center is simple but surprisingly useful: bring together in a single spot all the Windows 7 configuration options that are directly or indirectly related to notebooks. Whether you want to change the screen orientation on your Tablet PC, adjust settings before a presentation, or change power options, it's all just mere mouse clicks away.

Figure 14.1

The Mobility Center offers a smorgasbord of information and controls for notebook-related features.

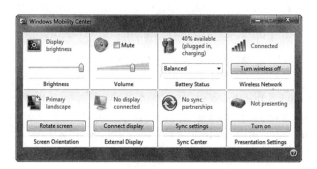

The Mobility Center is loaded with information on eight key notebook areas, as well as controls that let you adjust these features when the mood strikes you:

- ◆ **Brightness.** The current brightness setting of your notebook screen (if your machine supports this feature, that is). Use the slider to adjust the brightness.

- ◆ **Volume.** The current notebook speaker volume. Use the slider to adjust the volume to your liking, or click **Mute** to knock off the notebook's racket entirely.

◆ **Battery Status.** The current charge level of the notebook battery. Use the drop-down list to select one of three power plans: Balanced, Power saver, or High performance (see "Better Battery Life Through Power Management" below for the details on these plans).

◆ **Wireless Network.** The wireless connection status (Connected or Disconnected) and the signal strength if connected.

◆ **Screen Orientation.** The current orientation of the Tablet PC screen. Click **Rotate screen** to rotate the screen by 90 degrees in the counterclockwise direction.

◆ **External Display.** The current status of the external monitor connected to your notebook or docking station.

◆ **Sync Center.** The current synchronization status of your offline files. Click the **Sync settings** button to synchronize your notebook's offline files.

◆ **Presentation Settings.** The current presentation status. Click **Turn on** to activate Windows 7's notebook presentation settings. (Want to know more? Of course you do, so check out "Setting Up Your Notebook for a Presentation," later in this chapter.)

Note, too, that Microsoft is letting PC manufacturers get their not-all-that-grubby hands on the Mobility Center, so your version of the Mobility Center window may be tricked out with features specific to your notebook.

Better Battery Life Through Power Management

When using batteries to run your notebook computer on an airplane or some other no-power-outlet-in-sight location, it's natural to worry. That's because the battery can last only so long, so you have a limited amount of time to work or play before your electronic world goes dark. Windows 7 can help relieve some of that worry thanks to its *power management* features. For example, one of these features enables the system to shut down idle components (such as the hard disk and monitor) to prevent them from gobbling up battery power unnecessarily. Another

def•i•ni•tion

Power management refers to those Windows 7 features that enable you to monitor and manage the power consumption of devices, particularly notebook computer batteries and your hard disk and monitor.

feature lets you monitor how much power is left in the battery. This section takes you on a tour of these and other Windows 7 power-management landmarks.

Keeping an Eye on Battery Life

Keeping watch over your remaining battery life is crucial, and that's probably why Windows 7 gives you not one, not two, but *three* ways to do it:

◆ **Use the Mobility Center.** You saw earlier that the new Mobility Center doo-hickey includes a Battery Status section (flip back to Figure 14.1 if you don't believe me) that gives you estimates on both the time and percentage remaining on the battery.

◆ **Eyeball the taskbar's Power icon.** When you're running under battery power, you see the Power icon shown in Figure 14.2. When the battery is fully charged, the icon is white from top to bottom; as the battery gradually loses its steam, the level of white in the icon falls. For example, when there is 50 percent of battery life remaining, the icon shows as half white and half gray.

Figure 14.2

The Power icon tells you how much juice is left in your battery.

The Power icon

◆ **Point at the Power icon.** If deciphering the amount of white in the Power icon is just a bit too vague for you, you can get a less hieroglyphic reading by moving your mouse pointer over the Power icon. As you can see in Figure 14.3, Windows 7 raises a small banner that shows the time and percentage of power remaining.

Figure 14.3

Point the mouse at the Power icon to get a more detailed readout of the battery status.

41% remaining

Power to the People: Specifying a Power Plan

As I mentioned earlier, Windows 7 cheerfully shuts down some system components in an effort to keep your battery on its feet longer. This is controlled by your current *power plan*, a power management configuration that specifies which bits and pieces get shut down and when Windows 7 shuts them down. Windows 7 has three power plans to choose from:

♦ **Power saver.** Devices such as the screen and hard disk are powered down after a short idle interval. For example, on battery power, Windows 7 turns off the notebook display after 2 minutes.

♦ **High performance.** Devices are powered down only after a longer idle interval, which improves performance because you're less likely to have to wait for them to start up again. For example, on battery power, Windows 7 turns off the notebook hard disk after 10 minutes.

♦ **Balanced.** The middle road (more or less) between the Power saver and High performance plans. For example, on battery power, Windows 7 turns off the notebook display after 5 minutes.

The default power plan is Balanced, but Windows 7 again gives you three methods to change it:

♦ **Via the Mobility Center.** In the Battery Status section, use the drop-down list to select a power plan.

♦ **Via the Power icon.** Click the **Power** icon to see the banner shown in Figure 14.4, and then click either **Balanced** or **Power** saver. (Sadly, the High performance power plan isn't available using this method.)

Figure 14.4

*Click the **Power** icon and then click a power plan.*

♦ **Via the Power Options window.** Click the **Power** icon and then click **More power options** to display the Power Options window shown in Figure 14.5, then click a power plan option. (If you're looking for that elusive High performance plan, you have to click **Show additional plans** to make it come out of hiding.)

Figure 14.5

*Double-click the **Power** icon to display the Power Options window.*

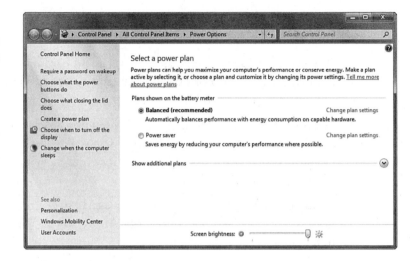

Cobbling Together Your Own Power Plan

If you're feeling different drummerish, you don't have to accept the default configuration for any of the power plans. Windows 7 offers a few different options for each plan, and you're free to play around with them to concoct a plan that suits the way you work. Here's how:

1. In the Power Options window, click **Change plan settings** beside the plan you want to mess with. The Edit Plan Settings window shows up. Figure 14.6 shows the Edit Plan Settings window for the Balanced power plan.

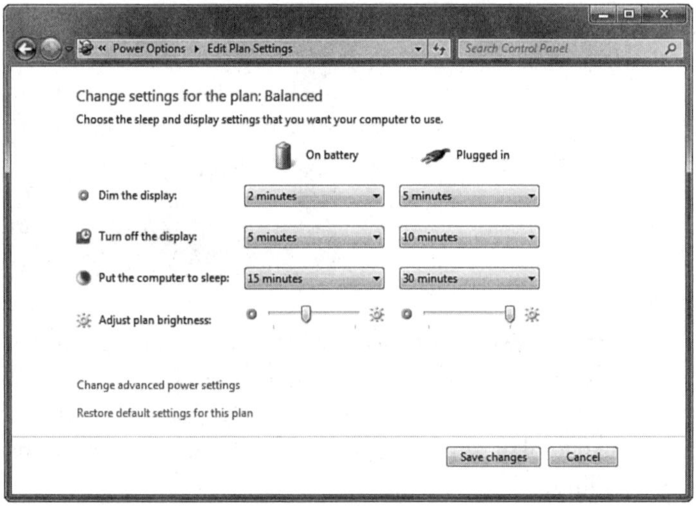

Figure 14.6

Use the Edit Plan Settings window to customize your own personal power plan.

2. In the **On battery column,** use the **Dim the display** list to select when you want Windows 7 to reduce screen brightness.

3. In the **On battery column,** use the **Turn off the display** list to select when you want Windows 7 to shut down the display.

4. In the **On battery column,** use the **Put the computer to sleep** list to select when you want Windows 7 to put your notebook into sleep mode.

5. In the **On battery column,** use the **Adjust plan brightness** slider to set the standard screen brightness.

6. Repeat steps 2 to 5 to configure the same options in the **plugged in** column.

7. Click **Save changes.**

Configuring Your Notebook's Power Buttons

Most newer notebooks enable you to configure three "power buttons": closing the lid, the on/off button, and the sleep button. (On some notebooks, there isn't a separate sleep button. Instead, you tap the on/off button quickly.) When you activate these buttons, they put your system into sleep or hibernate mode, or turn it off altogether.

Follow these steps to configure these buttons for power management:

1. In the Power Options window, click **Choose what the power buttons do.** The System Settings window shows up.

2. In each of the following three sections, select a power management option for running **On battery** and **Plugged in:**

   ♦ **When I press the power button:** Choose Do nothing, Sleep, Hibernate, or Shut down.

   ♦ **When I press the sleep button:** Choose Do nothing, Sleep, or Hibernate.

   ♦ **When I close the lid:** Choose Do nothing, Sleep, Hibernate, or Shut down.

3. Click **Save changes.**

Setting Up Your Notebook for a Presentation

The portability of a notebook or other mobile computer means that these machines are now the first choice as the source of content for presentations from the boardroom to the conference room. That's the good news. The bad news is that there are always a few chores you need to (or should) tend to before starting your presentation:

♦ Turn off your screen saver. The last thing you want is your screen saver kicking in while you're spending some extra time explaining a point.

♦ Turn off system notifications, including alerts for incoming e-mail messages and instant messaging posts. Your viewers don't want to be interrupted by these distractions.

♦ Adjust the speaker volume to an acceptable level.

♦ Select an appropriate desktop wallpaper image. Your desktop may be visible before or after the presentation, if only briefly. Even so, you probably want a wallpaper that invokes a professional image, or you may prefer a blank desktop.

If you're a regular presenter, changing all these settings before each presentation and reversing them afterwards is a time-consuming chore. However, Windows 7 comes with a feature called Presentation Settings that promises to take most of the drudgery out of this part of presenting. The Presentation Settings feature is a collection of configuration options, including screen blanking, system notifications, speaker volume, and desktop wallpaper. You use Presentation Settings to specify the configuration options you want to use during a presentation. Once you've done that, you can then use Presentation Settings to turn those options on (and off) with just a few mouse clicks.

Windows Wisdom

If you happen to have the Mobility Center on-screen, a quicker way to open the Presentation Settings dialog box is to click the projector icon in the Presentation Settings section.

To configure the Presentation Settings, follow these steps:

1. Select **Start, Control Panel, Hardware and Sound.**

2. Under the **Windows Mobility Center** heading, click **Adjust settings before giving a presentation.** Windows 7 displays the Presentation Settings dialog box shown in Figure 14.7.

3. Use the following controls to set up your notebook for presentations:

◆ **Turn off the screen saver.** Activate this check box to prevent the screen saver from kicking in.

◆ **Set the volume to.** Activate this check box and then use this slider to set the volume level you want.

◆ **Show this background.** Activate this check box and then click **Browse** to select a background (or click **None**).

4. Click **OK** to save the settings.

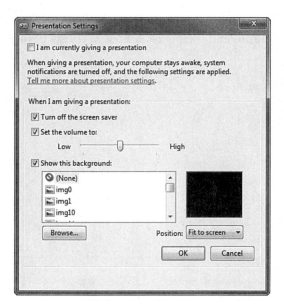

Figure 14.7

Use the Presentation Settings dialog box to set up a computer configuration to use when you're giving a presentation.

When it's time to take center stage and make your presentation, you have two ways to switch over to your saved settings:

◆ Open the Mobility Center and select **Turn on** in the Presentation Settings section. (Select **Turn off** when you're done.)

◆ Open the Presentation Settings dialog box, activate the **I am currently giving a presentation** check box, and click **OK**. (Deactivate this check box after the applause has subsided and you're ready to leave.)

The Least You Need to Know

◆ Select **Start, Control Panel, Adjust commonly used mobility settings** (it's under the Hardware and Sound heading) to try out Windows 7's new Mobility Center feature.

◆ When running your notebook on batteries, be sure you use the taskbar's Power icon to keep a close eye on the battery level.

◆ Click the **Power** icon to select a different power plan.

◆ Double-click the **Power** icon to open up the Power Options window.

◆ To configure your preferred presentation settings, select **Start, Control Panel, Hardware and Sound,** and then click **Adjust settings before giving a presentation.**

Part 4

Windows 7 on the Internet

For years, lots of pontificating pundits frowned on computers because they saw them as noninteractive machines that served to encourage anti-social behavior. Boy, did they get that wrong! As proof, you need look no further than the hundreds of millions of people who are on the Internet. These people aren't clamoring to listen to cheesy MIDI music. They want to connect. They want to exchange e-mail epistles; they want to natter in newsgroups; they want to chin-wag in chat rooms. In other words, computers have become interactive machines that encourage socializing. Who'da thunk it? If you want to get in on all this fun, the four chapters in Part 4 will tell you everything you need to know.

Chapter 15

Getting onto the Internet

In This Chapter

- How to choose an Internet service provider
- What you need to know to get an account and start surfing
- Understanding the difference between dial-up and broadband
- Getting connected to the Internet
- Getting disconnected from the Internet

The Internet's tentacles have insinuated themselves into every nook and cranny of modern life. Businesses from corner-hugging mom-and-pop shops to continent-straddling corporations are online; web pages are now counted in the billions; and people send far more e-mail messages than postal messages.

It truly is a wired (which, remember, is just "weird" spelled sideways) world, and if you feel like you're the only person left who isn't online, this chapter will help. I'll tell you exactly what you need to make it happen, and then I'll take you through the connection process, step by finicky step.

What to Look For in an Internet Service Provider

The route to the Internet isn't a direct one. Instead, you can only get there by engaging the services of a middleman or, more accurately, a middle company: an *Internet service provider* (ISP for short).

An ISP is a business that has negotiated a deal with the local telephone company or some other behemoth organization to get a direct connection to the Internet's highways and byways. These kinds of connections cost thousands of dollars a month, so they're out of reach for all but the most well-heeled tycoons. The ISP affords it by signing up subscribers and offering them a piece of the ISP's Internet connection. After you have an account with an ISP, the connection process works as follows:

def•i•ni•tion

An **Internet service provider** (ISP) takes your money in exchange for providing an Internet account, which you need in order to get online.

1. You use your modem to connect to the ISP.

2. The ISP's computer verifies that you're one of their subscribers.

3. The ISP's computer sets up a connection between your computer and the Internet.

4. You go, girl (or boy, as the case may be)!

So before you can do anything on the Internet, you have to set up an account with an ISP and then you need to give Windows the details. Before we get to that, let's take a second to run through a few pointers to bear in mind when deciding which ISP to use.

The first thing you have to decide is what type of connection you want, which will affect the kind of ISPs you check out. There are three basic connection types:

- **Dial-up.** This type of connection uses your computer's modem to dial a phone number that connects the modem to an ISP's system. In general, dial-up connections are slow, but cheap.

- **Broadband.** This type of connection uses a special external modem to connect to the ISP. Broadband connections are usually a bit more expensive than dial-up, but they are many times faster. Most folks use broadband these days.

- **Wireless.** This type of connection uses wireless networking technology to connect to a nearby device that has an Internet connection already set up (which is usually a broadband connection).

The next few sections take you through some specific ISP pointers for each type of connection, but here are four general ones to bear in mind when you're ISP shopping:

♦ Connection speeds are measured in either thousands of bits per second—usually abbreviated as kbps—or millions of bits per second—usually abbreviated as mbps. (A bit is the fundamental unit of information that computers deal with. For example, it takes eight bits to define a single character, such as "a" or even "ä.")

♦ Make sure the ISP offers a local or toll-free number for technical support.

♦ I recommend dealing with only large ISPs. There are still plenty of fly-by-night operations out there, and they're just not worth the hassle of dropped connections, busy signals, lack of support, going belly-up when you most need them, and so on.

♦ If you can't decide between two or more ISPs, see what extra goodies they offer: space for your own web pages, extra e-mail accounts, Internet software bundles, and so on.

Doing It with Dial-Up

Here are some things to mull over if you're thinking about a dial-up connection:

♦ Most ISPs charge a monthly fee, which typically ranges from $5 to $30. Decide in advance the maximum that you're willing to shell out each month.

♦ When comparing prices, remember that ISP plans usually trade off between price and the number of hours of connection time. For example, the lower the price, the fewer the hours you get.

♦ It's important to note that most plans charge you by the minute or by the hour if you exceed the number of hours the plan offers. These charges can be exorbitant (a buck or two an hour), so you don't want to get into that. Therefore, you need to give some thought to how much time you plan to spend online. That's hard to do at this stage, I know, but you just need to ballpark it. If in doubt, get a plan with a large number of hours (say, 100 or 150). You can always scale it back later on.

> **Windows Wisdom**
>
> Most people find that they spend a ton of time on the Internet for the first few months as they discover all the wonders and weirdness that's available. After they get used to everything, their connection time drops dramatically.

◆ Most major ISPs offer an "unlimited usage" plan. This means you can connect whenever you want for as long as you want, and you just pay a set fee per month (usually around $20). This is a good option to take for a few months until you figure out how often you use the Internet.

◆ All modems made in the past few years support a faster connection speed called 56K (or sometimes V.90), which offers a maximum speed of 56 kbps. If you have such a modem (if you're not certain, it's probably safe to assume that you do), make sure the ISP you choose also supports 56K (almost all of them do nowadays).

Look Out!

A dial-up connection to the Internet is just like making any other phone call, which means that anyone trying to call *you* will get a busy signal.

◆ Make sure the ISP offers a local access number to avoid long-distance charges. If that's not an option, make sure they offer access via a toll-free number. (Note: watch out for extra charges for the use of the toll-free line.) Even better, some nationwide ISPs offer local access in various cities across the land. This is particularly useful if you do a lot of traveling.

If you use a dial-up Internet connection, your telephone and modem will probably share the same line. In this case, you don't have to switch the cable between the phone and the modem all the time. Instead, it's possible to get a permanent, no-hassle setup that'll make everyone happy. The secret is that all modems have two telephone cable jacks in the back:

◆ **Line jack.** This one is usually labeled "Line" or "Telco," or has a picture of a wall jack.

◆ **Telephone jack.** This one is usually labeled "Phone" or has a picture of a telephone.

Follow these directions to set things up:

1. Run a phone cable from the wall jack to the modem's line jack.

2. Run a second phone cable from the telephone to the modem's telephone jack.

This setup lets you use the phone whenever you need it—the signal goes right through the modem (when you're not using it, of course)—and lets you use the modem whenever you need it.

Heading Down the Broadband Highway

Most people use broadband nowadays for a simple reason: it's way faster than dial-up. Depending on the connection speed, it can be anywhere from four or five times faster to 20, 30, or even 50 times faster. That's a lot of faster. (Another broadband bonus: you don't tie up your phone line when you're connected.) Here are some things to put on your "Broadband Shopping Notes" list:

◆ Most ISPs charge a monthly fee, which typically ranges from $15 to $60.

◆ Broadband requires a different kind of modem, which you usually rent from the ISP. Make sure you find out what the rental fee will be.

◆ When comparing prices, remember that broadband ISP plans usually trade off between price and connection speed. For example, a cheap plan might get you a 256 kbps connection, while a more expensive plan might max out at 5 mbps.

◆ When you look at the broadband speed, you'll almost always see two numbers, one higher than the other. The higher rate is the *download speed*, which is the speed at which stuff from the Internet is sent to your computer; the lower rate is the *upload speed*, which is the speed at which you send stuff from your computer to the Internet. Most Internet connections spend way more time downloading than uploading, so the download speed is really the one to watch.

◆ It's important to note that most plans put a monthly limit on the amount of data you can send back and forth, or the *bandwidth*. If you exceed that amount, you get charged extra (be sure to find out how much!).

I mentioned earlier that broadband uses a special ISP-supplied modem. Here are the basics for getting it set up:

◆ Run a phone cable from the wall jack to the port in the back of the modem.

◆ Run a networking cable from the network port in the back of the modem to the network card port in the back of your computer.

Going Wireless

If you want to set up a wireless Internet connection for your computer, this isn't something you get from an ISP, at least not directly. Instead, you need to establish an Internet connection—this is almost always a broadband connection—and then set it up on a separate device.

This separate device is usually a wireless router or gateway. Here's how to set things up:

♦ Run a phone cable from the wall jack to the port in the back of the broadband modem.

♦ Run a networking cable from the network port in the back of the modem to the special port (labeled "Internet" or "WLAN" or something similar) in the back of the wireless router.

If you haven't yet configured the wireless router or gateway for Internet access, see the manual that came with the device for instructions on how to proceed.

Getting Ready to Rumble: Gathering Information

As you'll see in just a sec, you can build your Internet connection with your bare hands, but you need to gather some raw material first. Whether it's a dial-up or broadband connection to your Internet account, you need to have the proper bits of information from your ISP. In the bad old days (way back in the previous century), you needed reams of the most obscure and incomprehensible gobbledygook you'd ever laid eyes on. Things are much more civilized nowadays (insert prayer to higher power of choice here), so you need to have just the following tidbits to *log on*:

♦ For a dial-up connection, you need the phone number you have to dial to connect to the ISP.

♦ For dial-up and broadband, you need the user name (which might also be called your log-on name) and password that you use to log on to the ISP.

♦ For a wireless connection, you need to know the name of your wireless network (sometimes called the SSID) and the security key or password, if the network requires one.

def•i•ni•tion

To **log on** means to provide your ISP with your user name and password, and so gain access to the wonder that is the Internet.

With that info at your side, you're now ready to set up the account.

Getting Started on Your Road to the Internet

Depending on who set up your computer, there's a chance your computer is already Net-friendly. To find out, click the **Internet Explorer** icon in the taskbar (it's the fancy-schmancy "e" icon to the right of the Start button) to crank up the Internet

Explorer web browser. If you end up on a web page, then your Internet connection is a going concern. If you see the sad message that "Internet Explorer cannot display the webpage," you've got a few hoops that you still need to jump through.

There's a good chance that your ISP sent you some kind of CD that contains the bits and pieces you need to get your connection running. If so, insert the CD and follow whatever instructions come your way to let the ISP handle all the hard stuff for you.

No CD? No problem. Whether your Internet path is a dial-up road or a broadband highway, you start things off by following these steps:

1. Select **Start, Control Panel** to get the Control Panel window on-screen.

2. Select **Network and Internet** to open the Network and Internet windows.

3. Under the **Internet Options** icon, click **Connect to the Internet.** At long last, you see the three choices you've been waiting for: Wireless, Broadband, and Dial-up, as shown in Figure 15.1.

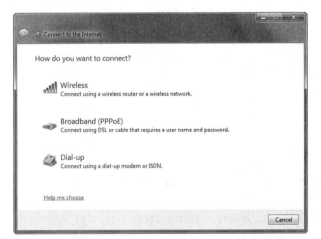

Figure 15.1

The inevitable fork in the Internet road: select Wireless, Broadband, or Dial-up.

4. Click the connection type you long for:

   ♦ **Dial-up.** If you click this type, you see a dialog box with the long-winded name, Type the information from your ISP. You use this dialog box to type in your ISP's phone number, and your user name and password. Figure 15.2 shows a completed version of this dialog box.

Windows Wisdom

For dial-up and broadband connection, you can save yourself having to type the password every time you log on by activating the **Remember this password** check box.

Figure 15.2

Use the dialog box with the long name to type in the info your ISP sent you.

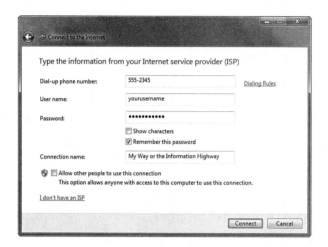

◆ **Broadband.** If you click this type, you see a dialog box that's almost a carbon copy of the one in Figure 15.2. The only difference is that you don't have to type in the dial-up phone number.

◆ **Wireless.** If you click this type, Windows 7 displays a list of nearby wireless networks. Click your network and then type in the security key or password, if you're asked for one.

5. Click **Connect.** Windows 7 creates the new connection and then takes it for a test drive.

If all goes well, you'd think there'd be music and fireworks because, hey, you're on the Internet! But, alas, no. You just get a rather ho-hum dialog box that says **You are connected to the Internet** (not even any exclamation points!), shown in Figure 15.3. If you're not quite ready to do the Internet thing right away, you should disconnect your dial-up connection, as described a bit later in the "Severing the Connection" section.

Figure 15.3

You see this dialog box if your Internet connection was a success.

Making the Connection

Windows 7 is considerate enough to establish a connection to the Internet automatically after you set up your account. If you're using a broadband connection, then you'll probably want to keep it running full-time, for convenience. You can't do that with dial-up, so you need to disconnect after you're done, and then reconnect later when you're looking for more Internet action.

To reconnect to the Internet, you have a couple of choices:

◆ **Making the connection by hand:** Click the **Network** icon in the taskbar's notification area (see Figure 15.4), click the Internet connection you created, click **Connect,** and then click **Dial.**

◆ **Starting an Internet program:** If you launch a program that requires an Internet connection—such as Internet Explorer or Windows Live Mail—Windows 7 displays the Dial-up Connection dialog box shown in Figure 15.5. Click **Connect** to make things happen.

> **Windows Wisdom**
>
> For even faster service in the future, activate the **Connect automatically** check box. This tells Windows 7 to bypass the Dial-up Connection dialog box and make the connection without pestering you.

Figure 15.4

*Click the **Network** icon, click your connection, and then click **Connect**.*

Figure 15.5

Now when you launch Internet-friendly programs such as Internet Explorer or Windows Live Mail, Windows 7 automatically prompts you to connect to the Internet.

Severing the Connection

When you've stood just about all you can stand of the Internet's wiles, you can log off by clicking the **Network** icon in the notification area, clicking your connection, and then clicking **Disconnect,** as shown in Figure 15.6.

Figure 15.6

Now when you launch Internet Explorer or Windows Mail, Windows 7 automatically prompts you to connect to the Internet.

The Least You Need to Know

◆ If you'll be setting up your connection by hand, your ISP should provide you with the settings and data you need: the access phone number (for dial-up) and your user name and password.

◆ To have both your phone and your modem available for use, run a phone cable from the wall jack to the modem's line port, and run a second cable from the phone to the modem's telephone jack.

◆ Making the leap to the Internet is as easy as clicking the cute little **Network** icon in the taskbar's notification area, clicking your connection, and then clicking **Connect.**

◆ To return to the real world, click your old friend the **Network** icon in the notification area, click your connection, and then click **Disconnect.**

Chapter 16

Wandering the Web with Internet Explorer

In This Chapter

- Using Internet Explorer to navigate web pages
- Saving web pages to your Favorites list
- Searching for the information you need
- Figuring out these newfangled tabs
- Dealing with file downloads
- Subscribing to RSS feeds (whatever they are)

Whether you're 19 or 90, a world traveler or a channel surfer, I don't think I'm going out on a limb when I say that you've probably never seen anything quite like the World Wide Web. We're talking here about an improbably vast conglomeration of the world's wit, wisdom, and weirdness. Arranged in separate pages of information, the web is home to just about every conceivable topic under the sun. If someone's thought of it, chances are someone else has a web page about it.

See Also

If you haven't yet signed up with an Internet service provider, it means you've skipped ahead in this book (and I've caught you!). To learn about signing up with an ISP, check out Chapter 15.

So the web is definitely worth a look or three. This chapter helps you get those looks by showing you how to use the Windows 7 Internet Explorer program, which is designed to surf (to use the proper web verb) websites. You'll learn all the standard page navigation techniques, and you'll learn all the features that Internet Explorer offers for making your online journeys more efficient and pleasant.

Cranking Up Internet Explorer

Assuming you have your Internet connection on the go, the most straightforward way to get Internet Explorer up and surfing is to click the **Internet Explorer** icon in the taskbar (it's the "e" with the swooshy thing around it, usually right beside the Start button). If you don't see that icon for some reason, you can also select **Start, All Programs, Internet Explorer.**

The first time you launch Internet Explorer, you may have to wrestle with the Set Up Windows Internet Explorer 8 Wizard. You can click the **Ask me later** button if you really don't feel like dealing with a wizard right now, but he'll just keep coming back, believe me, so it's better to get the whole setup rigmarole over with now. Here's what happens:

1. In the initial wizard dialog box, click **Next.** The Turn on Suggested Sites dialog box appears. Suggested Sites is an Internet Explorer 8 feature that displays a list of websites that are similar to whatever website you're currently viewing.

2. If Suggested Sites sounds like a good idea (you'll probably find it at least occasionally useful), select the **Yes, turn on Suggested Sites** option, and then click **Next.** The Choose your settings dialog box appears.

3. Select the **Use express settings** option (it's way faster than configuring everything by hand), and then click **Finish.** Internet Explorer throws up the Welcome to Internet Explorer page, which is seriously uninteresting.

4. Press **Ctrl+W** to close the page.

That's it. Now it's on with the web show.

Getting to Know Internet Explorer's Nuts and Bolts

There's a good chance that you'll now arrive at the MSN.com website, shown in Figure 16.1. (You may end up at a different site if your version of Windows 7 comes with custom Internet settings.) Note that this screen changes constantly, so don't sweat it if the one you see looks different than the one shown in Figure 16.1.

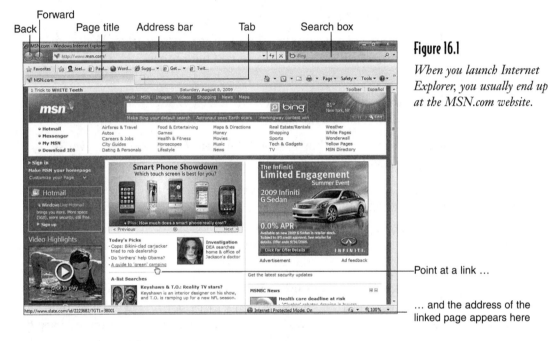

Figure 16.1

When you launch Internet Explorer, you usually end up at the MSN.com website.

MSN.com is Microsoft's Internet starting point. (This kind of site is known as a *portal* in the web trade.) With its colorful layout, generous graphics, and loads of links, MSN.com is a typical example of the professionally designed pages that the big-time sites offer.

Hacking Windows

If you don't like MSN.com (or whatever you have as Internet Explorer's default start page), it's easy to change it. First, surf to the page that you want to use as the new start page. Then select the **Tools, Internet Options** command to lure the Internet Options dialog box out into the open. In the General tab, click **Use current.** If you decide later on that you prefer Internet Explorer's default home page, open the Internet Options dialog box once again, but this time click **Use default.** If you'd rather not see any page at startup (useful if you want to launch Internet Explorer while you're not connected to the Internet, or if you like the restful, calming effect of the blank "page" that shows up), open the Internet Options dialog box and click **Use blank.**

Before I show you how to use this page to see more of the web, let's take a minute or two and get our bearings by checking out the main features of the Internet Explorer window (most of which I've pointed out in Figure 16.1):

◆ **Page title.** The top line of the screen shows you the title of the current web page. The title also appears in the tab, which is a new Internet Explorer feature. See "One-Window Browsing: Surfing with Tabs," later in this chapter to learn why these tab things are such a big hairy deal.

◆ **Address bar.** This area shows you the address of the current page. Web page addresses are strange beasts, indeed. I'll help you figure them out a bit later in this chapter.

◆ **Back and Forward.** You use these buttons to return to sites you've visited, as I explain in excruciating detail a bit later.

◆ **Search box.** You use this text box to search for websites (as explained ever so carefully in this chapter's "Order Out of Chaos: Searching for Sites" section).

> **Windows Wisdom**
>
> When you surf to another page, Internet Explorer may pause for a while and then display a message that says **This page cannot be displayed**. This often means that the website is kaput or down temporarily. However, I've found that Internet Explorer displays this message for no good reason a lot of the time, and that pressing **F5** to refresh the page will bring the program to its senses.

◆ **Content area.** This area below the tab takes up the bulk of the Internet Explorer screen. It's where the body of each web page is displayed. You can use the vertical scrollbar to see more of the current page.

◆ **Links.** The content area for most web pages also boasts a link or two (or 10). These links come in two flavors: images and text (the latter are usually underlined or in a different color than the rest of the text). When you put the mouse pointer over a link, Internet Explorer does two things (see Figure 16.1): it changes the pointer into a hand with a pointing finger, and it displays, in the status bar, the address of the linked page.

Web Page Navigation Basics

With that brief introduction out of the way, it's time to start wandering the web. This section runs through a few techniques for getting from one page to another.

The most straightforward method is to click any link that strikes your fancy. Click the link, and you're immediately (depending on the speed of your Internet connection) whisked to the other page.

How can I tell what's a link and what isn't?

That, unfortunately, is not as easy as it used to be. Originally, link text appeared underlined and in a different color. That's still the usual case for a link these days, but you can also get nonunderlined links, as well as images that are links. The only real way to be sure is to park your mouse pointer over some likely looking text or an image, and then watch what happens to the pointer. If it changes into the hand with a pointing finger (see Figure 16.1), then you know for sure that you've got a link on your hands.

Windows Wisdom

Internet Explorer also assumes that most web addresses are of the form http://www. whatever.com. Therefore, if you type just the "whatever" part and press **Ctrl+Enter,** Internet Explorer automatically adds the http://www. prefix and the .com suffix. For example, you can get to my Word Spy site (http://www.wordspy.com) by typing "wordspy" and pressing **Ctrl+Enter.**

What if I know the address of the page I want to peruse?

Easy money. Here's what you do:

- ◆ Click inside the Address bar, delete the existing address, type in the address you want to check out, and then press **Enter.**

- ◆ If the address is one that you've visited recently, use the Address bar's drop-down list to select it.

Why the heck are web addresses so, well, weird?

Probably because they were created by geeks who never imagined they'd be used by normal people. Still, they're not so bad after you figure out what's going on. Here's a summary of the various bits and pieces of a typical web address (or *URL*, which is short for Uniform Resource Locator, another geekism):

http://www.mcfedries.com/cigwin7/index.asp

http://	This strange combination of letters and symbols tells the browser that you're entering a web address. Note that the browser assumes every address is a web address, so you don't need to include this part if you don't want to.
www.mcfedries.com	This is what's known as the domain name of the server computer that hosts the web page (www.mcfedries.com is my web server).
/cigwin7/	This is the web server directory in which the web page makes its home. Web directories are pretty similar to the folders you have on your hard drive.
index.asp	This is the web page's file name.

Ugh. Is there any easier way to get somewhere?

If you're not sure where you want to go, the default start page—it's called MSN.com—has lots of choices. For example, click any of the categories near the top (Autos, Careers & Jobs, and so on) to see lots of links related to that topic.

What if I jump to one page and then decide I want to double back to where I was?

That's a pretty common scenario. In fact, you'll often find that you need to leap back several pages, and then leap forward again. Fortunately, Internet Explorer makes this easy, thanks to its Back and Forward toolbar buttons (which I helpfully pointed out back in Figure 16.1). Here's what you can do with them:

◆ Click **Back** to return to the previous page.

◆ Click **Forward** to move ahead to the next page.

◆ To jump directly to any page you've visited recently, drop down the Forward button's list (that is, click the downward-pointing arrow just to the right of the Forward button) and click the page you want.

◆ What if you want to go forward or back to a page but you also want to keep the current page at hand? No worries: Press **Ctrl+N** to open up a fresh copy of the Internet Explorer window. You can then use that copy to leap to whatever page you want.

> **Windows Wisdom**
>
> After you've used Internet Explorer for a while, it will often "suggest" an address after you've typed in a few characters. If you see the address you want in the list that appears, use the down arrow key to highlight the address, and then press **Enter** (or click **Go**).

Techniques for Efficient Web Gallivanting

The paradox of the web is that even though it doesn't really exist anywhere (after all, where is the amorphous never-never land of cyberspace?), it's still one of the biggest earthly things you can imagine. There aren't hundreds of thousands of pages, or even millions of them for that matter. No, there are *billions* of web pages. (Of course, if you ignore all the pages that are devoted to *Battlestar Galactica*, then, yes, there are only a few hundred thousand pages.)

To have even a faint hope of managing just a tiny fraction of such an inconceivably vast array of data and bad MIDI music, you need to hone your web browsing skills with a few useful techniques. Fortunately, as you'll see in the next few sections, Internet Explorer has all kinds of features that can help.

Saving Sites for Subsequent Surfs: Managing Your Favorites

One of the most common experiences that folks new to web browsing go through is to stumble upon a really great site, and then not be able to find it again later. They try to retrace their steps, but usually just end up clicking links furiously and winding up in strange Net neighborhoods.

If this has happened to you, the solution is to get Internet Explorer to do all the grunt work of remembering sites for you. This is the job of the Favorites feature, which holds "shortcuts" to web pages and even lets you organize those shortcuts into separate folders.

Here's how you tell Internet Explorer to remember a web page as a favorite:

1. Navigate to the page that has struck your fancy.

2. Click **Favorites** (the star icon pointed out in Figure 16.2) and then select **Add to Favorites** to get the Add a Favorite dialog box on-screen.

> **Windows Wisdom**
>
> You can display the Add a Favorite dialog box in no time at all by pressing **Ctrl+D**. If you want to add the site to the Favorites Bar (pointed out in Figure 16.2), click the **Add to Favorites Bar** icon (also pointed out in Figure 16.2).

Add to Favorites Bar

Pin the Favorites Center

Favorites Bar

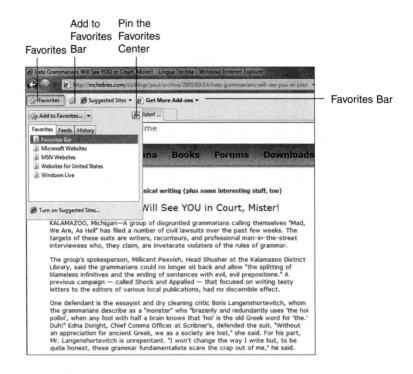

Favorites Bar

Figure 16.2

*Click the **Add to Favorites** button to get things going.*

3. The Name text box shows the name of the page, which is what you'll select from a menu later on when you want to view this page again. If you can think of a better name, don't hesitate to edit this text.

4. Click **Add** to finish.

After you have some pages lined up as favorites, you can return to any one of them at any time by clicking the **Favorites** icon, clicking the **Favorites** tab, and then clicking the page title.

If you need to make changes to your favorites, you can do a couple of things right from the Favorites list. Display the list and then right-click the item you want to work with. In the shortcut menu that slinks in, click **Rename** to change the item's name, or click **Delete** to blow it away. To change the address, click **Properties,** type the new address in the URL text box, and click **OK.**

For more heavy-duty adjustments, select the **Add a Favorite, Organize Favorites** command. Not surprisingly, this pushes the Organize Favorites dialog box into view. You get four buttons to play with:

> ### Windows Wisdom
>
> If you find yourself constantly reaching for the Favorites Center to get at your favorite pages, you might prefer to have the Favorites Center displayed full-time. You can do that by clicking the **Pin the Favorites Center** icon (see Figure 16.2). Internet Explorer then sets aside a chunk of real estate on the left side of the window to display the Favorites list.

◆ **New Folder.** Click this button to create a new folder. (Tip: If you click an existing folder and then click this button, Internet Explorer creates a subfolder.) Internet Explorer adds the folder and displays New Folder inside a text box. Edit the text and then press **Enter.**

◆ **Move.** Click this button to move the currently highlighted favorite into another folder. In the Browse For Folder dialog box that saunters by, highlight the destination folder, and then click **OK.**

◆ **Rename.** Click this button to rename the currently highlighted favorite. Edit the name accordingly and then press **Enter.**

◆ **Delete.** Click this button to nuke the currently highlighted favorite. When Windows 7 asks whether you're sure about this, click **Yes.**

When you're done, click **Done** (and say "Duh") to return to Internet Explorer.

Order Out of Chaos: Searching for Sites

Clicking willy-nilly in the hope of finding something interesting can be fun if you've got a few hours to kill. But if you need a specific tidbit of information *now*, then a click-click here and click-click there just won't cut the research mustard. To save time, you need to knock the web down to a more manageable size, and Internet Explorer's Search feature can help you do just that.

The idea is straightforward: you supply a search "engine" (as they're called) with a word or two that describes the topic you want to find. The search engine then scours the web for pages that contain those words, and presents you with a list of matches. Does it work? Well, it depends on which search engine you use. There are quite a few available, and some are better than others at certain kinds of searches. The biggest problem is that, depending on the topic you're looking for, the search engine might still return hundreds or even thousands of matching sites! You can usually get a more targeted search by adding more search terms and by avoiding common words. For example, suppose you want to know the airspeed velocity of an unladen swallow. If you search on just "swallow," you'll hit a wall of tens of millions of results. However, a search for "airspeed unladen swallow" will get you some pretty good results right off the bat.

A basic site search couldn't be easier: use the Search text box to type the word or phrase you want to find and then press **Enter.** Internet Explorer passes the search buck over to the Bing site, which then displays the results a few seconds later. As you can see in Figure 16.3, you get a series of links and descriptions. (Generally speaking, the higher the link is in the list, the more likely the page it points to matches your search text.) Clicking a link displays the page.

Figure 16.3

After the search is done, Internet Explorer displays a list of links to matching pages.

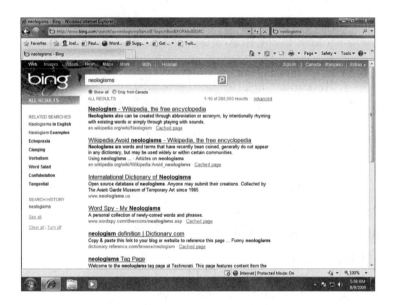

Internet Explorer uses Bing, which does a fine job of scouring the web, but you may want to try out a few other search engines to see which one you like best. For example, pretty much the entire world uses Google, so you might want to try it to see what all the fuss is about. Here are the steps to plod through to add what Internet Explorer calls a "search provider" (do not, I repeat do *not*, use the phrase "search provider" in public):

1. Click the downward-pointing arrow on the right side of the Search box, and then select **Find More Providers.** Internet Explorer whisks you away to the Search Providers web page.

2. Locate the search engine you want to try out, and then click its **Add to Internet Explorer** button. The Add Search Provider dialog box shows up to ask if you're sure you want to go through with this.

3. Say "Yuh-huh" and click **Add.**

To use your new search engine, type your search text, click the downward-pointing arrow on the right side of the Search box, and then click the search engine.

Hacking Windows

If you like one of the new search engines more than Live Search, tell Internet Explorer that you want to use it as the default search engine (which means you don't have to select it from the list each time you open Internet Explorer). Click the downward-pointing arrow on the right side of the Search box, and then select **Manage Search Providers.** Select the search engine, select **Set as default,** and then click **Close.**

One-Window Browsing: Surfing with Tabs

I mentioned in passing earlier in this chapter that you can keep the current site in Internet Explorer and surf to a different site by pressing Ctrl+N to open a new Internet Explorer window. That's a neat trick, but it's not unusual to use it *too* often and end up with a half-dozen or more Internet Explorer windows crowding the desktop. That's a lot of windows to wield.

Fortunately, the Time of Many Windows may soon be a thing of the past. That's because Internet Explorer comes with a nifty feature called *tabs* that lets you browse multiple sites in a *single* window. Sweet!

The way it works is that you create a new tab in the current window, and you then use that tab to display a different web page. How do you create a new tab? Like so: press **Ctrl+T** or click the **New Tab** button, pointed out in Figure 16.4. You then type the address you want and press **Enter** to load the page into the new tab.

Figure 16.4

The newest version of Internet Explorer lets you surf sites using tabs.

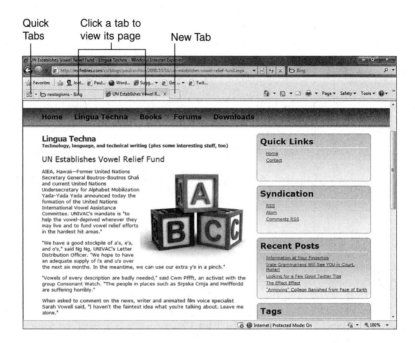

Here are a few tab techniques you can use to impress your friends:

- If you see a link that you want to load into a separate tab, right-click the link and then select **Open in New Tab.**

- To view a page that you have loaded in another tab, click the tab.

- To see miniversions—called *thumbnails*, in the trade—of all the pages you have open in tabs, click the **Quick Tabs** button (pointed out in Figure 16.4). Click a thumbnail to jump to that tab.

- To get rid of a tab, click it and then click the **"X"** that appears on the right side of the tab.

Dealing with Files in Internet Explorer

As you click your way around the web, you find that some links don't take you to other pages but are, instead, tied directly to a file. In this case, Internet Explorer makes you jump through some or all of the following hoops:

1. In most cases, after you click the link to the file, you see the File Download—
   Security Warning dialog box, which asks whether you want to run or save the
   file. It's much safer to save the file, so click **Save.**

> **Windows Wisdom**
>
> Windows 7 provides every user with a Downloads folder. So why doesn't Windows
> 7 do the smart thing and select Downloads for you automatically when the Save As
> dialog box appears? Beats me. Anyway, it's a good idea to use Downloads just so
> you know where all your downloaded stuff resides. In the Save As dialog box, click the
> arrow beside your user name and then click **Downloads.**

---

2. Windows 7 then displays the Save As dialog box so that you can choose where
   you want the file saved. Select a location and then select **Save.**

3. If you elected to save the file, you'll eventually see the Download Complete dialog box, which offers three buttons:

   ◆ **Run.** Click this button to launch the downloaded file.

   ◆ **Open Folder.** Click this button to open a window that displays the con-
     tents of the folder into which you saved the file. This is a good choice if
     you want to do something other than launch the file (such as rename it or
     sic your antivirus program on it).

   ◆ **Close.** Click this button to put off dealing with the file until later.

Look Out! _____

You need to be careful about downloading files because they can contain viruses
that wreck your system. To be safe, you should only download from reputable
sites, or from sites that you trust explicitly. If you plan on living dangerously and downloading files willy-nilly, at least get yourself a good antivirus program—such as McAfee
(www.mcafee.com) or Norton (www.symantec.com)—and use it to check each file you
download.

Feed Me: Subscribing to RSS Feeds

Some websites—particularly these blogs that everyone's talking about nowadays—
regularly add new content. That's awfully nice of them, but it does mean that you

have to check the site often if you want to keep up with the latest. You can avoid this hassle altogether by turning the tables and having the site tell *you* when it has posted something new. You can perform this trick if the site has a feature called Real Simple Syndication, or RSS, which enables you to subscribe to the "feed" that the site sends out. This feed contains the most recent wit and wisdom that has been added to the site.

So far so good, but you need a "feed reader" to get the site's feed and display the shiny new content. That's the bad news. The good news is that Internet Explorer 7 now has feed-reading capabilities built right in, so you can subscribe to and read RSS feeds right from the comfort of your browser.

> ### Windows Wisdom
>
> Got a ton of feeds to get through? Keep the Feeds list on-screen all the time by pressing **Ctrl+J**. (When you're done, press **Ctrl+J** again to remove the Feeds list.)

How do you know if a site has an RSS feed or two? Keep an eye on Internet Explorer's Feeds button. When it lights up a bright orange, it means it has detected a feed on the site. Drop down the **Feeds** list as shown in Figure 16.5, and then click the feed you want to check out. Internet Explorer then displays the feed. If it looks interesting, click **Subscribe to this feed** and then click **Subscribe** in the dialog box that appears.

Figure 16.5

The Feeds button lights up if a site has one or more RSS feeds.

Feeds

To view a feed after you have subscribed to it, follow these steps:

1. Click the **Favorites** button.

2. Click the **Feeds** tab. Internet Explorer displays the Feeds list, as shown in Figure 16.6.

3. Click the feed you want to see.

Figure 16.6

Use the Feeds list to see a list of the RSS feeds you've subscribed to.

The Least You Need to Know

◆ To start Internet Explorer, click the **Internet Explorer** icon in the taskbar. (Alternatively, select **Start, All Programs, Internet Explorer.**)

◆ To surf to another page, either click a link or type an address in the Address bar and then press **Enter.** Use the toolbar's **Back** button to return to the previous page, and use the **Forward** button to head the other way.

◆ To scour the web for a particular topic, type a word or two in the Search box and press **Enter.**

◆ Click the **Favorites** button and then click the **Add to Favorites** command (or press **Ctrl+D**) to save a page to the Favorites list.

♦ Click the **Favorites** button to view your Favorites, Feeds, and History lists.

♦ To create a new tab, press **Ctrl+T** or click the **New Tab** button. You can also right-click a link and then click **Open in New Tab.**

17

Sending and Receiving E-Mail with Windows Live Mail

In This Chapter

- Giving Windows 7 your e-mail account particulars
- How to compose and send an e-mail message
- Working with the Windows 7 Contacts list
- Handling attachments
- How to get and read incoming messages
- Folders, signatures, and other message techniques

The world passed a milestone of sorts a few years ago when it was reported that, in North America at least, more e-mail messages are sent each day than postal messages. Now, e-mail message volume is several times that of "snail mail" (as regular mail is derisively called by the wired set), and the number of e-notes shipped out each day is counted in the *billions*.

The really good news is that e-mail has become extremely easy to use because e-mail programs have become much better over the years. As you see in this chapter, shipping out messages and reading incoming messages is a painless affair thanks to the admirable e-mail capabilities of Windows Live Mail.

Getting Started with Windows Live Mail

As you might have guessed from the "Live" portion of its name, Windows Live Mail is part of Windows Live Essentials, which is the collection of those programs that Microsoft decided to leave out of Windows 7. To learn how to install it, hike back to Chapter 6 and read the section titled "Installing Windows Live Essentials Programs."

Once that's done, you fire up the program by selecting **Start, All Programs, Windows Live, Windows Live Mail.**

Setting Up Your Internet E-Mail Account

Before Windows Live Mail loads for the first time, it calls in the Add an E-mail Account Wizard to handle the various steps required to divulge the details of the e-mail account you have with your ISP (Internet service provider). There are two possible routes here: the high (easy) road, and the low (hard) road.

The High Road: Quick Account Setup

Windows Live Mail understands that many (perhaps even most) e-mail accounts are really straightforward; with just a bit of information it can glean the underlying details of the account. This process is relatively foolproof with well-known e-mail providers such as Microsoft's Hotmail, and it seems to work okay with other companies, too.

In this scenario, all you need to know is your e-mail address and your password. You enter that data in the Add an E-mail Account wizard's initial dialog box, plus the display name you want to use (this is the name people see when you send them a message). Click **Next,** read the instructions (if any) that the wizard tells you to follow to complete the setup, and then click **Finish.**

The Low Road: Configuring an Account By Hand

If the wizard can't configure your e-mail account automatically, then you've got to roll up your sleeves and do it yourself. Here's a rundown of the information you should have at your fingertips:

◆ Your e-mail address.

◆ The type of server the ISP uses for incoming e-mail: *POP3, IMAP,* or *HTTP.*

◆ The Internet name used by the ISP's incoming *mail server* (this often takes the form mail.*provider*.com, where *provider* is the name of the ISP). Note that your ISP might call this its *POP3 server.*

◆ The Internet name used by the ISP's outgoing mail server (this is almost always the same as the incoming e-mail server). Some ISPs call this their *SMTP server.*

◆ Whether your ISP's outgoing mail server requires authentication (most do, nowadays).

def•i•ni•tion

The acronyms and abbreviations are thick on the ground in this section. You don't have to understand them to send and receive e-mail, but here's what they mean just in case you're interested: **POP3** stands for Post Office Protocol version 3; **IMAP** stands for Internet Message Access Protocol; and **SMTP** stands for Simple Mail Transfer Protocol.

def•i•ni•tion

A **mail server** is a computer that your ISP uses to store and send your e-mail messages.

◆ Whether your ISP requires you to use special port numbers. You can think of ports as communications channels, and Windows Live Mail and your ISP must be tuned in to the same channel for things to work. If you don't have any info on this, then your ISP probably uses the standard port numbers and so you don't have to sweat this part.

◆ The user name and password for your e-mail account. (These are almost always the same as your Internet log-on name and password.)

Here's what happens:

1. In the initial wizard dialog box, enter your address in the **E-mail address** text box and your password in the **Password** text box.

2. Use the **Display Name** text box to type the name you want other folks to see when you send them a message (most people just use their real name) and then click **Next.**

3. Use the **My incoming mail server is a *X* server** list to specify the type of e-mail server your ISP uses; most are **POP3.**

4. Use the **Incoming server** text box to enter the name of the server that your ISP uses for incoming mail. Also, change the **Port** value if your ISP uses a port other than the one shown.

5. Use the **Login ID** text box to enter your e-mail username (this should already be filled in for you) or address (whichever one you're supposed to use to log in).

6. Use the **Outgoing** server text box to enter the name of the server that your ISP uses for outgoing mail. Also, change the **Port** value if your ISP uses a port other than the one shown.

7. Activate the **My outgoing server requires authentication** check box if your ISP's outgoing mail server does the authentication thing.

8. Click **Next** to get your account set up.

9. Click **Finish.**

The Lay of the Windows Live Mail Land

By default, Windows Live Mail is set up to go online and grab your waiting messages when you launch the program. We'll get there eventually, so for now just close the Connect dialog box if it shows up.

At long last, the Windows Live Mail window shows itself, and it looks much like the one in Figure 17.1.

Figure 17.1

Use Windows Live Mail to ship and receive Internet e-mail messages.

The Folder pane on the left lists the various storage areas that come with Windows Live Mail. I talk about folders in more detail later in this chapter. For now, here's a quick summary of what the default folders are all about:

◆ **Quick views.** This section offers special "views" of your messages, such as Unread E-mail, which shows you all the messages that you haven't read yet.

◆ **Inbox.** This folder is where Windows Live Mail stores the e-mail messages that you receive.

◆ **Drafts.** This folder stores messages that you're in the middle of composing and have saved.

◆ **Sent items.** This folder stores a copy of the messages that you've sent.

◆ **Junk e-mail.** This folder is the Siberia to which Windows Live Mail exiles suspected spam messages. See the section in Chapter 18 titled, "Using the Junk Mail Filter to Can Spam."

◆ **Deleted items.** This folder stores the messages that you delete.

◆ **Outbox.** This folder stores messages that you've composed but haven't sent yet.

The Outbox: Sending an E-Mail Message

Let's begin the Windows Live Mail tour with a look at how to foist your e-prose on unsuspecting colleagues, friends, family, and *Brady Bunch* cast members. This section shows you the basic technique to use, and then gets a bit fancier in discussing the Address Book, attachments, and other Windows Live Mail sending features.

The Basics: Composing and Sending a Message

Without further ado (not that there's been much ado to this point, mind you), here are the basic steps to follow to fire off an e-mail message to some lucky recipient:

1. Click the **New** button in the toolbar. (Keyboard fans will be pleased to note that pressing **Ctrl+N** also does the job.) You end up with the New Message window on-screen, as shown in Figure 17.2.

Figure 17.2

You cobble together an e-mail message in the New Message window.

Formatting bar

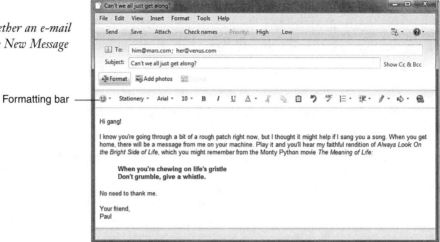

2. In the **To** text box, type in the e-mail address of the recipient. (It's perfectly acceptable to enter multiple addresses in this text box. Use a semicolon [;] or a comma [,] to separate each address.)

3. The address you put in the To box is the "main" recipient of the message. However, it's common to shoot a copy of the message off to a secondary recipient. To do that, click **Show Cc and Bcc** and then enter their e-mail address in the Cc text box. (Again, you can enter multiple addresses, if you're so inclined.)

   There's also a *blind courtesy* (or *carbon*) *copy* (Bcc), which delivers a copy of the message to a specified recipient. However, none of the other recipients see that person's address anywhere. Click **Show Cc and Bcc** (if you didn't do that already) and type the address in the **Bcc** text box.

4. Use the Subject line to enter a subject for the message. (The subject acts as a kind of title for your message. It's the first thing the recipient sees, so it should accurately reflect the content of your message, but it shouldn't be too long. Think *pithy*.)

5. Decide what type of message you want to send. You have two choices, both of which are commands on the Format menu:

   ◆ **Rich Text (HTML).** Choose this command to include formatting in your message. This enables you to make your message look its best. However, your recipient might have problems if his or her e-mail program doesn't support this formatting, although most do these days. (Just so you know,

HTML stands for Hypertext Markup Language. It's a series of codes used to format characters and things, and it's used to create web pages. Don't worry, you don't have to know anything about HTML to use this feature.)

◆ **Plain Text.** Choose this command to send out the message without any formatting. This makes life easier for your recipient if he or she doesn't have an e-mail program that supports formatting. If you're not sure what your recipient is using, choose this command.

6. Use the large, empty area below the Subject line to type in the message text (also known as the *message body*).

7. If you chose the Rich Text (HTML) format, after you're inside the message text area, notice that the buttons on the Formatting bar suddenly come alive, as do more of the Format menu commands. Use these buttons and commands to change the font, format paragraphs, add a background image, apply stationery, and more.

8. When your message is fit for human consumption, you have two sending choices:

◆ **If you're working online.** Click the **Send** toolbar button (or try **Alt+S** on for size). Windows Live Mail sends the message, no questions asked.

◆ **If you're working offline.** Click the **Send** toolbar button or press **Alt** and then select **File, Send later.** In this case, Windows Live Mail coughs up a dialog box that tells you the message will bunk down in the Outbox folder until you're ready to send it. This is good because it means you can compose a few messages before connecting to the Internet. When you're ready to actually ship the messages, click the **Sync** toolbar button or press **F5.**

> ### Windows Wisdom
>
> Windows Live Mail has a Spelling command on the Tools menu (as well as a Spelling toolbar button). It's a good idea to run this command before foisting your message on the recipient. It just takes a sec, and if the spell checker finds an error or two, you'll save yourself a bit of embarrassment.

Note that after your message is Net-bound, Windows Live Mail also is kind enough to save a copy of it in the Sent Items folder. This is handy because it gives you a record of all the missives you launch into cyberspace.

Easier Addressing: Using the Contacts List

If you find yourself with a bunch of recipients to whom you send stuff regularly (and it's a rare e-mailer who doesn't), you soon grow tired of entering their addresses by hand. The solution is to toss those regulars into the Contacts list. That way, you can fire them into the To or Cc lines with just a few mouse clicks.

Here's how you add someone to the Contacts list:

1. In Windows Live Mail, click the **Contacts** button. (Keyboard diehards can get their kicks by pressing **Ctrl+Shift+C.**)

2. In the Contacts window that reports for duty, click the **New** toolbar button. (Alternatively, press **Ctrl+Shift+C.**) The Contacts window conjures up the Properties dialog box shown in Figure 17.3.

Figure 17.3

Use this dialog box to spell out the particulars of the new recipient.

3. In the **Quick add** tab, enter the person's first and last names.

4. Use the **Personal e-mail** text box to enter the recipient's address.

5. Fill in the person's phone number and company name, as well as the fields in the other tabs, if you feel like it.

6. When you're done, click **Add contact** to add the new recipient.

Windows Wisdom

If you want to send a message to a particular set of recipients, you can organize them into a *category* and then specify the category name in the To line. To create a category, open the Contacts window and then click **Create a category** (or press **Ctrl+Shift+G**). Enter a category name, click each contact you want in the category, and then click **Save**.

After you have some folks in your Contacts list, Windows Live Mail gives you a ton of ways to get them a message. Here's my favorite method:

1. In the New Message window, click **To.** Windows Live Mail displays the Send an E-mail dialog box.

2. Click the contact name.

3. Click **To** (or **Cc** or **Bcc**).

4. Click **OK.**

Inserting Attachments and Other Hangers-On

Most of your messages will be text-only creations (perhaps with a bit of formatting tossed in to keep things interesting). However, it's also possible to send entire files along for the ride. Such files are called, naturally enough, *attachments*. They're very common in the business world, and it's useful to know how they work. Here goes:

1. In the New Message window, click the **Attach** toolbar button. The Open dialog box rears its head.

2. Find the file you want to attach and then highlight it.

3. Click **Open.** Windows Live Mail returns you to the New Message window where you see a new Attach box that includes the name of the file.

def•i•ni•tion

An **attachment** is a separate file that accompanies an e-mail message.

As you can see, adding attachments isn't that hard. However, that doesn't mean you should bolt an attachment or two onto every message you send. Adding attachments can greatly increase the size of your message, so it may take the recipient quite a while to download your message, which won't be appreciated, I can tell you. Some ISPs put an upper limit on the size of a message, so it's also possible that your recipient may never see your note. Use common sense and only attach files when it's absolutely necessary.

The Inbox: Getting and Reading E-Mail Messages

Some people like to think of e-mail as a return to the days of *belles-lettres* and *billets-doux* (these people tend to be a bit pretentious). Yes, it's true that e-mail has people writing again, but this isn't like the letter writing of old. The major difference is that e-mail's turnaround time is usually much quicker. Instead of waiting weeks or even months to get a return letter, a return e-mail might take as little as a few minutes or a few hours.

So if you send out a message with a question or comment, chances are you get a reply coming right back at you before too long. Any messages sent to your e-mail address are stored in your account at your ISP. Your job is to use Windows Live Mail to access your account and grab any waiting messages. This section shows you how to do that and shows you what to do with those messages after they're safely stowed on your computer.

Getting Your Messages

Here are the steps to stride through to get your e-mail messages:

1. Click the **Sync** toolbar button (or press **F5**).

2. Windows Live Mail connects to the Internet (if necessary), accesses your mail account, absconds with any waiting messages, and then stuffs them into the Windows Live Mail Inbox folder. Disconnect from the Internet if you no longer need the connection.

3. If it's not already displayed, click the **Inbox** folder so you can see what the e-postman delivered.

When you're working online, Windows Live Mail automatically checks for new messages every 30 minutes. You can change that by clicking the **Menus** icon (it's in the toolbar, to the left of the Help question mark icon) and then **Options.** In the General tab, use the spin box that's part of the **Check for new messages every *X* minute(s)** option to set the checking interval.

Reading Your Messages

Figure 17.4 shows the Inbox folder with a few messages. The first thing to notice is that Windows Live Mail uses a bold font for all messages that you haven't read yet. You also get info about each message organized with the following half-dozen columns:

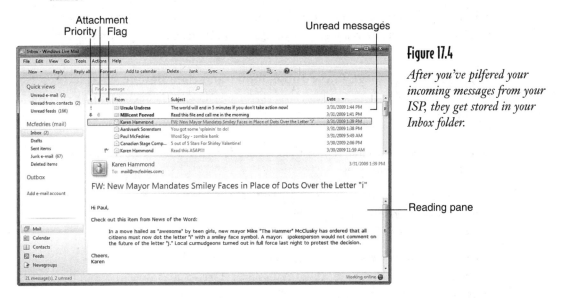

Figure 17.4

After you've pilfered your incoming messages from your ISP, they get stored in your Inbox folder.

- ◆ **Priority.** This column tells you whether the sender set up the message with a priority ranking. If you see a red exclamation mark, it means the message was sent with high priority (this is the "Handle this pronto, buster!" symbol); if you see a blue, downward-pointing arrow, it means the note was sent with low priority (this is the "Handle this whenever, man" symbol).

- ◆ **Attachment.** If you see a paper clip icon in this column, it means the message is accompanied by a file attachment. See the "Attending to Attachments" section later in this chapter.

- ◆ **Flag.** If you want to remind yourself to deal with a message, you can "flag" it for a future follow-up (a sort of digital string-tied-to-the-finger thing). You do this by highlighting the message and then selecting the **Actions, Flag Message** command (or just click inside the Flag column). This adds a flag icon in this column.

- ◆ **From.** This column tells you the name (or occasionally, just the e-mail address) of the person or company that sent you the message.

- **Subject.** This column shows you the subject line of the message, which will, hopefully, give you a brief description of the contents of the message.

- **Date.** This column tells you the date and time the message was received.

Windows Live Mail offers two methods for seeing what a message has to say:

- **Highlight the message in the Inbox folder.** Windows Live Mail displays the text of the note in the reading pane. After about five seconds, Windows Live Mail removes the bolding from the message to indicate that it has been read.

- **Highlight the message in the Inbox folder and then double-click it.** (For the heck of it, you also can press **Ctrl+O** or just **Enter.**) This method opens the message in its own window.

To read other messages, either repeat these procedures or use any of the following Windows Live Mail techniques:

- **To read the previous message in the list:** Press **Alt** and then select **View, Previous or next message, Previous Message.** (**Ctrl+<** works, as well; if you have the message window open, click the **Previous** toolbar button.)

- **To read the next message in the list:** Press **Alt** and then select **View, Previous or next message, Next Message.** (**Ctrl+>** also does the job; if you have the message window open, click the **Next** toolbar button.)

- **To read the next *unread* message:** Press **Alt** and then select **View, Previous or next message, Next Unread Message** (or press **Ctrl+U**).

- **To read the next unread *conversation:*** Press **Alt** and then select **View, Previous or next message, Next Unread Conversation** (or press **Ctrl+Shift+U**).

def•i•ni•tion

A **conversation** is a series of messages with the same subject line. It's also known as a *thread* in e-mail circles.

If you plan on using the Next Unread Conversation command, you first have to group all the messages from the same conversation. To do that, **Press Alt** and then activate the **View, View by Conversation** command.

Attending to Attachments

As I mentioned earlier, if you get a message that has one or more files tied to it, you see a paper clip icon in the Inbox folder's Attachment column. You also see a paper clip icon in the upper-left corner of the reading pane. Windows Live Mail gives you a few ways to handle any attachments in the current message:

◆ **Saving the file.** Press **Alt** and then select **File, Save Attachments** to convince the Save Attachments dialog box to drop by. If there are multiple files, use the Attachments To Be Saved list to highlight the ones you want to save. Use the Save To text box to specify where you want the files to be stored (click **Browse** to choose the folder from a dialog box). Then click **Save** to dump the file (or files) onto your hard disk.

◆ **Saving the file from the reading pane.** Right-click the file in the upper-left corner of the reading pane, click **Save as,** and follow the steps I just took you through.

◆ **Opening the file.** If you just want to see what's in the file, you can open it. To do that, right-click the file in the upper-left corner of the reading pane, and then click **Open.**

> **See Also**
>
> Although Windows Live Mail makes it easy to deal with attachments, you should never just blithely open an attached file because you might end up infecting your computer with a virus. To learn more about this and how to protect yourself from virus attachments, see Chapter 18.

What to Do with a Message After You've Read It

This section gives you a rundown of all the things you can do with a message after you've read it. In each case, you either need to have a message highlighted in the Inbox folder, or you need to have the message open. Here's the list:

◆ **Ship out a reply.** If you think of a witty retort, you can e-mail it back to the sender by clicking the **Reply** toolbar button. (The keyboard route is **Ctrl+R.**)

◆ **Ship out a reply to every recipient.** If the note was foisted on several people, you might prefer to send your response to everyone who received the original. To do that, click the **Reply all** button. (The keyboard shortcut is **Ctrl+Shift+R.**)

◆ **Forward the message to someone else.** To have someone else take a gander at a message you received, you can forward it by clicking the **Forward** button. (Keyboard dudes and dudettes can press **Ctrl+F.**)

Windows Wisdom

A forwarded message contains the original message text, which is preceded by an "Original Message" header and some of the message particulars (who sent it, when they sent it, and so on). If you want your recipient to see the message exactly as you received it, press **Alt** and then use the **Actions, Forward As Attachment** command instead.

◆ **Move the message to some other folder.** If you find your Inbox folder getting seriously overcrowded, you should think about moving some messages to other folders. The easiest way to go about this is to drag the message from its current folder and drop it on the other folder in the Folders list. If that's too easy, press **Alt** and then select **Edit, Move to folder** (or press **Ctrl+Shift+V**). In the Move dialog box that shows up, highlight the destination folder and then click **OK.** (You can create a new folder by clicking the **New Folder** button, entering a name for the folder in the New Folder dialog box, and then clicking **OK.**)

◆ **Delete the message.** If you don't think you have cause to read a message again, you might as well delete it to keep the Inbox clutter to a minimum. To delete a message, either press **Alt** and then select **Edit, Delete,** or click the **Delete** button. (A message also can be vaporized by pressing **Ctrl+D** or by dragging it to the Deleted Items folder.) Note that Windows Live Mail doesn't get rid of a deleted message completely. Instead, it just dumps it in the Deleted Items folder. If you later realize that you deleted the message accidentally (insert forehead slap here), you can head for **Deleted Items** and then move it back into the Inbox.

Manufacturing New Message Folders

Right out of the box, Windows Live Mail comes with the six prefab folders that I described earlier in this chapter. Surely that's enough folders for anyone, right?

Maybe not. Even if you're good at deleting the detritus from your Inbox folder, it still won't take long before it becomes bloated with messages and finding the note you need becomes a real needle-in-a-haystack exercise. What you really need is a way to organize your mail. For example, suppose you and your boss exchange a lot of e-mail. Rather than storing all her messages in your Inbox folder, you could create a separate folder just for her messages. You could also create folders for each of the Internet mailing lists you subscribe to, for current projects on the go, or for each of your regular e-mail correspondents. There are, in short, 1,001 uses for folders, and this section tells you how to create your own.

> **Windows Wisdom**
>
> You can save yourself a step or two by heading for the Folder pane and right-clicking the folder in which you want the new folder to appear. Then click **New Folder**, enter the folder name, and click **OK**.

To create a new folder, follow these steps:

1. Press **Alt** and then select the **File, Folder, Create new folder** command to display the Create Folder dialog box. (Attention, keyboardists: pressing **Ctrl+Shift+D** also gets you where you want to go.)

2. In the **Select the folder** list, highlight the folder within which you want the new folder to appear. For example, if you want your new folder to be inside your inbox, click the **Inbox** folder.

3. Use the **Folder name** text box to enter the name of the new folder.

4. Click **OK**.

Setting Up a Signature

In e-mail lingo, a *signature* is a chunk of text that appears at the bottom of all your messages. Most people use their signature to give contact information, and you often see sigs (that's the hip short form) adorned with witty quotations or sayings. Windows Live Mail even lets you create multiple signatures, so you can tailor them to various audiences.

Here are the steps to plow through to create a signature or two:

1. Select the **Menus, Options** command. The Options dialog box climbs into the ring.

2. Display the **Signatures** tab.

3. Click **New.** Windows Live Mail adds a new item to the Signatures list.

4. Use the **Text** box to compose the signature.

> **Windows Wisdom**
>
> The "default signature" is the first signature you create. To set up some other signature as the default, highlight it in the Signatures list, and then click **Set as Default.**

5. Annoyingly, Windows Live Mail gives each signature a boring name such as Signature #1. A more meaningful name would be nice, so click the signature in the Signatures list, click **Rename,** enter a snappier name, and then press **Enter.**

6. Repeat steps 3 through 5 to create more signatures, if you so desire.

7. If you want Windows Live Mail to tack on the default signature to all your messages, activate the **Add signatures to all outgoing messages** check box. If you don't want the signature to show up when you reply to a message or forward a message to someone, leave the **Don't add signatures to Replies and Forwards** check box activated.

8. When you're done, click **OK** to return to Windows Live Mail.

If you elected not to add your signature automatically, it's easy enough to toss it into a message that you're composing. In the New Message window, move the cursor to where you want the text to appear, and then select **Insert, Signature.** (If you have multiple signatures defined, a submenu with a list of the sigs slides out. Select the one you want to use.)

The Least You Need to Know

♦ To start Windows Live Mail, select **Start, All Programs, Windows Live, Windows Live Mail.**

♦ To compose a message, click the **New** button, enter the address and a Subject line, fill in the message body, and then either click **Send** (if you're online) or press **Alt** and then select **File, Send later** (if you're offline).

♦ To receive messages, click the **Sync** button.

♦ Make liberal use of folders to organize your messages. You create new folders by pressing **Alt** and then selecting the **File, Folder, New** command (or by pressing **Ctrl+Shift+D**).

♦ If you want to finish your messages with a flourish, create a signature by selecting **Menus, Options** and displaying the **Signatures** tab.

Chapter 18

Your Net Safety Net

In This Chapter

- ◆ Keeping hackers and other miscreants out of your system
- ◆ Guarding against nasty e-mail viruses, spam, and other useless messages
- ◆ Maintaining e-mail privacy
- ◆ Foiling phishing
- ◆ Blocking those annoying pop-up windows
- ◆ Watching the big security picture with the Security Center

The Internet is a more cosmopolitan place now than in its relatively lawless beginnings. However, although the Net is no longer the digital equivalent of the Wild West, we've progressed only to about the level of Al Capone's Chicago of the 1930s. In other words, although most of your Internet dealings will be safe and pleasant, there are plenty of cyberhoodlums and e-gangsters roaming the Net's dark streets and alleyways. You need to exercise some caution to avoid the Internet's version of muggings and extortion.

Fortunately, the situation is not so grim that you can't easily protect yourself. As you'll see in this chapter, avoiding viruses, spam scams, system intruders, and other Internet bad guys is a relatively simple combination of common sense and the prudent tweaking of a few settings.

Squashing Spyware with Windows Defender

If you access the Net using a broadband—cable modem or digital subscriber line (DSL)—service, chances are you have an "always on" connection, which means there's a much greater chance that a malicious hacker could find your computer and have his or her way with it. You might think that with millions of people connected to the Internet at any given moment, there would be little chance of a nefarious user finding you in the herd. Unfortunately, one of the most common weapons in a black-hat hacker's arsenal is a program that runs through millions of addresses automatically, looking for "live" connections. The problem is compounded by the fact that many cable systems and some DSL systems use addresses in a narrow range, thus making it easier to find always-on connections.

> **Windows Wisdom**
>
> It pays to take a second and check that Windows Firewall is actually on the job. Select **Start, Control Panel, System and Security, Check firewall status.** In the Windows Firewall window, make sure the Windows Firewall state shows On. If it doesn't, click **Turn Windows Firewall on or off** and then select **Turn on Windows Firewall.**

However, having a hacker locate your system isn't a big deal as long as he or she can't get into your system. There are two ways to prevent this: one is to turn on Windows Firewall, which blocks unauthorized access to your computer and which is (thankfully) activated by default in Windows 7.

In recent years, a new threat to our PCs has emerged. It's called *spyware*, and it's a nasty bit of digital business that threatens to deprive a significant portion of the online world of their sanity. Spyware refers to a program that surreptitiously monitors your computer activities—particularly the typing of passwords, PINs, and credit card numbers—or harvests sensitive data on your computer, and then sends that information to an individual or a company via your Internet connection.

You might think that having Windows Firewall between you and the bad guys would make spyware a problem of the past. Unfortunately, that's not true. These programs piggyback on other legitimate programs that you actually *want* to download, such as file-sharing programs, download managers, and screen savers. To make matters even worse, most spyware embeds itself deep into a system and removing it is a delicate and time-consuming operation beyond the abilities of even the most experienced users. Some programs actually come with an "uninstall" option, but it's nothing but a ruse, of course. The program appears to remove itself from the system, but what it actually does is reinstall a fresh version of itself when the computer is idle. A pox on all their houses!

All this means that you need to buttress Windows Firewall with an anti-spyware program that can watch out for these unwanted programs and prevent them from getting their hooks into your system. Happily, Windows 7 comes with just such a program, and it has an appropriate (and hopefully accurate!) name: Windows Defender.

Out of the box, Windows 7 sets up Windows Defender to protect your system from spyware nastiness in two ways:

- Windows Defender scans your system for spyware infestations every day at 2 A.M.

- Windows Defender runs in the background full-time to watch out for spywarelike activity. If it detects a spyware fiend trying to sneak in the back door, Windows Defender terminates the brute with extreme prejudice.

As with Windows Firewall, what you need to do is check to make sure that both of these protection features are turned on. Here's how:

1. Click **Start,** type defend in the Start menu's Search box, and then click **Windows Defender** in the search results.

2. Select **Tools** to display the Tools and Settings window.

3. Select **Options** to open the Options window.

4. Select **Automatic scanning** and then activate the **Automatically scan my computer** check box. While you're here, you can also monkey with the scan schedule (**Frequency, Approximate time,** and **Type**).

> **Windows Wisdom**
>
> Feel free to run a scan on your computer right now, if you like. Launch Windows Defender and then click **Scan** to do a quick scan. If you want a more thorough check, pull down the **Scan** list and select **Full Scan.**

5. Select **Real-time protection** and then activate the **Use real-time protection** check box.

6. Click **Save.**

Working with E-Mail Safely and Securely

E-mail is by far the most popular online activity, but it can also be the most frustrating in terms of security and privacy. E-mail viruses are legion, spam gets worse every day, and messages that should be secret are really about as secure as if they were written on the back of a postcard. Fortunately, it doesn't take much to remedy these and other e-mail problems, as you'll see over the next few sections.

Protecting Yourself Against E-Mail Viruses

Until just a few years ago, the primary method that computer viruses used to propagate themselves was the floppy disk. A user with an infected machine would copy some files to a floppy, and the virus would surreptitiously add itself to the disk. When the recipient inserted the disk, the virus copy would come to life and infect yet another computer.

When the Internet became a big deal, viruses adapted (as viruses are wont to do) and began propagating either via malicious websites or via infected program files downloaded to users' machines.

Over the past couple of years, however, by far the most productive method for viruses to replicate has been the humble e-mail message. Melissa, I Love You, BadTrans, Sircam, Klez ... the list of e-mail viruses is a long one, but they all operate more or less the same way—they arrive as a message attachment, usually from someone you know. When you open the attachment, the virus infects your computer and then, without your knowledge, uses your e-mail program and your address book to ship out messages with more copies of itself attached. The nastier versions will also mess with your computer; the soulless beasts might delete data or corrupt files, for example.

You can avoid getting infected by one of these viruses by implementing a few commonsense procedures:

◆ Never open an attachment that comes from someone you don't know.

◆ Even if you know the sender, if the attachment isn't something you're expecting, assume the sender's system is infected. Write back and confirm that he or she sent the message.

◆ Some viruses come packaged as "scripts"—miniature computer programs—that are hidden within messages that use the Rich Text (HTML) format. This means that the virus can run just by viewing the message! If a message looks suspicious, don't open it, just delete it. (Note that you'll need to turn off the Windows Live Mail reading pane before deleting the message. Otherwise, when you highlight the message, it will appear in the preview pane and set off the virus. Click **Menus** and then click **Layout**, deactivate the **Show the reading pane** check box, and click **OK**.)

◆ Install a top-of-the-line antivirus program, particularly one that checks incoming e-mail. Also, be sure to keep your antivirus program's virus list up-to-date. As you read this, there are probably dozens, maybe even hundreds, of morally challenged scum-nerds designing even nastier viruses. Regular updates will help you keep up. Here are some security suites to check out:

Norton Internet Security (www.symantec.com/index.jsp)

McAfee Internet Security Suite (http://mcafee.com/us)

Avast! Antivirus (www.avast.com)

AVG Internet Security (http://free.grisoft.com/)

Besides these general procedures, Windows Live Mail also comes with its own set of virus protection features. Here's how to use them:

1. In Windows Live Mail, click **Menus** and then click **Safety options.**

2. Display the **Security** tab.

3. In the **Virus Protection** section of the dialog box, you have the following options:

    ◆ **Select the Internet Explorer security zone to use.** You use the security zones to determine whether scripts inside HTML-format messages are allowed to run. If you choose Internet Zone, scripts are allowed to run; if you choose Restricted Sites Zone, scripts are disabled. Restricted Sites Zone is the default setting, and it's the one I highly recommend.

    ◆ **Warn me when other applications try to send mail as me.** As I mentioned earlier, it's possible for programs and scripts to send e-mail messages without your knowledge. When you activate this check box, Windows Live Mail displays a warning dialog box when a program or script attempts to send a message behind the scenes.

    ◆ **Do not allow attachments to be saved or opened that could potentially be a virus.** When you activate this check box, Windows Live Mail monitors attachments to look for file types that could contain viruses or destructive code. If it detects such a file, it halts the ability to open or save that file, and it displays a note at the top of the message to let you know about the unsafe attachment.

4. Click **OK.**

5. Click **Menus** and then click **Options** to switch to the Options dialog box.

6. In the Read tab, activate the **Read all messages in plain text** check box.

7. Click **OK.**

Using the Junk Mail Filter to Can Spam

Spam—unsolicited commercial messages—has become a plague upon the earth. Unless you've done a masterful job at keeping your address secret, you probably receive at least a few spam e-mails every day, and it's more likely that you receive a few dozen. The bad news is most experts agree that it's only going to get worse. And why not? Spam is one of the few advertising mediums where the costs are substantially borne by the users, not the advertisers.

The best way to avoid spam is to not get on a spammer's list of addresses in the first place. That's hard to do these days, but there are some steps you can take:

- Never use your actual e-mail address in a newsgroup account. The most common method that spammers use to gather addresses is to harvest them from newsgroup posts. One common tactic is to alter your e-mail address by adding text that invalidates the address but is still obvious for other people to figure out:

    user@myisp.remove_this_to_e-mail_me.com

- When you sign up for something online, use a fake address if possible. If you need or want to receive e-mail from the company and so must use your real address, make sure you deselect any options that ask if you want to receive promotional offers. Alternatively, enter the address from a free web-based account (such as a Hotmail account), so that any spam you receive will go there instead of to your main address.

- Never open suspected spam messages, because doing so can sometimes notify the spammer that you've opened the message, thus confirming that your address is legit. For the same reason, you should never display a spam message in the Windows Live Mail preview pane. As described earlier, shut off the preview pane before highlighting any spam messages that you want to delete.

- Never, I repeat, *never*, respond to spam, even to an address within the spam that claims to be a "removal" address. By responding to the spam all you're doing is proving that your address is legitimate, so you'll just end up getting *more* spam.

If you do get spam despite these precautions, the good news is that Windows Live Mail comes with a Junk E-mail feature that can help you cope. Junk E-mail is a *spam filter*, which means that it examines each incoming message and applies sophisticated tests to determine whether the message is spam. If the tests determine that the message is probably spam, the e-mail is exiled to a separate Junk E-mail folder. It's not perfect (no spam filter is), but with a bit of fine-tuning as described in the next few sections, it can be a very useful anti-spam weapon.

Setting the Junk E-Mail Protection Level

Filtering spam is always a tradeoff between protection and convenience. That is, the stronger the protection you use, the less convenient the filter becomes, and vice versa. This inverse relationship is caused by a filter phenomenon called the *false positive*. This is a legitimate message that the filter has pegged as spam and so (in Windows Live Mail's case) moved the message to the Junk E-mail folder. The stronger the protection level, the more likely it is that false positives will occur, so the more time you must spend checking the Junk E-mail folder for legitimate messages that need to be rescued. Fortunately, Windows Live Mail gives you several Junk E-mail levels to choose from, so you can choose a level that gives the blend of protection and convenience that suits you.

To set the Junk E-mail level, click **Menus and then click Safety options.** Windows Live Mail displays the Safety Options dialog box. The Options tab gives you four choices for the Junk E-mail protection level:

- ◆ **No Automatic Filtering.** This option turns off the Junk E-mail filter. Choose this option only if you use a third-party spam filter or if you handle spam using your own message rules.

- ◆ **Low.** This is the default protection level and it's designed to move only messages with obvious spam content to the Junk E-mail folder. This is a good level to start with—particularly if you get only a few spams a day—because it catches most spam and has only a minimal risk of false positives.

- ◆ **High.** This level handles spam aggressively and so only rarely misses a junk message. On the downside, the High level also catches the occasional legitimate message in its nets, so you need to check the Junk E-mail folder regularly to look for false positives. Use this level if you get a lot of spam—a few dozen messages or more each day.

Windows Wisdom

If you get a false positive in your Junk E-mail folder, click the message and then select **Actions, Junk e-mail, Mark as not junk.**

◆ **Safe List Only.** This level treats all incoming messages as spam, except for those messages that come from people or domains in your Safe Senders list (see "Specifying Safe Senders," below). Use this level if your spam problem is out of control (a hundred or more spams each day) and if most of your nonspam e-mail comes from people you know or from mailing lists you subscribe to.

If you hate spam so much that you never want to even *see* it, much less deal with it, activate the **Permanently delete suspected junk e-mail instead of moving it to the Junk E-mail folder** check box.

Look Out!

Spam is so hair-pullingly frustrating that you may be tempted to activate the **Permanently delete suspected junk e-mail instead of moving it to the Junk E-mail folder** check box out of sheer spite. I don't recommend this, however. The danger of false positives is just too great, even with the Low level, and it's not worth missing a crucial message.

Specifying Safe Senders

If you use the Low or High Junk E-mail protection level, you can reduce the number of false positives by letting Windows Live Mail know about the people or institutions that regularly send you mail. By designating these addresses as Safe Senders, you tell Windows Live Mail to automatically leave their incoming messages in your Inbox and never to redirect them to the Junk E-mail folder. And certainly if you use the Safe Lists Only protection level, you must specify some Safe Senders because Windows Live Mail treats everyone else as a spammer!

Your Safe Senders list can consist of three types of addresses:

◆ Individual e-mail addresses of the form *someone@somewhere.com*. All messages from these individual addresses will not be treated as spam.

◆ Domain names of the form *@somewhere.com*. All messages from any address within that domain will not be treated as spam.

♦ Your Contacts list. You can tell Windows Live Mail to treat everyone in your Contacts list as a Safe Sender, which makes sense since you're unlikely to be spammed by someone you know.

You can specify a Safe Sender either by entering the address by hand (using the Safe Senders tab in the Junk E-mail Options dialog box) or by using an existing message from the sender (right-click the message, select **Junk e-mail,** and then select either **Add sender to safe senders list** or **Add sender's domain to safe senders list**).

Blocking Senders

If you notice that a particular address is the source of much spam or other annoying e-mail, the easiest way to block the spam is to block all incoming messages from that address. You can do this using the Blocked Senders list, which watches for messages from a specific address and relegates them to the Junk E-mail folder.

As with Safe Senders, you can specify a Blocked Sender either by entering the address by hand (using the Blocked Senders tab in the Junk E-mail Options dialog box) or by using an existing message from the sender (right-click the message you want to work with, select **Junk e-mail,** and then select either **Add sender to blocked senders list** or **Add sender's domain to blocked senders list**).

Caveat Surfer: Internet Explorer and Security

Tons of people are flocking to the web, and tons of content providers are waiting for them there. Still, many people view the web as an essentially scary and untrustworthy place. There are many reasons for this, but one of the biggest is the security issue.

Internet Explorer offers quite a number of features that tackle this issue directly. The Internet Explorer window gives you visual cues that tell you whether a particular document is secure. For example, Figure 18.1 shows Internet Explorer displaying a secure web page. Notice how a lock icon appears to the right of the address, and that the address of a secure page uses **https** up front rather than **http.** Both of these features tell you that the web page has a security certificate that passed muster with Internet Explorer.

Figure 18.1

An example of a secure web document.

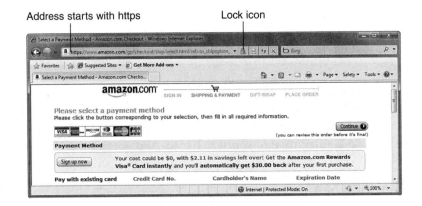

Address starts with https — Lock icon

Avoiding the Lures of Scammers with the SmartScreen Filter

Phishing refers to creating a replica of an existing web page to fool you into submitting personal info, financial data, or a password. It's a whimsical word for a serious bit of business, but the term comes from the fact that Internet scammers are using increasingly sophisticated lures as they "fish" for your sensitive data.

The most common ploy is to copy the web page code from a major site—such as AOL or eBay—and use that code to set up a replica page that appears to be part of the company's site. You receive a fake e-mail with a link to this page, which solicits your credit card data or password. When you submit the form, it sends the data to the scammer while leaving you on an actual page from the company's site so you don't suspect a thing.

A phishing page looks identical to a legitimate page from the company because the phisher has simply copied the underlying source code from the original page. However, no spoof page can be a perfect replica of the original. Here are four things to look for:

♦ **Weirdness in the address.** A legitimate page will have the correct domain—such as aol.com or ebay.com—while a spoofed page will have only something similar—such as aol.whatever.com or blah.com/ebay.

♦ **Weirdness in the addresses associated with page links.** Most links on the page probably point to legitimate pages on the original site. However, there may be some links that point to pages on the phisher's site.

♦ **Text or images that aren't associated with the trustworthy site.** Many phishing sites are housed on free web hosting services. However, many of these services place an advertisement on each page, so look for an ad or other content from the hosting provider.

◆ **No lock icon.** A legitimate site would only transmit sensitive financial data using a secure connection, which Internet Explorer indicates by placing a lock icon in the Address box, as described earlier. If you don't see the lock icon with a page that asks for financial data, then the page is almost certainly a spoof.

If you watch for these things, you'll probably never be fooled into giving up sensitive data to a phisher. However, phishing attacks are becoming legion, so we need all the help we can get. To that end, Internet Explorer 8 comes with a new tool called the SmartScreen Filter. This filter alerts you to potential phishing scams by doing two things each time you visit a site:

◆ Analyzing the site content to look for known phishing techniques (that is, to see if the site is "phishy").

◆ Checking to see if the site is listed in a global database of known phishing sites.

Phishing has become such a problem that Internet Explorer doesn't even bother to ask you whether you want to use the SmartScreen Filter; it just turns it on by default. To make sure the SmartScreen Filter is on, select **Safety, SmartScreen Filter,** and, if you see the **Turn On SmartScreen Filter command, click it.** In the Microsoft Phishing Filter dialog box that shows up, make sure the **Turn on SmartScreen Filter** option is activated, and then click **OK.**

> ### Windows Wisdom
>
> If you turn off the automatic SmartScreen Filter checks, you can still check for phishing site by site. After you navigate to a site that you want to check, select **Safety, SmartScreen Filter, Check This Website.**

Here's how the SmartScreen Filter works:

◆ If you come upon a site that Internet Explorer knows is a phishing scam, it changes the background color of the Address bar to red and displays a Phishing Website message in the Security Report area (just to the right of the address). It also blocks navigation to the site by displaying a separate page that tells you the site is a known phishing scam. A link is provided to navigate to the site if you so choose.

◆ If you come upon a site that Internet Explorer thinks is a potential phishing scam, it changes the background color of the Address bar to yellow and displays a Suspicious Website message in the Security Report area.

Click the Suspicious Website text and Internet Explorer displays a security report with a link that enables you to report the site. If you're sure this is a scam site, be sure to report it to help improve the database of phishing sites and prevent others from giving up sensitive data.

Covering Your Tracks: Deleting Your Browsing History

Internet Explorer 8 makes it much easier to delete your browsing history. In previous versions you had to make separate deletions for temporary files, cookies, visited addresses, saved form data, and saved passwords. In Internet Explorer 8, you do this:

1. Select **Safety, Delete Browsing History** (or press **Ctrl+Shift+Delete**) to display the Delete Browsing History dialog box, shown in Figure 18.2.

Figure 18.2

Use the Delete Browsing History dialog box to choose what web stuff you want to blow away.

2. If you don't want to save the files associated with sites on your Favorites list, deactivate the Preserve Favorites Website Data check box.

3. Activate the check box beside each type of data you want to smite:

   ◆ **Temporary Internet files.** These are copies of text, images, media, and other content from the pages you've visited recently. Internet Explorer stores all this data so that the next time you view one of those pages, it can retrieve data from the cache and display the site much more quickly. This is clearly a big-time privacy problem because it means that anyone can examine the cache to learn where you've been surfing.

◆ **Cookies.** These are small text files that sites store on your computer. Most cookies are benign, but they can be used to track your activities online.

◆ **History.** This is a list of addresses of the sites you've visited in the past 20 days, as well as each of the pages you visited within those sites. Again, this is a major privacy accident just waiting to happen, because anyone sitting at your computer can see exactly where you've been online over the past 20 days.

◆ **Form data.** This refers to the AutoComplete feature, which stores the data you type in forms and then uses that saved data to suggest possible matches when you use a similar form in the future. This is definitely handy, but it also means that anyone else who uses your computer can see your previously entered form text.

◆ **Passwords.** This is another aspect of AutoComplete, and Internet Explorer uses it to save form passwords. Sure it's nice and convenient, but it's really just asking for trouble because it means that someone sitting down at your computer can log on to a site, a job made all the easier if you activated the site option to save your username!

◆ **InPrivate Filtering Data.** This is information that Internet Explorer 8 gathers to detect when third-party providers are supplying data to the sites you visit. For more information, see the next section.

4. Click **Delete.**

Your Own Private Web: InPrivate Browsing and Filtering

Deleting your browsing history is a handy technique, for sure, but you have to remember to do it, and it's a distressingly all-or-nothing affair. That is, when you delete form data, passwords, history, cookies, or the cache files, you delete *all* of them (unless you preserve the cookies and cache files for your favorites). This is a problem because you often only want to remove the data for a single site or a few sites.

Fortunately, Internet Explorer 8 implements a single new feature that solves these problems: InPrivate browsing. When you activate this feature, Internet Explorer stops storing private data when you visit websites. It no longer saves temporary Internet files, cookies, browsing history, form data, and passwords.

To use InPrivate browsing, select **Safety, InPrivate Browsing** (or press **Ctrl+Shift+P**). Internet Explorer opens a new browser window as shown in Figure 18.3. Notice two things in this window that tell you InPrivate browsing is activated:

◆ You see [InPrivate] in the title bar.

◆ You see the InPrivate icon in the address bar.

Figure 18.3

When you activate InPrivate browsing, Internet Explorer 8 opens a new window and displays indicators in the title bar and address bar.

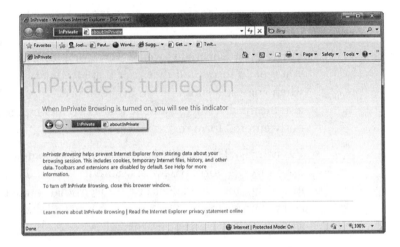

A similar idea is InPrivate filtering. When you visit a website, it's possible that the site loads some of its content from a third-party provider. It could be an ad, a map, a YouTube video, or an image. That's not a terrible thing once in a while, but if a particular third-party company provides data for many different sites, that company could conceivably build up a profile of your online activity.

What InPrivate filtering does is watch out for these third-party providers and track the data they provide. If the InPrivate feature detects that a third-party site is providing data quite often to the sites you visit, InPrivate will begin blocking that site's content so that it can't build up a profile of your activity.

InPrivate filtering is off by default. To turn it on, select **Safety, InPrivate Filtering** (or press **Ctrl+Shift+F**).

Blocking Pop-Up Windows

One of the most annoying things on the web are those ubiquitous pop-up windows that infest your screen with advertisements when you visit certain sites. (A variation on the theme is the "pop under," a window that opens "under" your current browser window, so you don't know it's there until you close the window.) Pop-up windows can also be dangerous because some unscrupulous software makers have figured out ways to use them to install spyware on your computer without your permission. They're nasty things, any way you look at them.

Fortunately, Microsoft has given us a way to stop pop-ups before they start. It's called the Pop-up Blocker and it looks for pop-ups and prevents them from opening. Follow these steps to use and configure the Pop-up Blocker:

1. In Internet Explorer, select **Tools, Pop-up Blocker.**

2. In the menu that appears, if you see the command **Turn On Pop-up Blocker,** it means the feature is turned off, so select this command to turn it on, and then select **Yes** when Internet Explorer asks if you're sure. (If you see Turn Off Pop-up Blocker, instead, all is well.)

3. Select **Tools, Pop-up Blocker, Pop-up Blocker Settings** to display the Pop-up Blocker Settings dialog box. You have the following options:

    ◆ **Address of website to allow.** Use this option when you have a site that displays pop-ups you want to see. Enter the address and then click **Add.**

    ◆ **Play a sound when a pop-up is blocked.** When this check box is activated, Internet Explorer plays a brief sound each time it blocks a pop-up. If this gets annoying after a while, deactivate this check box.

    ◆ **Show Information Bar when a pop-up is blocked.** When this check box is activated, Internet Explorer displays a yellow bar below the tabs each time it blocks a pop-up, just so you know it's working on your behalf.

    ◆ **Blocking Level.** Use this list to choose how aggressive you want Internet Explorer to be with pop-ups. Medium should work fine, but if you still get lots of pop-ups, switch to High.

4. Click **Close.**

Pop-up Blocker, now on the case, monitors your surfing and steps in front of any pop-up window that tries to disturb your peace. Figure 18.4 shows the yellow Information bar that appears under the tabs to let you know when a pop-up was thwarted. If you want to see the pop-up anyway, click the Information bar and then click **Temporarily Allow Pop-ups** in the menu that appears.

Figure 18.4

When the Pop-up Blocker is active, it displays a yellow information bar each time it blocks a pop-up ad.

Information bar

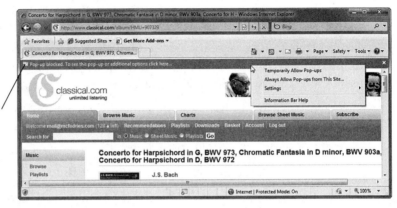

The Least You Need to Know

♦ To guard against e-mail–borne viruses, never open attachments that come from strangers, and double-check with friends before opening unexpected attachments they send your way.

♦ To cut down on the spam you receive, don't use your real address in a newsgroup; use a fake address whenever possible when signing up for things online, and never respond to spam or even open suspected spam messages.

♦ Only submit sensitive data (such as your credit card number) to a secure site (that is, one that has a lock icon in the status bar).

♦ To access the security settings in Windows Live Mail, click the **Menus** icon and then click **Safety Options.**

Part 5

Windows 7 at the Shop: Customizing, Maintaining, and Troubleshooting

According to media guru Marshall McLuhan, "The mark of our time is its revulsion against imposed patterns." This shameless name- and quote-dropping is meant not to impress, but to introduce the main theme of Part 5: customizing Windows 7. The look and feel of Windows 7 certainly qualifies as an "imposed pattern," and it was designed by Microsoft to be suitable for a typical user. However, if the notion of being "typical" fills you with fear and loathing, then you've come to the right place, because the four chapters coming up will show you how to refurbish Windows 7 to suit your tastes and the way you work. This part also proffers a few pointers on keeping Windows running smoothly and on fixing problems that crop up.

Chapter 19

Refurbishing the Desktop

In This Chapter

- ◆ Messing with the desktop background
- ◆ Redoing the desktop colors
- ◆ Adding and changing desktop icons
- ◆ Loading gadgets onto the Windows 7 desktop
- ◆ Monkeying around with the display's screen resolution

For most of its history, the PC has maintained a staid, nay, *dull* exterior. Fortunately, the Nuthin'-but-Beige school has given way in recent years to some almost-stylish machines cavorting in gunmetal gray or shiny black exteriors. And with PCs set to invade our living rooms and family rooms in the coming computer-as-the-center-of-the-media-universe revolution, it's likely that colorful and truly stylish machines will become the norm before too long.

That's a good thing because lots of people don't like the same old same old. These rugged individualists want to express themselves, and that's hard to do with beige (unless you call it ecru, instead). The same goes for the Windows 7 desktop. Yes, when you were installing Windows 7 or setting up your new computer, you probably had the chance to pick out a nifty desktop background, but maybe now you prefer a different scene or even a solid color. If so, you'll see in this chapter that Windows 7 offers plenty of ways to make your mark with a custom desktop color or background.

Why Customize?

Yo, Geek Boy! Changing the desktop sounds great and everything, but most of the time I can't even see it. Isn't all this just a waste of time?

Hey, who're you calling a geek? It's actually not a waste of time because many of the changes you make to the desktop apply to Windows 7 as a whole. For example, you can change the colors of window titles and borders, alter the font used in the taskbar, and change the overall size of the screen area. You'll learn all about these and many more customization options in this chapter.

You launch most of these customizations from the friendly confines of the Personalization window. To get this window on the desktop, use either of the following techniques:

♦ Right-click an empty section of the desktop and then click **Personalize** in the shortcut menu.

♦ Select **Start, Control Panel, Appearance and Personalization, Personalization.**

Changing the Desktop Background

It's true that the desktop is usually hidden, particularly if, like me, you prefer to run your programs maximized. Still, there are plenty of times when the desktop is visible, such as at startup and when you close your programs. And on many Windows 7 systems, you can get a quick peek at the desktop by hovering your mouse over the **Show Desktop** button that's hunkered down on the far right of the taskbar.

If that's enough of an excuse for you to tweak the look of the desktop, then you'll enjoy this section where I show you how to change the desktop background or color.

Wallpaper is an image or design that covers some or all of the desktop. (Before you ask, no, I'm not sure why Microsoft calls it "wallpaper" when you're supposed to be thinking that your screen is like the top of a desk. It's either a mixed metaphor or the Microsoft offices have a *very* strange interior designer.) You can choose one of the prefab wallpapers that come with Windows 7, one of your own pictures, or a solid color.

Here's how it works:

1. In the Personalization window, select **Desktop Background** to arrange a rendezvous with the Desktop Background window.

2. Use the **Picture location** list to select the collection of wallpaper images you want to view, such as **Windows Desktop Background;** select **Pictures Library** to see the contents of your Pictures library; or select **Solid Colors** to apply a simple color to the desktop.

> ### Windows Wisdom
> If you want to use multiple images and create a desktop slide show, activate the check box for each image you want to use, and then use the **Change every list** to set how often you want to see a new picture.

3. Click the image or color you want to use.

4. If you choose an image, select one of the following **Picture position** options:

   ◆ **Fill.** Displays a single copy of the image extended on all sides so it fills the entire desktop. As it extends the picture, Windows keeps the ratio of width to height the same, so this usually means that part of the image gets cut off.

   ◆ **Fit.** Displays a single copy of the image extended until either the width of the picture fits the width of the screen, or the height of the picture fits the height of the screen. Use this position if you want to display all of the image without distortion and without cutting off any of the image.

   ◆ **Stretch.** Displays a single copy of the image extended on all sides so it fills the entire desktop. In this case, Windows doesn't keep the ratio of the width to height, so your picture may end up a bit distorted.

   ◆ **Tile.** Displays multiple copies of the image repeated so they fill the entire desktop. Choose this option for small images.

   ◆ **Center.** Displays a single copy of the image in the center of the screen. This is a good choice for large images.

> ### Windows Wisdom
> The Windows 7 list of approved images isn't the only wallpaper game in town. There's no problem using some other image if that's what you'd prefer. To do this, click the **Browse** button to promote the Browse dialog box, find and highlight the image file, and then click **Open**.

5. Click **OK** to plaster the wallpaper onto the desktop.

Populating the Desktop

On most systems, the Windows 7 desktop is a rather Spartan affair with just one measly icon: the Recycle Bin. Gone are the old standbys such as the My Computer icon and the Internet Explorer icon. This was a conscious design choice on Microsoft's part because they'd prefer that you make the Start menu your Windows starting point.

However, if you miss having a satisfyingly cluttered desktop, there's nothing to stop you from tossing as many knickknacks on there as can fit. You can fill out the desktop with Windows 7's desktop icons, your own program shortcuts, and gadgets. The next few sections take you through these desktop shenanigans.

Windows Wisdom

Windows 7 also enables you to sort your desktop icons. Right-click the desktop, click **Sort By,** and then click a sort order: **Name, Size, Item type** (this is, by type of file), or **Date modified** (that is, by date). Felix Unger–types can keep things in apple-pie order all the time by clicking **View** and then activating the **Auto Arrange icons** command and the **Align icons to grid** command.

Adding Desktop Icons

To get your desktop repopulation program underway, click the **Change desktop icons** link in the Personalization window. The Desktop Icon Settings dialog box that jumps aboard is where you deal with the Windows 7 built-in desktop icons.

In the Desktop icons section, use the check boxes to add icons such as User's Files and Computer to the desktop. If you want to change the icon displayed by Windows 7, highlight it in the list and then click **Change Icon** (see "Changing an Icon" below for the details).

Adding Program Shortcuts

Windows 7's paltry half-dozen-minus-one ready-made desktop icons aren't going to do much to solve your desktop underpopulation problem. If you really want to have icons cheek-by-jowl on the desktop, you need to roll up your sleeves and toss a bunch of them on there yourself. You can create "shortcuts" for your favorite programs or documents, and double-clicking any shortcut will then launch the associated program or document, without any further fuss or fanfare. Creating these shortcuts isn't quite as easy as pie, but it's pretty darn close:

1. You have two ways to get the desktop-shortcut-creation party started:

    ◆ If you want to create a shortcut for a program, select **Start** to unwrap the Start menu.

    ◆ If you want to create a shortcut for a file, select **Start, Documents** (or whatever other library is appropriate, such as Pictures or Music).

2. Find the icon for which you want to create the shortcut.

3. Right-click the icon and then click **Send To, Desktop (create shortcut).** Windows 7 plops a new shortcut icon on the desktop.

Note that you can change the icon if the default one that Windows 7 uses isn't to your liking. To get started, right-click the shortcut, click **Properties,** and then click **Change Icon.** The next section takes you on the rest of the journey.

Changing an Icon

In several places throughout this book (including the previous two sections), you learn how to customize an object by changing its icon. How you get started depends on the object you're working with. However, in all cases you eventually end up at the Change Icon dialog box shown in Figure 19.1.

Here are some notes about working with this dialog box:

◆ In Windows 7, icons are usually stored in groups within executable files, particularly .exe and .dll files. Files with the .ico extension are pure icon files.

◆ If the icon you want isn't displayed in the Change Icon dialog box, use the Look for icons in this file text box to enter the name of an icon file and then press **Tab.** Here are a few suggestions:

%SystemRoot%\system32\shell32.dll

%SystemRoot%\system32\Pifmgr.dll

%SystemRoot%\explorer.exe

◆ If you're not sure about which file to try, click the **Browse** button and choose a file in the dialog box that appears.

◆ Click the icon you want to use, then click **OK.**

Figure 19.1

The Change Icon dialog box lists the icons that are available in an executable or icon file.

Adding Gadgets

To close your look at the do-it-yourself desktop, I'll show you how to tinker with the *gadgets* that Windows 7 lets you play with on the desktop. A gadget is a kind of miniprogram that performs a specific function. It might be a clock that you can set to a different time zone, a slide show of the images in your Pictures folder, a calendar, or a game. You can add these and many other gadgets to the desktop.

> **Windows Wisdom**
>
> Windows 7 ships with a relatively paltry collection of gadgets. You can see a lot more of them (hundreds, in fact) by clicking the **Get more gadgets online** link, which takes you to the Microsoft Gadgets website.

To get your gadget workshop open for business, use either of the following techniques:

- ◆ Right-click an empty section of the desktop and then click **Gadgets** in the shortcut menu.

- ◆ Select **Start, Control Panel, Appearance and Personalization, Desktop Gadgets.**

This buys you a ticket to the Gadgets window, shown in Figure 19.2. Click a gadget and then click **Show details** to get more info about it. If you like what you see, click and drag the icon and drop it onto the desktop.

Screen Saver Silliness

In olden times (say, 10 years ago), monitors weren't as good as they are today, and most of us struggled along using ugly DOS screens. One of the problems people faced was leaving their monitors on too long and ending up with some DOS hieroglyphics burned permanently into the screen (this is usually referred to, not surprisingly, as *burn-in*). To prevent this from happening, some genius came up with the idea of a *screen saver:* a program that automatically kicks in after the computer is idle for a few minutes. The screen saver displays some kind of moving pattern on the screen that helps prevent burn-in. However, with a simple touch of a key or jiggle of a mouse, the normal screen returns, unharmed and none the worse for wear.

Nowadays, it's pretty tough to burn an image into your screen. Improvements in monitor quality and the graphical nature of Windows have made such a fate much more difficult (although not impossible). Curiously, though, screen savers are still around and are, in fact, flourishing. The reason: most of them are just plain cool. Who cares about preventing burn-in when you can watch wild, psychedelic patterns or your favorite cartoon every few minutes?

Windows Wisdom

Most folks use screen savers for the fun factor, but they have a practical side, as well. For example, if you set up the screen saver to kick in very soon (say, after just one minute), then it's useful for hiding your screen when you're not at your desk. Also, as you'll see in this section, you can secure your computer by adding a password to the screen saver.

There are scads of commercial screen savers on the market, and Windows 7 comes equipped with some of its own. To try them out, first select **Screen Saver** in the Personalization window to open the Screen Saver Settings dialog box. Now drop down the Screen saver list, and select a screen saver.

You can also choose the following options:

♦ **Wait.** This spin box controls the amount of time your computer must be inactive before the screen saver starts doing its thing. You can enter a number between 1 and 9,999 minutes.

♦ **On resume, display logon screen.** Activate this check box to have Windows 7 display the log-on screen when you stop the screen saver. This means you have to log on to Windows again.

Windows Wisdom

Having to log on again each time your screen saver kicks in sounds like a hassle, but it's actually an effective security feature. If you leave your desk for a while, any snoop who tries to gain access to your computer will run smack dab into the log-on screen and be foiled. Of course, you must set up your Windows 7 user account with a password (see Chapter 11) for this to stop anyone with the IQ of a trained monkey or better.

♦ **Preview.** Click this button to give the screen saver a trial run. To return to the dialog box, move your mouse or press any key.

♦ **Settings.** Click this button to set various options for the screen saver (note, however, that some screen savers don't have any options). The Settings dialog box that appears depends on which screen saver you chose. Choose the options you want, and then click **OK** to return to the Personalization window.

Changing the Desktop Colors and Fonts

It's possible to redo much more of the Windows 7 interface (as the geeks like to call the stuff you see on your screen) than just the desktop background. Among many other things, you can change the font, color, and size of icon titles; the color of window title bars, scrollbars, and backgrounds; and the fonts and colors used in dialog boxes. This section shows you how to do it.

You begin by clicking **Window Color** in the Personalization window. How you proceed from here depends on your computer's graphics capabilities. You'll see one of the following two things on your screen:

♦ **The Window Color and Appearance window.** You see this window if your computer has a reasonably muscular graphics system. In this case, head for the following section, "Choosing a Glass Color Scheme."

♦ **The Window Color and Appearance dialog box.** You see this dialog box if your computer has an old or scrawny graphics system. In this case, you need to jump down to the section "Choosing a Regular Color Scheme."

Windows Wisdom

If your computer's graphics are particularly underpowered, stuff may appear slowly on your screen if you go with the default color theme, which is called Windows 7 Basic. In the Personalization window, drop down to Windows Classic, instead, and you should notice a performance boost.

Choosing a Glass Color Scheme

Systems with decent graphics hardware get to eyeball one of Windows 7's most striking features: the "glass" interface that makes the Start menu, the taskbar, and window and dialog box title bars and borders semitransparent. Why does the world need such an effect, I hear you ask? Windows 7 flacks will tell you that it helps people like you and me to focus more on the content of a window rather than the window itself. That just might be true, but the effect sure is striking, so what the heck?

The Window Color and Appearance window is simplicity itself, as you can see in Figure 19.3. Just click the color you prefer. If you don't like the glass effect, you

---

Hacking Windows

If Windows 7's built-in colors don't do it for you, create your own. Click **Show color mixer** to display three sliders: Hue, Saturation, and Brightness. Play with these sliders to come up with a color you like.

can nix it by deactivating the **Enable transparency** check box. If you leave this check box on, you can also use the Color intensity slider to change the amount of transparency. (The further to the right you drag the slider, the less transparent your windows become.) Note, too, that you can also click **Advanced appearance settings** to get the Window Color and Appearance dialog box to rise and shine, which means you can join in the fun of the next section.

Figure 19.3

You see the Window Color and Appearance window if your computer is equipped with a graphics system that can handle the nifty "glass" effect.

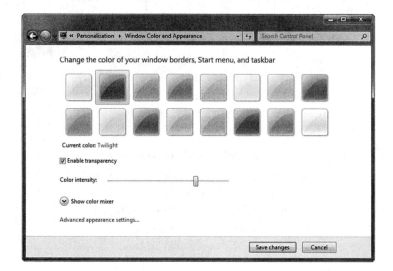

Choosing a Regular Color Scheme

If your computer isn't so good with the graphics, you get to mess with the Window Color and Appearance dialog box, which shows several fake windows and a bunch of doodads to play with. Here's what you do:

1. Use the **Item** list to choose which element of the screen you want to play with.

2. Use the following techniques to customize the selected element:

   ◆ If it's possible to change the size of the item, the **Size** spin box beside the Item list will be enabled. Use this spin box to adjust the size to taste.

   ◆ If it's possible to change the color of the item, the **Color 1** button will be enabled. Use this color palette control to choose the color you want.

◆ Some screen elements (such as the Active Title Bar item) can display a color *gradient*, where one color fades into another. In this case, you use the **Color 1** button to pick the first color and the **Color 2** button to pick the second color.

◆ If the item has text, use the **Font** list to change the typeface. You also can adjust the font using the **Size** list, the **Color** button, and the **Bold** and **Italic** buttons.

3. Repeat steps 1 and 2 until you've customized all the items you want.

4. Click **OK** to return to the Personalization window.

Saving Your Custom Theme

After you make changes to the Windows 7 theme, you might want to save those changes so you can apply them easily later on. Good idea! Here's how:

1. In the Personalization window's My Themes area, click **Unsaved Theme.**

2. Click **Save theme,** to open the Save Theme As dialog box.

3. Enter a cute or witty name for your theme.

4. Click **OK** to return to the Personalization window. You've now saved your custom theme, which means you can return to it any time you like (by selecting it in the My Theme lists) if you change the color scheme later on.

Changing the Display Settings

The next bit of desktop decoration I'll put you through relates to various display settings. Again, these are options that apply not just to the desktop, but to everything you see on your screen. To see these settings, you've got a couple of ways to go:

◆ If you've got the Personalization window open, click **Display** and then click **Change display settings.**

◆ Right-click the desktop and then click **Screen resolution.**

Either way, the Screen Resolution window that fades in is shown in Figure 19.4.

Figure 19.4

The Screen Resolution window lets you muck around with your display.

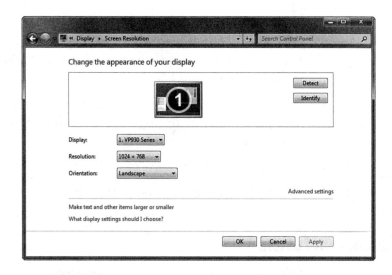

The **Resolution** slider determines the number of pixels used to display stuff on the screen. I've mentioned pixels before, but it's worth repeating myself here: a *pixel* is an individual pinpoint of light. All the colors you see on your screen are the result of thousands of these pixels getting turned on and set to display a specific hue.

The lowest screen area value is 800 × 600. This means that Windows 7 uses pixels arranged in a grid that has 800 columns and 600 rows. That's nearly half a million pixels for your viewing pleasure! The number of higher screen area values you can pick depends on your monitor and on your video adapter. Here are some notes:

- The more pixels you use (that is, the higher you go on the Resolution slider), the smaller things will look on the screen.

- In general, you should tailor the screen area value with the size of your monitor. If you have a standard 14- or 15-inch monitor, try 800 × 600; for 17- or 19-inch monitors, head up to 1,024 × 768; if you're lucky enough to have a 21-inch behemoth, go for 1,600 × 1,200 (if your video adapter will let you).

- If you have an older game or other program that has to be run at 640 × 480, it should change the resolution on its own when you start it. If it doesn't, right-click the program's icon in the Start menu and then click **Properties.** In the Compatibility tab, activate the **Run in 640 × 480 screen resolution** check box.

When you've made your changes, click **OK.** If you choose a different resolution, Windows 7 changes the setting and then asks whether you want to keep it. Click **Yes.** If things don't look right for some reason, click **No** to return to your normally scheduled display settings.

Look Out!

If your display goes haywire when Windows 7 applies the new settings, it probably means that you tried some combo that was beyond the capabilities of your adapter/monitor team. Your screen likely will be unreadable, but don't panic. Windows 7 will automatically reset the display after 15 seconds.

The Least You Need to Know

◆ To open the Personalization window, either right-click the desktop and then click **Personalize,** or select **Start, Control Panel, Appearance and Personalization, Personalization.**

◆ Most wallpaper images are small, so you need to use the Tile option to get the fill effect. For larger images, use either Center or Fit to Screen.

◆ To add a gadget, right-click the desktop, click **Gadgets,** and then drag a gadget onto the desktop.

◆ Try to use a screen resolution value that matches your monitor. For most monitors, 1,024 × 768 is ideal.

Chapter 20

Revamping the Start Menu and Taskbar

In This Chapter

- Changing Start menu settings
- Adding your own shortcuts to the Start menu
- Quick taskbar tweaks
- Customizing the notification area

You probably deal with the Start menu and taskbar dozens of times a day, clicking this, dragging that. If you could just figure out some ways to perform these chores more quickly and more efficiently, you'd probably save yourself lots of time for more interesting pursuits.

Well, then, you've come to the right chapter! Here's where you'll stumble upon all kinds of useful settings, options, tips, and techniques that not only let you customize the Start menu and taskbar, but that let you customize these Windows bits to make yourself more productive.

A Smart Start: Reconstructing the Start Menu

The Start menu is your royal road to Windows 7 riches, as well as to the programs installed on your machine. Because you use this road a lot during the course of a day, you'll probably want to make it as short and as straight as possible. Fortunately, Windows 7 gives you lots of ways to customize the Start menu to do this and to suit the way you work.

Toggling Some Start Menu Settings On and Off

The Windows 7 Start menu boasts a number of settings that you can turn on and off. These settings enable you to, among other things, add the Favorites list as a submenu, display the Control Panel icons as a submenu, and customize the power button.

To get to these settings, you have a couple of ways to go:

- Select **Start, Control Panel, Appearance and Personalization, Taskbar and Start Menu.**

- Right-click the **Start** button and then click **Properties.**

Either way, the Taskbar and Start Menu Properties dialog box comes off the bench. Now display the **Start Menu** tab.

The first thing we'll tweak is the Start menu's power button, which is the button that displays Shut Down in the lower right corner of the Start menu. Click that button and Windows closes itself up and then turns off your computer. That's a neat trick, but what if you don't turn off your computer that often? For example, you might find that you more often restart your computer, or put it to sleep, or use the Lock command to batten down the Windows hatches when you leave your desk.

Whatever the case, wouldn't it be nice to convert the handy Shut Down button into, say, a Restart button or a Lock button? You asked for it, you got it! In the Start Menu tab, click the **Power button action** list and then click the command you prefer: Switch User, Log Off, Lock, Restart, Sleep, or Shut Down.

The Start Menu tab is also home to two long-winded check boxes:

- **Store and display recently opened programs in the Start menu.** When this check box is activated, Windows keeps track of the programs you fire up, and it uses the Start menu to display a list of the ones you use most frequently. That's darn handy, but if you'd rather not see this list (say, for privacy reasons), go ahead and deactivate this check box.

♦ **Store and display recently opened items in the Start menu and the taskbar.**
When this check box is activated, Windows keeps track of the documents you
open, and it uses each program's jump list (which I mentioned back in Chapter 2)
to display a list of the files you check out most frequently. Again, this is usually a
good thing, but if you'd prefer your jump lists to remain unpopulated, deactivate
this check box.

To move on with things, click the Start Menu tab's **Customize** button. This gets you
up close and personal with the Customize Start Menu dialog box, shown in Figure 20.1.

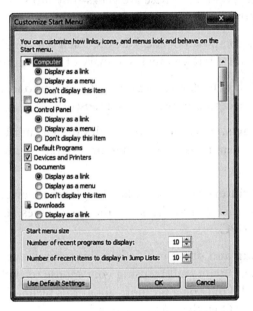

Figure 20.1

*The Customize Start Menu
dialog box is bursting with
Start menu settings.*

What you're dealing with at the top of the
dialog box is a long list of check boxes and
options that control the structure and behavior of the icons on the right side of the Start
menu (the folders and Windows 7 features).
The items that deal with folders—Control
Panel, Documents, Downloads, Games, Music,
Personal Folder (the icon with your user name),
Pictures, Recorded TV, and Videos—offer the
same set of three option buttons:

Windows Wisdom

Setting up folders such as Control
Panel and Documents as menus
is a faster way to work, but
what if you need to see those
windows in the future? That's no
problem. What you need to do
is right-click the icon and then
click **Open** in the shortcut menu.

- **Display as a link.** This option means that when you click the folder icon in the Start menu, Windows 7 opens the folder in a window.

- **Display as a menu.** This option means that when you click the folder icon in the Start menu, a submenu slides out to display the contents of the folder.

- **Don't display this item.** This option means that the folder icon doesn't appear in the Start menu.

(Note that there's also a System Administrative Tools item that offers three similar, but differently worded, options. These are geeks-only tools, so it's unlikely that you'll want to bother with this one.)

The rest of the list is composed of check boxes. Each one toggles a particular Start menu feature on and off. Here's a quick summary of the features:

- **Connect To.** This check box toggles the Connect To icon on and off. You use this icon to connect to the Internet or a network.

- **Default Programs.** This check box toggles the Default Programs icon on and off. You use this icon to associate different programs with different action and file types.

- **Devices and Printers.** This check box toggles the Devices and Printers icon on and off. You use this icon to check out the devices (yes, the printers, too) that are attached to your PC.

- **Enable dragging and dropping.** When this setting is activated, it enables you to rearrange Start menu stuff by using your mouse to click and drag the icons here and there. I'll tell you a bit more about this technique later in this chapter; see "Adding Your Own Start Menu Icons."

- **Favorites menu.** This check box toggles the icon for the Favorites submenu on and off the Start menu.

- **Help.** This check box toggles the Help and Support icon on and off.

- **Highlight newly installed programs.** With this setting lit up, Windows 7 monitors the Start menu to see if some program adds its own icons or a submenu to the All Programs menu. If it does, Windows 7 displays a notice letting you know and it highlights the new icons or submenu.

- **Homegroup.** This check box toggles the icon for the Homegroup folder on and off. This folder shows you the computers and devices in your homegroup.

◆ **Network.** This check box toggles the icon for the Network folder on and off. This folder shows you the computers and devices on your network.

◆ **Open submenus when I pause on them with the mouse pointer.** When this setting is activated, you can open a submenu just by placing your mouse pointer over the menu item. If you deactivate this check box, you can only open a submenu by clicking the menu item.

◆ **Recent Items.** This check box toggles the icon for the Recent Items folder on and off. Recent Items displays a list of the last 15 files you worked on in any program.

◆ **Run command.** This check box toggles the icon for the Run command on and off.

◆ **Search other files and libraries.** These options determine whether Windows looks outside of your personal file library when you search using the Search box. You can tell it not to search elsewhere; to search elsewhere as well as your PC's Public folder; or to search elsewhere, but not in the Public folder.

◆ **Search programs and Control Panel.** Deactivate this check box to tell Windows 7 not to search your installed programs or the Control Panel when you run a search from the Search box.

◆ **Sort All Programs menu by name.** This check box toggles the alphabetic sorting of items in the All Programs menu on and off.

◆ **Use large icons.** This check box determines the relative size of the icons that appear in the programs section (the left half) of the Start menu. Deactivate this check box if you raise the number of programs Windows 7 displays on the Start menu, as described next.

Next up in the Customize Start Menu dialog box is the **Number of recent programs to display** spin box, which you can use to adjust the number of icons that appear in the Start menu's programs section. Recall that this section displays icons for the most recent programs you fired up. You can use the spin box to set the maximum number of these icons that appear in this section. Enter a number from 0 to 30.

Along a similar vein, there's the **Number of recent items to display in Jump lists** spin box, which you can use to adjust the maximum number of files that Windows 7 displays in its jump lists. Enter a number from 0 to 60.

Hacking Windows _____

If you want to give an icon a permanent place in the Start menu's programs section, click **Start** to open the Start menu, right-click the icon, and then click **Pin to Start Menu**. Windows 7 moves the icon up into the top part of the menu and displays the icon title in bold. (Note that you can do this with any icon on the All Programs menus as well.) If you change your mind about the icon, you can return it to normal by right-clicking it and then clicking **Unpin from Start Menu**. If you want to remove a single program icon from the Start menu, click **Start** to open the Start menu, right-click the icon, and then click **Remove from this list.**

That's all he wrote for the Customize Start Menu dialog box, so click **OK** to return to the Taskbar and Start Menu Properties dialog box, and then click **OK** to put all the new settings into effect.

Adding Your Own Start Menu Icons

Most new users just assume the arrangement of icons on the Start menu is a permanent part of the Windows 7 landscape. They're right, to a certain extent. Everything on the main Start menu can only be messed with by using the techniques from the previous section.

What *is* a bit surprising is that the menus that appear when you click **All Programs** are completely open for customization business. You can add icons, move them around, rename them, delete them, and more. I show you how to do all of this in this section.

Let's begin by learning how to add an icon to the Start menu. You usually don't have to worry about this when you install an application. That's because most of today's programs are hip to the Start menu, so they'll add an icon or three during their installation procedure. However, there are two cases when you'll need to add an icon yourself:

♦ If you want easy access to a particular document that you use often.

♦ If you installed an older program that isn't Start-menu savvy.

It's important to bear in mind that the icons you're working with here are *shortcuts* to documents or programs. A shortcut is a teensy file whose sole mission in life is to act as a pointer to some other file. For example, when you launch a shortcut for a document, the shortcut tells Windows 7 the location of the *actual* document. Windows 7 then finds the document and opens it for you.

Here's how you add an icon to the Start menu:

1. Use Windows Explorer to find the document you want to work with or the file that runs the program you want to add.

2. Click and drag the document or file from Windows Explorer and hover it over the **Start** button. After a second or two, the Start menu pops up.

3. Drag the file up into the Start menu.

4. Do one of the following:

    ◆ If you want to make the icon a part of the Start menu's permanent program icon section (at the top of the Start menu), drag it up into the Start menu, wait until the little banner says Pin to Start Menu (see Figure 20.2), and then drop it.

Windows Wisdom
If you click and drag the document or file from My Computer and then drop it on the **Start** button, Windows 7 automatically pins a shortcut to the document or file to the "permanent" part of the Start menu's programs section.

Figure 20.2

When you see the Pin to Start Menu banner, go ahead and drop the icon to create a Start menu shortcut for it.

♦ If you want the icon to appear in the All Programs menu, press and hold down the **Alt** key and then drag the file over top of **All Programs,** wait a beat until the menu appears, and then drag the file into the All Programs menu. If you want it to appear in one of the All Programs submenus, drag the file over the submenu, wait until the submenu appears, drag the file into the submenu, and then drop it inside the submenu. Oh, and you can release **Alt** now, too.

Windows Wisdom
Remember that the icons you delete are only shortcuts that point to the original program file or document. You're not deleting the originals.

What about the opposite procedure, when you need to get rid of something on the Start menu? I'm glad you asked. If the icon is on the main Start menu, right-click it and then click **Remove from this list.** If the icon resides in the All Programs area, display the icon you want to remove, right-click it, and then click **Delete.**

Easy Start Menu Maintenance

To close out your look at customizing the Start menu, here are a couple of tips and techniques that can make this part of your life even easier:

♦ **Right-click convenience.** You can perform many maintenance chores right from the Start menu itself. Right-click a Start menu icon, and you'll get a menu with all kinds of useful commands, including Cut, Copy, Delete, and Rename. (The actual roster of commands depends on the icon. The largest collection is found with the icons on the All Programs menu.)

♦ **Drag-and-drop rearranging.** You can move things around in the All Programs menu by using your mouse to click and drag the icons directly. You can drop them higher or lower on the same menu, or even drop them onto another menu altogether.

Renovating the Taskbar

Like the Start menu, the taskbar also seems to be a nonmalleable feature of the Windows 7 countryside. If that were true, however, then this chapter would end right about here. The fact that you still have a few pages left to slog through tells you that, indeed, the taskbar is readily malleable. Not only that, but most of the taskbar customizations you'll see over the next few sections are practical timesavers and not mere "Hey, Ma, look what I can do!" tricks (although feel free to show off these techniques to any handy family member).

Unlocking the Taskbar

When Microsoft was testing Windows with new users, they found that people often ended up with inadvertently customized taskbars that they didn't know how to fix. For example, it's quite easy to accidentally resize the taskbar while trying to resize a window (as you see a bit later). To prevent this kind of faux customization (and the confusion it creates), Windows 7 comes with its taskbar locked so that it can't be moved or sized. Here's how to unlock it so that you can manhandle the taskbar on purpose:

1. Right-click an empty section of the taskbar.

2. In the shortcut menu that appears, look for the **Lock the Taskbar** command. If there's a checkmark beside it, click the command to remove the checkmark and unlock the taskbar.

Taskbar Travels: Moving and Sizing the Taskbar

The taskbar, recumbent on the bottom of the screen, seems quite comfy. However, that position might not be comfy for *you*, depending on the ergonomics of your desk and chair. Similarly, you might have a program where you need to maximize the available vertical screen space, so you might not appreciate having the taskbar usurp space at the bottom of the screen. These are mere molehills that can be easily leapt by moving the taskbar to a new location:

1. Right-click an empty section of the taskbar and then click **Properties.** Our old friend the Taskbar and Start Menu Properties dialog box reappears.

2. Click the **Taskbar screen location** list, and then click the location you prefer: Left, Right, Top, or Bottom.

3. Click **OK.** Windows 7 tosses the taskbar to the new location.

What if you're not so much interested in moving the taskbar as in resizing it? For example, if you're feeling particularly frisky, you might end up with a truckload of programs on the go. However, each of those programs claims a bit of taskbar turf. Eventually, the taskbar reaches its maximum capacity and it sprouts little up and down arrows to the right of the icons, as pointed out in Figure 20.3. Click the down arrow to see the icons for your other running programs, and then click the up arrow to return to the original batch of icons.

Figure 20.3

Who can tell what each of these taskbar buttons represents?

Click these arrows to see your other taskbar icons

That extra click to get to the icon you need is a real hassle and flies in the face of the taskbar's one-click convenience. The way you fix that is by expanding the taskbar from its single-row setup to a setup that has two or more rows. Here's how:

1. Move the mouse pointer so that it rests on the top edge of the taskbar. The pointer changes into a vertical two-headed arrow.

2. Click and drag the edge of the taskbar up slightly. After you travel a short distance, a second taskbar row springs into view, as shown in Figure 20.4.

Figure 20.4

To see the button text, stretch the taskbar into this two-row configuration.

3. Keep dragging the taskbar up until the taskbar is the size you want, and then release the mouse button.

If you've moved the taskbar to the left or right side of the screen, dragging the outer edge only increases the width of the taskbar—it doesn't create new rows.

Some Useful Taskbar Options

The next round of taskbar touchups involves a small but useful set of properties, which can be displayed by using either of the following techniques:

♦ Select **Start, Control Panel, Appearance and Personalization, Taskbar and Start Menu.**

♦ Right-click an empty section of the taskbar and then click **Properties.**

This reunites you with the Taskbar and Start Menu Properties dialog box. This time, however, you'll be dealing with the **Taskbar** tab.

The Taskbar appearance group controls the look and feel of the taskbar. As you play with the settings in this group, keep an eye on the fake taskbar that appears just above the Lock the taskbar check box. This will give you some idea of how the taskbar will change based on the settings you toggle on and off. Here's a summary of the available check boxes:

- **Lock the taskbar.** This check box toggles the taskbar lock on and off.

- **Auto-hide the taskbar.** If you activate this check box, Windows 7 shrinks the taskbar to a teensy blue strip that's barely visible along the bottom of the screen. This gives a maximized window more room to stretch its legs. When you need the taskbar for something, just move the mouse pointer to the bottom of the screen. Lo and behold, the full taskbar slides into view. When you move the mouse above the taskbar, the taskbar sinks back whence it came.

- **Use small icons.** When this option is activated, the taskbar icons convert into smaller versions, which is a great way to get more icons crammed into a single taskbar row.

- **Taskbar location on screen.** As I described in the previous section, you use this list to move the taskbar to a different location.

- **Taskbar buttons.** The items in this list determine how and whether Windows 7 combines taskbar icons. As you know, when you run a program, Windows 7 adds a button for the program to the taskbar. The default value is **Always combine, hide labels,** which means that Windows 7 reduces clutter by combining similar taskbar buttons into a single button. For example, if you have two or three instances of Internet Explorer on the go, they'll get grouped into a single button. If you choose **Combine when taskbar is full** instead, then Windows 7 only does the combining thing once the taskbar becomes completely filled with buttons. To forego all this combining malarkey, choose **Never combine.**

Click **OK** to put your settings into effect.

Getting Control of the Notification Area

The notification area on the right side of the taskbar is blissfully low on icons in Windows 7. (If you've used previous versions of Windows, you might have ended up with a notification area festooned with a ridiculous number of icons.) In Windows 7, no matter how many of your installed programs try to run roughshod over the notification area, you'll always see *only* the following icons: Volume, Network, Action Center, and (if you have a notebook PC) Power. Sweet!

That doesn't mean all your other notification area icons are gone for good, they're just permanently hidden, although in two different ways:

   ◆ Some icons are visible, but to see them you have to click the upward-pointing arrow on the left side of the notification area (see Figure 20.5).

   ◆ Some icons are completely hidden, but you do see any notification messages displayed by those icons.

Figure 20.5

In Windows 7, you have to click the arrow to see your other notification area icons.

This new setup simplifies things considerably and gives you more taskbar breathing room, but there are times when it's not so convenient. For example, if you frequently control a program by right-clicking its tray icon, you either have that extra click to get at the icon, or you can't get at it at all. Fortunately, you can customize the notification area to show an icon right in the tray, hide it in the extra menu, or remove it completely and see just its notifications. Here's how:

1. Click the notification area arrow and then click **Customize.** (You can also right-click the taskbar, click **Properties,** and then click **Customize.**) The Notification Area Icons window appears, as shown in Figure 20.6.

2. For each icon, click the **Behaviors** list to choose one of the following options:

   ◆ **Show icon and notifications.** Choose this option to add the icon to the main notification area.

   ◆ **Hide icon and notifications.** Choose this option to shuffle the icon off to the notification area's extra menu.

   ◆ **Only show notifications.** Choose this option to completely remove the icon from the main notification area. Windows 7 will still display the icon's notifications, however.

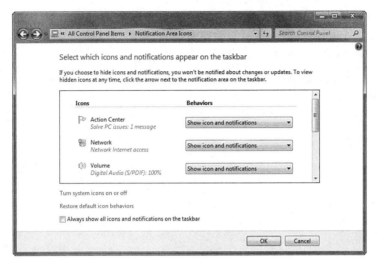

Figure 20.6

Use the Notification Area Icons window to set up the notifications area to suit your style.

3. Click the **Turn system icons on or off** link. The System Icons window appears. The system icons are the four (or five) icons I mentioned earlier: Clock, Volume, Network, Action Center, and (if you're running Windows 7 on a notebook PC), Power.

4. Deactivate the check box for each system icon you don't use.

5. Click **OK** to return to the Notification Area Icons window.

6. Click **OK.**

The Least You Need to Know

◆ The Start menu and taskbar options are available by selecting **Start, Control Panel, Appearance and Personalization, Taskbar and Start Menu,** or by right-clicking the **Start** button or an empty stretch of the taskbar and then clicking **Properties.**

◆ To add Start menu stuff, click and drag a document or program file from Windows Explorer, hover the mouse over the **Start** button, and then drop it on the menu you want.

◆ To make direct Start menu modifications, display the Start menu and then right-click any command.

◆ Before embarking on any taskbar modifications, be sure to unlock it first. The quickest route is to right-click an empty part of the taskbar and then deactivate the **Lock the Taskbar** command.

◆ To mess around with the notification area, click the notification area arrow and then click **Customize.**

Chapter 21

Maintaining Your System in Ten Easy Steps

In This Chapter

◆ Maintain your hard disk by checking for errors, monitoring free space, deleting unnecessary files, and defragmenting files

◆ Set up your system for easier recovery by creating restore points, backing up your files, and creating a full system backup

◆ Keep your system up-to-date by checking for updates and solutions to problems

◆ Set up a maintenance schedule to keep your system running in peak form without burdening your schedule

We tend to forget that computers are mechanical devices that can fail at any time, or can simply wear out over time. In other words, the data you've stored on your computer is at risk *right now*. Not months or years from now. *Now*. This doesn't mean you should just sit around and wait for your computer to start sucking mud. ("Sucking mud" is a colorful phrase used by programmers to refer to a crashed machine. Legend has it that the phrase comes from the oilfield lament, "Shut 'er down, Ma, she's a-suckin' mud!")

No, what you *should* be doing is a little proactive system maintenance to help prolong your machine's life and to help propel your system to new heights of efficiency and speed. This chapter can help by showing you the Windows 7 tools that can get you in what I like to call "ounce of prevention mode" (and to avoid what I call "pound of cure mode" down the road). In particular, I give you a step-by-step plan for maintaining your system and checking for the first signs of problems.

Step 1—Check Your Hard Disk for Errors

You see later in this chapter that you should back up your files frequently because all hard disks eventually go to the Great Computer in the Sky. However, it's possible to avoid a premature hard disk death (as well as lost files and otherwise-inexplicable system crashes) by regularly checking your disk for errors. (By "regularly," I mean about once a week or so.) Here's how you do it:

1. Shut down any programs that are on the loose.

2. Select **Start, Computer** to open the Computer window.

3. Right-click your hard disk and select **Properties.**

4. In the dialog box that appears, display the **Tools** tab.

5. Click the **Check Now** button. This gets you an appointment with the Check Disk dialog box.

6. Check Disk offers two checking options:

   ◆ **Automatically fix file system errors.** Activate this check box to have Windows 7 handle the dirty work of fixing any file problems that it finds. This gives you one less thing to fret about, so activating this option is a good idea.

def•i•ni•tion

A **sector** is a tiny piece of a disk, and Windows 7 uses a disk's sectors as mini-storage bins that hold bits of your files. A "bad" sector is one that has gone wonky for some reason, so it can no longer be used to store anything reliably.

   ◆ **Scan for and attempt recovery of bad sectors.** Activate this option to have Check Disk examine the physical surface of the disk for corruption. This is a good idea because a lot of bad *sectors* means not only that you might not be able to store files reliably, but also that your hard disk might be heading for a crash. Note, however, that this slows down the check considerably, so you should probably use this option only once a month or so.

7. Click **Start** to get the Check Disk show on the road.

8. If any errors are found (and you didn't activate the **Automatically fix file system errors** option), you'll see a dialog box alerting you to the bad news. Follow the instructions provided.

9. When the check is done, a dialog box lets you know. Click **OK.**

Remember that Check Disk can take quite a while under some circumstances, so only run the program at the end of the day or when you know you won't be needing your computer for a while.

Step 2–Check Free Disk Space

Ever wonder how much free space you have left on your hard disk? It's easy enough to find out:

1. Select **Start, Computer** to get reunited with the Computer window.

2. Click your hard disk.

As you can see in Figure 21.1, the Details pane shows you how much free space you have left to work with. (You also see the amount of free space if you select **View, Tiles** to switch to Tiles view, as shown in Figure 21.1.)

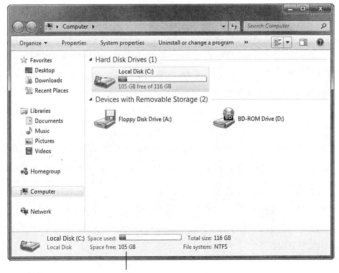

Figure 21.1

Highlight your hard disk in the Computer window to see how much disk real estate is left to be developed.

Make sure this number doesn't get too low

> ### Windows Wisdom
>
> How do you know when your hard disk is getting low on disk space? It depends. If it's the disk where Windows 7 is stored, then you should never let that disk get much below 200 megabytes (MB) of free space. If it's some other disk that you use to store programs and files, start getting worried when the free space drops to around 100 MB. If the free space is measured in gigabytes (GB), then don't worry because there are about 1,000 megabytes in every gigabyte, so you have plenty of room.

Step 3—Delete Unnecessary Files

If you find that your hard disk is getting low on free space, you should delete any unneeded files and programs. Here are a few methods you can use to perform a spring cleaning on your hard disk by hand:

- **Uninstall programs you don't use.** If you have an Internet connection, you know it's easier than ever to download new software for a trial run. Unfortunately, that also means it's easier than ever to clutter your hard disk with unused programs. You should uninstall these and other rejected applications (see Chapter 6).

- **Delete downloaded program archives.** Speaking of program downloads, your hard disk is probably also littered with zip files or other downloaded archives. For those programs you use, you should consider moving the archive files to a removable medium for storage. For programs you don't use, consider deleting the archive files.

- **Delete application backup files.** Applications often create backup copies of existing files and name the backups using either the .bak or .old extension. Use Windows 7's Search utility to locate these files and delete them (as described in Chapter 5).

Once you've completed these tasks, you next should run the Disk Cleanup utility, which can automatically remove several other types of files, including the following:

- **Temporary Internet files.** These are copies of web pages that Internet Explorer keeps on hand so that the pages view faster the next time you visit them. Saying goodbye to these files will slow down some of your surfing slightly, but it will also rescue lots of disk space.

- ◆ **Recycle Bin.** These are the files that you've deleted recently. Windows 7 stores them in the Recycle Bin for a while just in case you delete a file accidentally. If you're sure you don't need to recover a file, you can clean out the Recycle Bin and recover the disk space.

- ◆ **Temporary files.** These are "scratch pad" files that some programs use to doodle on while they're up and running. Most programs are courteous enough to toss out these files, but a program or computer crash could prevent that from happening. You can delete these files at will.

- ◆ **Thumbnails.** These are copies of your pictures files that Windows 7 uses to quickly display thumbnail versions of those files. If you delete the thumbnails, Windows 7 will just re-create them as it needs them.

Note that you may not have all of these types of files on your system, so if you don't see some of them when you run Disk Cleanup, don't sweat it.

Follow these steps to use Disk Cleanup to trash any or all of these kinds of files:

1. Windows 7 offers you three different routes to get started:

    - ◆ In the Computer folder, select the hard disk and then click **Properties.** In the dialog box that beams up, click the **Disk Cleanup** button.

    - ◆ Select **Start, Control Panel, System and Security,** and then under **Administrative Tools,** click **Free up disk space.**

    - ◆ Select **Start, All Programs, Accessories, System Tools, Disk Cleanup.**

2. If you used either of the last two paths and you have multiple hard disks, the Select Drive dialog box will ask you which one you want to work with. Use the Drives list to pick out the drive and then click **OK.**

3. Either way, you end up at the Disk Cleanup window shown in Figure 21.2. Activate the check box beside each type of file you want to blow to kingdom come.

4. Click **OK.** Disk Cleanup asks whether you're sure.

5. Click **Yes.**

Figure 21.2

Use Disk Cleanup to obliterate all kinds of more or less useless files from your hard disk.

Step 4—Defragment Your Hard Disk

With its 3D-ish icons, "glass" effects, and slick desktop, Windows 7 surely presents a polished surface to the world. However, when it's just kicking around at home, Windows 7 is a bit of a slob. I'm thinking, in particular, about how Windows 7 stores files on your hard disk. It's actually remarkably casual about the whole thing, and tosses bits and pieces of each file wherever it can find room. This doesn't matter much at first, but after a while you end up with files that are scattered willy-nilly all over your hard disk. This is a problem because it means that to open a file, Windows 7 has to make lots of little, time-consuming trips to the far corners of the hard disk in order to gather up all those disparate chunks.

def•i•ni•tion

A hard disk is said to be **fragmented** when pieces of its files are scattered in various places throughout the disk.

This is why computers that feel nice and zippy when you first take them out of the box seem to get more sluggish over time. In geek terms, the problem is that the files on your hard disk have become *fragmented*. The solution is to run the Windows 7 Disk Defragmenter program, which will rearrange the contents of your hard disk so that each file's hunks are arranged consecutively (or *contiguously*, as the geeks like to say). Don't worry, though: your documents and programs don't get changed in any way and your disk contents will look exactly the same when you view them in My Computer.

The good news about all this defragmentation stuff is that Windows 7 is set up to automatically defragment your hard disk every day. (The default time is 1 A.M., so that may be why you haven't noticed, insomniacs excepted.) Therefore, you probably won't ever have to worry about it. However, it's a good idea to check that the Automatic Defragmenter is on the job, which you'll do in the following steps:

1. You can get underway by using any of the following techniques:

    ♦ In the Computer window, click the hard disk and then click **Properties.** In the dialog box that gets piped in, display the **Tools** tab and click the **Defragment Now** button.

    ♦ Select **Start, Control Panel, System and Security,** and then under **Administrative Tools,** click **Defragment your hard drive.**

    ♦ Select **Start, All Programs, Accessories, System Tools, Disk Defragmenter.**

2. In the Disk Defragmenter window that results, click **Configure Schedule.** The Disk Defragmenter: Modify Schedule dialog box shows up.

3. Make sure the **Run on a schedule** check box is activated, as shown in Figure 21.3.

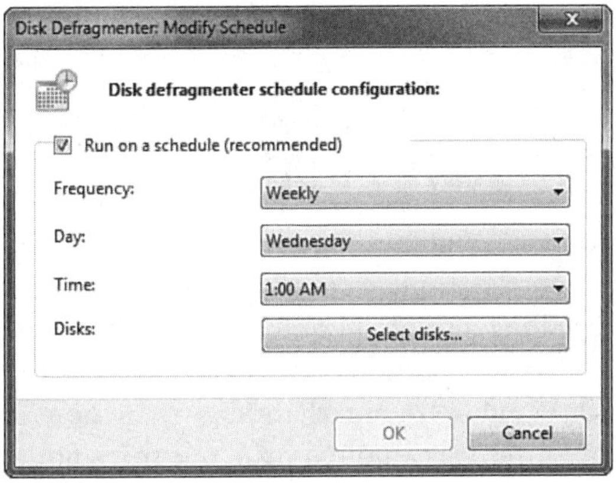

Figure 21.3

Make sure the Automatic Defragmenter is doing its defragmentation duty while you're asleep.

4. To change how often the Automatic Defragmenter does its thing, click the **Frequency** list and then select Daily, Weekly, or Monthly. (Weekly is probably best for most people.)

5. If you chose either Weekly or Monthly, click the **Day** list and choose the day of the week or month you want the defragment to run.

6. Click the **Time** list and choose the time of day you want the defragment to happen.

7. Click **OK.**

On the other hand, maybe you *want* to run a defragment anyway, just because you can. Hey, it's a free country. Before getting to the Disk Defragmenter details, here's a bit of prep work you need to do:

♦ Shut down all running programs.

♦ Run the Check Disk program to be sure there are no errors on your hard disk. In particular, be sure you activate the **Scan for and attempt recovery of bad sectors** check box.

♦ Use the methods I outlined in the previous section to get rid of any files you don't need.

With all that done, click **Defragment disk** in the Disk Defragmenter window. The defragmenting process might take some time, depending on the size of your disk and how severely fragmented it is. Because it's not unusual for a defragment job to take a couple of hours or more, consider running Disk Defragmenter just before you leave the office or go to bed.

Step 5—Set System Restore Points

One of the most frustrating of Windows experiences is to have your system sailing along without so much as an electronic hiccup, and then to have everything crash or become unstable after installing a program or a chunk of hardware. This all-too-common scenario means that some program component or device driver simply doesn't get along with Windows 7, and that the two are now at loggerheads. Uninstalling the program or device can often help, but that's not a foolproof solution.

To help guard against software or hardware installations that bring down the system, Windows 7 has a feature called System Protection. Its job is straightforward, yet clever: to take periodic snapshots—called *restore points*—of your system, each of which includes the current Windows 7 configuration. The idea is that if a program or device installation causes problems on your system, you use another feature called System Restore to revert your system to the most recent restore point before the installation.

System Protection automatically creates restore points at the following times:

See Also

I show you how to use System Restore to recover from a problem in Chapter 22. See the section titled "Recovering Using System Restore."

- ◆ Every 24 hours if you keep your computer on full-time. If you turn your machine off periodically, Windows 7 creates a restore point every 24 hours that the machine is running.

- ◆ Before installing an update via the Automatic Updates feature (discussed later in this chapter).

- ◆ Before installing certain applications. Some newer applications—notably Office 2000 and later—are aware of System Protection and ask it to create a restore point prior to installation.

- ◆ When you attempt to install a device driver that is "unsigned" (meaning that it can't be verified that the driver will work properly with Windows 7).

You can also create a restore point manually using the System Protection feature. Follow these steps:

1. Select **Start, System and Security, System, System protection.** The System Properties dialog box appears and displays the System Protection tab for you.

2. In the Protection Settings table, make sure you see On in the Protection column of your hard disk. If it says Off, instead, say "What the ...?", click **Configure,** activate the **Restore system settings and previous versions of files** check box, and then click **OK.**

3. Click **Create.** The System Protection dialog box appears.

4. Use the text box to enter a description for the new restore point and then click **Create.** System Protection creates the restore point and displays the Create Restore point: Success dialog box.

5. Click **Close** to return to the System Protection tab.

6. Click **OK.**

Windows Wisdom

Don't worry about creating too many restore points. Windows 7 restricts the amount of disk space restore points use, and if you bump up against that ceiling, Windows 7 automatically deletes the oldest restore points. If you want to give your system more room for restore points, click **Configure** and then drag the **Max Usage** slider.

Step 6—Back Up Your Files

Other than a few people who insist on living in It-Can't-Happen-to-Me Land, I think most folks get the "why" part of backing up. They know that computers crash all the time and that they can lose irreplaceable data if they don't have backups kicking around. However, many of those people just don't get the "how" part. That is, they'd like to run backups, but it's such a time-consuming chore that it just doesn't seem worth the hassle. For many people, backing up ranks just above root canal on the Top 10 Most Unpleasant Chores list. "Sorry, I'd like to do a backup, but I have to call the IRS to schedule an audit."

If backing up has always seemed like too much of a bother, wait until you get a load of Windows Backup, the backup program that comes with Windows 7. The big whoop about Windows Backup is that it uses a new feature called Automatic Backup that makes backing up your precious files about as painless and hassle-free as this stuff gets. You run through a relatively short and comprehensible wizard to configure Automatic Backup, and then Windows Backup handles everything for you behind the scenes. In fact, after the initial setup, you may never have to do *anything* with Windows Backup again, unless your system fails and you need to restore your files. How sweet does *that* sound (the Automatic Backup feature, that is, not the system failure)?

However (you knew there had to be a "however" coming soon), the price of this auto-mated backup business is that you need a backup destination with lots of free space. In fact, you need enough free space to hold the entire backup, because Windows Backup simply won't back up to a disk that doesn't have enough space.

So how much free space do you need? Well, the other thing about Windows Backup is that, at a minimum, it backs up the entire drive on which Windows 7 is installed. (You can exclude your documents from the backup, but that would just be silly.) Windows Backup does compress the backed-up data so that it doesn't take up too much space, but you're still probably looking at a minimum of 4 or 5 GB, and probably more.

Where on Earth are you going to find that kind of free space? Here are three good choices:

- ◆ **An external hard drive.** This is the easiest solution because you can buy 200 GB behemoths that plug into a USB port on your computer and are ready to go in seconds flat. These external hard drives are big enough to hold all your backup data and are fast enough that each backup won't take forever.

- ◆ **A recordable DVD drive.** Your best bet here is a rewritable DVD drive (DVD-RW or DVD+RW), which lets you write files to it multiple times, so Windows Backup can keep using it over and over. If you use one-time recording discs such as DVD-R or DVD+R, then you need to remember to put in a new disc after each backup, which defeats our goal of truly automated backups.

- ◆ **A network folder.** If you've got your computers talking to each other over a network, then you might have one machine with lots of extra hard disk space. If so, you could share a folder on that hard disk with the network and then use that shared folder as a backup spot.

Now that we've knocked the whole backup process down to size, let's whip out the brass tacks and get down to business. To get started, you have a couple of choices:

- ◆ Select **Start, Control Panel,** and then under the System and Security heading, click **Back up your computer.**

- ◆ Select **Start, All Programs, Maintenance, Backup and Restore.**

After a second or two, the Backup and Restore window punches in. Your first job is to configure the Automatic Backup features, which just takes a few steps:

1. Click **Set up backup.** The Set Up Backup Wizard pulls itself out of a hat.

2. The wizard first wants to know the backup destination. You have two choices (click **Next** when you're ready to move on):

   - ◆ **On a hard disk or CD/DVD drive.** In the list of drives, click the one you want to use.

   - ◆ **On a network.** Click **Save on a network** if you want to use a shared network folder. Your best bet here is to click the **Browse** button and then use the Browse for Folder dialog box to select the shared network folder.

3. Click **Next.** The What do you want to back up? dialog box appears.

4. Your best (and easiest) bet here is to select the **Let Windows choose** option, and then click **Next.** The Review your backup settings dialog box appears.

5. At this point you might want to configure your own backup schedule (this is where the "automatic" part of the backup process comes into play; see "Step 10—Set Up a Maintenance Schedule," later in this chapter, for some ideas on the proper schedule to choose). If so, click **Change schedule** and then go to work (click **OK** when you're done):

♦ **How Often.** Select Daily, Weekly, or Monthly.

♦ **What day.** If you selected Weekly or Monthly, select the day of the week or month on which you want the backups to occur.

♦ **What time.** Select the time of day you want the backup to run. (Choose a time when you won't be using your computer.)

6. That's about it. Click **Save settings and run backup** to give the wizard its walking papers. Windows Backup lets you know that it will perform a full backup of your system now.

7. If that's okay with you, click **Yes.**

8. Follow any instructions that appear on screen, particularly if Windows Backup asks you to insert a disc. Once the backup starts, click the **Backup in progress** icon in the notification area to watch the progress.

9. When the backup is done, click **Close.**

Step 7—Create a System Image Backup

If a system goes kaput, one of the most common reasons is a corrupted system file that Windows 7 requires to get itself out of bed in the morning. Therefore, you can often resurrect a seemingly dead system by repairing those mucked-up files. This sounds like it would be hard, but Windows 7 has a feature that makes it relatively easy. The safety net I'm talking about here is actually a complete backup of your Windows 7 installation; this is called a *system image* backup, and it's part of the System Recovery Options that I discuss in Chapter 22.

> **Windows Wisdom**
>
> If you've already set up Windows Backup and run your first backup, then you already have a system image stored away, because Windows Backup includes a system image in the initial backup by default.

It takes a long time to create a system image (at least several hours, depending on how much stuff you have), but it's worth it for the peace of mind.

Here are the steps to follow to create the system image:

1. Select **Start, Control Panel,** and then under the System and Security heading, click **Back up your computer.** (You can also select **Start, All Programs, Maintenance, Backup and Restore.**) The Backup and Restore window appears.

2. Click **Create a system image.** The Create a System Image Wizard drops by.

3. The wizard asks you to specify a backup destination. You have three choices (click **Next** when you're ready to continue):

   ◆ **On a hard disk.** Select this option if you want to use a disk drive on your computer. If you have multiple drives, use the list to select the one you want to use.

   ◆ **On one or more DVDs.** Select this option if you want to use DVDs to hold the backup.

   ◆ **On a network location.** Activate this option and then click **Select** to choose a shared folder on your network.

4. Click **Start backup.**

Step 8–Check for Updates

Windows 7 is a moving target. Oh, it might look stationary, but while you're busy learning where things are and how things work, the Microsoft programmers are busy fixing bugs, improving existing features, and adding new features. In previous versions, these changes were packaged into massive *service packs* that you could download from the web or get on CD. With Windows 7, however, Microsoft is taking a different tack and is going to have individual fixes and improvements available on a special website called Windows Update. In fact, you no longer even have to go that far because Windows 7 comes with a feature called Windows Update that will check for new Windows trinkets and then download and install them automatically.

Windows 7 should be set up with automatic updates already. However, automatic updates require that your computer be left on so that it can connect to the Internet. You might not want this for two reasons:

◆ You might not want to leave your computer on 24/7 because it wastes energy. (Although most modern computers are fairly energy efficient.)

◆ You might not want your computer to be connected to the Internet while you're not around to "supervise" the connection.

Whatever the reason, if you're not comfortable with Windows 7 automatically updating your system, here's how to turn it off:

1. Select **Start, All Programs, Windows Update** to run face-first into the Windows Update window.

2. Click **Change settings.**

3. Click the **Important updates** list and choose **Never check for updates.**

4. Select **OK.**

Now the responsibility falls on you to check for updates. Fortunately, the procedure is pretty close to painless:

1. Select **Start, All Programs, Windows Update** to return to the Windows Update window.

2. Click **Check for updates.** Windows Updates goes online and pokes around to see if there's anything new for your computer.

3. If you see "No important updates available," say "Yes!" and go do something else. Otherwise, you'll see a window similar to the one shown in Figure 21.4. Click **Install updates.**

4. Windows Update will let you know when the installation is complete, and in most cases you won't have to do anything else. Occasionally, however, you may need to restart your system to put the new updates into effect. In that case, click **Restart now** to make it so.

Figure 21.4

You see this version of Windows Update if there's at least one important update ready for you to install.

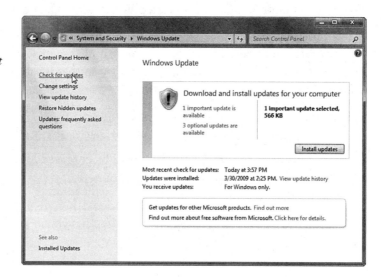

Step 9—Check for Solutions to Problems

Microsoft, bless their nerdy hearts, are constantly collecting information about Windows 7 from folks just like yourself. When a problem occurs, Windows 7 usually asks whether you want to report the problem to Microsoft and, if you do, they store these tidbits in a massive database. Engineers then tackle the "issues" (as they euphemistically call them) and hopefully come up with solutions.

The great news is that they then make these solutions available to anyone who goes looking for them. Windows 7 keeps a list of problems your computer is having, so you can tell it to go online and see if a solution is available. If there's a solution waiting, Windows 7 will grab it, install it, and fix your system. Nice!

Here are the steps to follow to check for solutions to problems:

1. Select **Start, Control Panel, Action Center.** (You can also click the **Action Center** icon in the notification area, and then click **Open Action Center.**)

2. Under the Maintenance heading, look for information on a problem your computer is having.

3. If a solution exists for your problem, click the solution to install it.

Step 10—Set Up a Maintenance Schedule

Maintenance is effective only if it's done regularly, but there's a fine line to be navigated here. If maintenance is performed too often, it can become a burden and interfere with more interesting tasks; if it's performed too seldom, it becomes ineffective. So how often should you perform the maintenance steps listed in this chapter? Here are some guidelines:

◆ **Checking your hard disk for errors.** Run a basic scan about once a week. Run the more thorough disk surface scan once a month. (The surface scan takes a long time, so run it when you won't be using your computer for a while.)

◆ **Checking free disk space.** Do this about once a month. If you have a drive in which the free space is getting low, check it about once a week.

◆ **Deleting unnecessary files.** If free disk space isn't a problem, run this chore about once every two or three months.

◆ **Defragmenting your hard disk.** How often you defragment your hard disk depends on how often you use your computer. If you use it every day, then Disk

Defragmenter's default daily schedule is just right for you. If your computer doesn't get heavy use, you probably need to run Disk Defragmenter only weekly or even monthly.

- **Setting restore points.** Windows 7 already sets regular system restore points, so you need only create your own restore points when you're installing a program or device or making some other major change to your system.

- **Backing up your files.** If you use your computer a lot, or if you're paranoid about losing any of your work, opt for a daily backup. If you use your computer less frequently and you're not all that concerned about losing work, a weekly schedule is probably best.

- **Creating system image backups.** These take a very long time, so either do them regularly once every month or two, or just wait until you've made major changes to your system.

- **Checking for updates.** If you've turned off automatic updating, you should check for Windows 7 updates about once a week.

- **Checking for solutions to problems.** You probably only need to check for solutions about once every couple of months. If your system is behaving erratically, check more often.

The Least You Need to Know

- Select a hard disk in the Computer folder and then click **Properties** to open the drive's Properties dialog box. In the **General** tab, click **Disk Cleanup** to remove unnecessary files; also, on the **Tools** tab, click **Check now** to run Check Disk; click **Defragment now** to run Disk Defragmenter; click **Backup now** to run Windows Backup.

- Bad hard disk sectors can cause all kinds of woes. Therefore, you should activate Check Disk's **Scan for and attempt recovery of bad sectors** check box about once a month or so.

- You should run Disk Cleanup every couple of weeks and Check Disk every week (and the bad-sector check every month).

- If you want your version of Windows 7 to always be up-to-date, be sure to turn on Windows Update's automatic updating feature and let it handle everything for you.

Troubleshooting and Recovering from Problems

In This Chapter

◆ Determining the source of a problem

◆ Using general troubleshooting strategies to solve common problems

◆ Troubleshooting problems using websites and newsgroups

◆ Using Windows 7 recovery tools: Last Known Good Configuration, System Restore, and System Recovery Options

A long time ago, somebody with way too much time on his or her hands proved mathematically that it's impossible to make any reasonably complex software program problem-free. As the number of variables increase, as the interactions of subroutines and objects become more complex, and as the underlying logic of a program grows beyond the ability of a single person to grasp all at once, errors inevitably creep into the code. Given the status of Microsoft Windows 7 as one of the most complex software packages ever created, it's certain that there are problems lurking in the weeds. The good news is that, if Windows 7 is like most of its predecessors, the great majority of these problems will be extremely obscure and will appear only under the rarest of circumstances.

However, this doesn't mean you're guaranteed a glitch-free computing experience. Far from it. The majority of computer woes are caused by third-party programs and devices, either because they have inherent problems themselves or because they don't get along well with Windows 7. Using software, devices, and device drivers designed for Windows 7 can help tremendously, as can the maintenance program I outlined in Chapter 21. Nonetheless, you need to know how to troubleshoot and resolve the computer problems that invariably will come your way. In this chapter, I help you do just that by showing you my favorite techniques for determining problem sources, and by taking you through all of the Windows 7 recovery tools.

Determining the Source of the Problem

One of the ongoing mysteries that all Windows 7 users experience at one time or another is what might be called the now-you-see-it-now-you-don't problem. This is a glitch that plagues you for a while and then mysteriously vanishes without any intervention on your part. (This also tends to occur when you ask a nearby user or someone from the IT department to look at the problem. Like the automotive problem that goes away when you take the car to a mechanic, computer problems will often resolve themselves as soon as a knowledgeable user sits down at the keyboard.) When this happens, most people just shake their heads and resume working, grateful to no longer have to deal with the problem.

Windows Wisdom

Software glitches are traditionally called *bugs*. There's a popular and appealing tale of how this sense of the word *bug* came about. As the story goes, in 1947 an early computer pioneer named Grace Hopper was working on a system called the Mark II. While investigating a problem, she found a moth among the machine's vacuum tubes, so from then on glitches were called bugs. A great story, to be sure, but this tale was *not* the source of the computer-glitch sense of "bug." In fact, engineers had already been referring to mechanical defects as "bugs" for at least 60 years before Ms. Hopper's actual moth came on the scene. As proof, the *Oxford English Dictionary* offers the following quotation from an 1889 edition of the *Pall Mall Gazette*:

"Mr. Edison, I was informed, had been up the two previous nights discovering 'a bug' in his phonograph—an expression for solving a difficulty, and implying that some imaginary insect has secreted itself inside and is causing all the trouble."

Unfortunately, most computer ills don't get resolved so easily. For these more intractable problems, your first order of business is to track down the source of the snag. This is, at best, a black art, but it can be done if you take a systematic approach. Over the years, I've found that the best method is to ask a series of questions designed to gather the required information and/or to narrow down clues to the culprit. Here are the questions:

- **Did you get an error message?** Unfortunately, most computer error messages are obscure and do little to help you resolve a problem directly. However, error codes and error text can help you down the road, either by giving you something to search for in an online database (see "Troubleshooting Using Online Resources," later in this chapter) or by providing information to a tech support person. Therefore, you should always write down the full text of any error message that appears.

Windows Wisdom

If the error message is lengthy and you can still use other programs on your computer, don't bother writing down the full message. Instead, while the message is displayed press the **Print Screen** key to place an image of the current screen on the clipboard. Then open Paint or some other graphics program, press **Ctrl+V** to paste the screen into a new image, and save the image. If you think you'll be sending the image via e-mail to a tech support employee or someone else who can help with the problem, consider saving the image using the JPEG format to keep the image size small.

If the error message appears before Windows 7 starts, but you don't have time to write it down, press the **Pause/Break** key to pause the startup. After you record the error, press **Ctrl+Pause/Break** to resume the startup.

- **Did you recently change any Windows settings?** If the problem started after you changed your Windows configuration, try reversing the change. Even something as seemingly innocent as starting the screen saver can cause problems, so don't rule anything out.

- **Did you recently change any application settings?** If so, try reversing the change to see if it solves the problem. If that doesn't help, check to see if an upgrade or patch is available. Also, some applications come with a "Repair" option that can fix corrupted files. Otherwise, try reinstalling the program.

- **Did you recently install a new program?** If you suspect a new program is causing system instability, restart Windows 7 and try using the system for a while

See Also

To learn how to uninstall a program, in Chapter 6, see the section titled "Giving a Program the Heave-Ho."

without running the new program. If the problem doesn't reoccur, then the new program is likely the culprit. Try using the program without any other programs running. You should also examine the program's "readme" file (if it has one) to look for known problems and possible workarounds. It's also a good idea to check for a Windows 7–compatible version of the program. Again, you can also try the program's "repair" option, or you can reinstall the program.

♦ **Did you recently upgrade an existing program?** If so, try uninstalling the upgrade.

♦ **Did you recently install a device driver that is not Windows 7-compatible?** Windows 7 allows you to install drivers that aren't Windows 7–certified, but it also warns you that this is a bad idea. Incompatible drivers are one of the most common sources of system instability, so whenever possible you should uninstall the driver and install one that is designed for Windows 7. Windows 7 automatically sets a system restore point before it installs the driver, so if you can't uninstall the driver, you should use that to restore the system to its previous state. (See "Recovering Using System Restore," later in this chapter.)

♦ **Did you recently apply an update from Windows Update?** Updates rarely make things worse (thankfully, since they're *supposed* to make things better), but nothing is certain in the Windows world. If your machine has been discombobulated since installing an update, try removing the update. Select **Start, Control Panel, Programs, View installed updates** to meet up with the Installed Updates window. Select the update that you want to trash and then select **Remove.**

♦ **Did you recently install a Windows 7 service pack?** If you installed a service pack and you elected to save the old system files, then you can uninstall the service pack using Control Panel's Installed Programs window (as described in Chapter 6).

General Troubleshooting Tips

Figuring out the cause of a problem is often the hardest part of troubleshooting, but by itself it doesn't do you much good. Once you know the source, you need to parlay that information into a fix for the problem. I discussed a few solutions in the previous section, but here are a few other general fixes you need to keep in mind:

♦ **Close all programs.** You can often fix flaky behavior by shutting down all your open programs and starting again. This is a particularly useful fix for problems caused by low memory or low system resources.

♦ **Log off Windows 7.** Logging off clears the memory and so gives you a slightly cleaner slate than merely closing all your programs.

♦ **Reboot the computer.** If problems exist with some system files and devices, logging off won't help because these objects remain loaded. By rebooting the system, you reload the entire system, which is often enough to solve many computer problems.

♦ **Turn off the computer and restart.** You can often solve a hardware problem by first shutting your machine off. Wait for 30 seconds to give all devices time to spin down and then restart.

♦ **Check connections, power switches, and so on.** Some of the most common (and some of the most embarrassing) causes of hardware problems are the simple physical things: making sure a device is turned on; checking that cable connections are secure; ensuring that insertable devices are properly inserted.

♦ **Use the troubleshooters.** Windows 7 comes with a few features called *troubleshooters* that are designed to tackle problems using simple, step-by-step procedures. Select **Start, Control Panel,** and then click the **Find and fix problems** link under the System and Security heading. The Troubleshooting window offers up a bunch of problem-solving tools for topics such as programs, hardware, system, and security.

Troubleshooting Using Online Resources

The Internet is home to an astonishingly wide range of information, but its forte has always been computer knowledge. Whatever problem you may have, there's a good chance that someone out there has run into the same thing, knows how to fix it, has posted the solution on a website or newsgroup, or would be willing to share it with you if asked. True, finding what you need is sometimes difficult, and you often can't be sure how accurate some of the solutions are. However, if you stick to the more reputable sites and if you get second opinions on solutions offered by complete strangers, then you'll find the online world an excellent troubleshooting resource. Here's my list of favorite online resources to check out:

- **Microsoft Product Support Services.** This is Microsoft's main online technical support site. Through this site you can access Windows 7 frequently asked questions, see a list of known problems, download files, and send questions to Microsoft support personnel. See *support.microsoft.com*.

- **Microsoft Knowledge Base.** The Microsoft Product Support Services site has links that enable you to search the Microsoft Knowledge Base, which is a database of articles related to all Microsoft products including, of course, Windows 7. These articles provide you with information about Windows 7 and instructions on using Windows 7 features. But the most useful aspect of the Knowledge Base is for troubleshooting problems. Many of the articles were written by Microsoft support personnel after helping customers overcome problems. By searching for error codes or keywords, you can often get specific solutions to your problems.

- **Microsoft TechNet.** This Microsoft site is designed for IT professionals and power users. It contains a huge number of articles on all Microsoft products. These articles give you technical content, program instructions, tips, scripts, downloads, and troubleshooting ideas. See *technet.microsoft.com*.

- **Windows Update.** Check this site for the latest device drivers, security patches, service packs, and other updates. See *windowsupdate.microsoft.com*.

- **Microsoft Security and Privacy.** Check this site for the latest information on Microsoft's security and privacy initiatives, particularly security patches. See *www.microsoft.com/security*.

- **Vendor websites.** All but the tiniest hardware and software vendors maintain websites with customer support sections that you can peruse for upgrades, patches, workarounds, frequently asked questions, and sometimes chat or bulletin board features.

- **Newsgroups.** Computer-related newsgroups exist for hundreds of topics and products. Microsoft maintains its own newsgroups via the msnews.microsoft.com server, and Windows Live Mail creates an account on that server for you automatically. Also, Usenet has a huge list of groups in the alt. and comp. hierarchies. Before asking a question in a newsgroup, be sure to search Google Groups to see if your question has been answered in the past. See *groups.google.com*.

Recovering from a Problem

Ideally, solving a problem will require a specific tweak to the system: a setting change, a driver upgrade, a program uninstall. But sometimes you need to take more of a "big picture" approach that reverts your system to some previous state in the hope that you'll leap past the problem and get your system working again. Windows 7 offers three tools that enable you to try this approach: Last Known Good Configuration, System Restore, and System Recovery Troubleshooter, which should be used in that order. The next four sections discuss these tools.

Booting Using the Last Known Good Configuration

Each time Windows 7 starts successfully, the system makes a note of the drivers and hardware configuration that were used. If you make driver or hardware changes and then find that the system won't start, you can tell Windows 7 to load using the configuration that worked the last time. (That is, the configuration that doesn't include your most recent hardware changes.) This is called the *Last Known Good Configuration*, and the theory is that by using the previous working configuration, your system should start since it's bypassing the changes that caused the problem. Here's how to start Windows 7 using the Last Known Good Configuration:

1. Restart your computer.

2. When the OS Choices menu appears, press **F8** to display the Windows Advanced Options Menu. (If your system doesn't display the OS Choices menu, press **F8** immediately after your system finishes the Power-On Self Test, which is usually indicated by a single beep.)

3. Select the **Last Known Good Configuration** option.

Recovering Using System Restore

The Last Known Good Configuration is most useful when your computer won't start and you suspect that a hardware change is causing the problem. You might think that you can also use the Last Known Good Configuration if Windows 7 starts but is unstable, and you suspect a hardware change is causing the glitch. Unfortunately, that won't work because once you start Windows 7 successfully, the hardware change is added to the Last Known Good Configuration. To revert the system to a previous configuration when you can start Windows 7 successfully, you need to use the System Restore feature.

I showed you how to use System Restore to set restore points in Chapter 21. Remember, too, that Windows 7 creates automatic restore points each time you start your system and when you perform certain actions (such as installing an uncertified device driver). To revert your system to a restore point, close all your running programs, then follow these steps:

Windows Wisdom

System Restore is available in safe mode. So if Windows 7 won't start properly, and if using the Last Known Good Configuration doesn't work, perform a safe mode startup (perform the steps in the previous section, except select **Safe Mode** in the list) and run System Restore from there. If you can't even boot in safe mode, you can run System Restore from the Windows 7 install disc. See "Recovering Using the System Recovery Options," later in this chapter.

---

1. Select **Start, All Programs, Accessories, System Tools, System Restore.**

2. The first dialog box you see depends on your system. If you have no recent updates, the first dialog box just gives you an overview of System Restore, so click **Next.** Otherwise, the first dialog box gives you two options:

   ◆ **Recommended restore.** Click this option to restore your system to the state it was in before the most recent update. This should work most of the time, so I recommend starting with this option. Click **Next** and skip to step 5.

   ◆ **Choose a different restore point.** Click this option if you know you want to use a different restore point or if you tried the most recent one and it didn't solve your problem. Click **Next.** The wizard conjures up the System Restore dialog box shown in Figure 22.1.

3. Click the restore point you want to restore. (Note that the Automatic Restore Point items are the restore points created automatically by Windows 7 each time you start your computer.)

4. Click **Next.** If you have multiple hard drives on your system, you see the Confirm Volumes to Restore dialog box.

5. Activate the check box for each disk you want to restore (it's probably safest to restore all the disks), and then click **Next.** System Restore displays a dialog box to confirm the restore point.

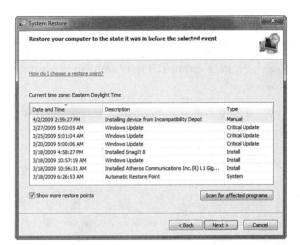

Figure 22.1

Use this window to choose the restore point you want to revert to.

6. Click **Finish.** System Restore, apparently a paranoid little program, once again asks you to confirm.

7. Click **Yes.** System Restore begins restoring the restore point. When it's done, it restarts your computer.

8. If you see the System Restore dialog box telling you that the restore was successful, clap your hands excitedly and then click **Close.**

> ### Windows Wisdom
>
> If restoring your system makes things worse or causes additional problems, you have a couple of choices. To undo the restore, launch System Restore, click **Next,** select the **Restore Operation** restore point, and click **Next.** Alternatively, you can run System Restore and revert the system to an even earlier restore point.

Recovering Using the System Recovery Options

If your system still won't start, all is not yet lost. Windows 7 comes with the System Recovery Options, a collection of tools available even if Windows 7 itself won't start. The idea is that you access these options when you boot your computer and then select the recovery tool you want to use.

To try this out, first follow these steps to get the System Recovery Options on the job:

1. Restart your computer.

2. When the OS Choices menu appears, press **F8** to display the Windows Advanced Options Menu. (If your system doesn't display the OS Choices menu, press **F8** immediately after your system finishes the Power-On Self Test, which is usually indicated by a single beep.)

3. Select the **Repair Your Computer** option. After a minute or two, System Recovery Options appears and prompts you to select a keyboard layout.

4. Say "Hunh?" and click **Next.** System Recovery Options prompts you to enter a user name and password.

5. Type your Windows 7 user name and password, and then click **OK.** The Choose a recovery tool dialog box appears, as shown in Figure 22.2.

Figure 22.2

System Recovery Options offers a fine selection of recovery tools.

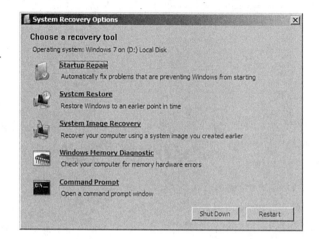

System Recovery Options comes with the following five tools to help get your system back on its feet:

♦ **Startup Repair.** This tool checks your system for problems that might be preventing it from starting. If it finds any, it attempts to fix them automatically.

♦ **System Restore.** This tool runs System Restore so that you can revert your system to a restore point (see "Recovering Using System Restore" earlier in this chapter).

♦ **System Image Recovery.** This tool restores your system using a system image backup, which you learned how to create in Chapter 21 (see the section "Step 7—Create a System Image Backup").

♦ **Windows Memory Diagnostic.** This tool checks your computer's memory chips for faults, which may be why your system isn't starting up. Click this option and then click **Restart now and check for problems.** If it finds a problem in your chips, then you'll need to take your machine into the shop and get the chips replaced.

- **Command Prompt.** This tool takes you to the Windows 7 command prompt, where you can type commands to do, well, *something*. Unfortunately, these commands are pretty advanced, so this tool isn't much use to you.

The Least You Need to Know

- If a problem occurs soon after you changed something on your computer—a Windows setting, a program, a device, and so on—try reversing that change to see if this fixes the error.

- You can often recover from problems just by either shutting down all running programs, logging off Windows 7, or rebooting the computer.

- Take advantage of online resources such as Microsoft Product Support Services (particularly the Knowledge Base), vendor websites, and newsgroups (particularly the Google Groups search engine).

- To recover from a more serious problem, use the following tools and techniques, in this order: Last Known Good Configuration, System Restore, and System Recovery Options.

Appendix

The Complete Idiot's Keyboard Command Reference

General Windows Keyboard Shortcuts

Press	To
Alt+Print Screen	Copy the active window's image to the Clipboard.
Print Screen	Copy the entire screen image to the Clipboard.
Ctrl+Alt+Delete	Display the Windows Security window.
Ctrl+Esc	Open the Start menu.
Ctrl+Z	Undo the most recent action.

Keyboard Shortcuts for Programs

Press	To
Working with Program Windows	
Alt+Esc	Cycle through the open program windows.
Alt+Tab	Cycle through thumbnails of the open program windows.
Alt+F4	Close the active program window.
F1	Display context-sensitive Help.
Working with Documents	
Ctrl+N	Create a new document.
Ctrl+O	Display the Open dialog box.
Ctrl+P	Display the Print dialog box.
Ctrl+S	Save the current file. If the file is new, display the Save As dialog box.

Keyboard Shortcuts for Working with Data

Press	To
Backspace	Delete the character to the left of the insertion point.
Delete	Delete the selected data or the character to the right of the insertion point.
Ctrl+A	Select all the data in the current window.
Ctrl+C	Copy the selected data.
Ctrl+X	Cut the selected data.
Ctrl+V	Paste the most recently cut or copied data.

Keyboard Shortcuts for Dialog Boxes

Hold Down	To
Tab	Move forward through the dialog box controls (check boxes, buttons, etc.).
Shift+Tab	Move backward through the dialog box controls.
Ctrl+Tab	Move forward through the dialog box tabs.
Alt+Down arrow	Display the list in a drop-down list box.
Spacebar	Toggle a check box on and off; select the active option button or command button.
Enter	Select the default command button or the active command button.
Esc	Close the dialog box without making any changes.

Keys to Hold Down While Dragging and Dropping

Hold Down	To
Ctrl	Copy the dragged object.
Ctrl+Shift	Display a shortcut menu after dropping a dragged object.
Esc	Cancel the current drag.
Shift	Move the dragged object.

Windows Explorer Keyboard Shortcuts

Press	To
+ (numeric keypad)	In the Folders list, display the next level of subfolders for the current folder.
– (numeric keypad)	In the Folders list, hide the current folder's subfolders.
* (numeric keypad)	In the Folders list, display all levels of subfolders for the current folder.

continues

Windows Explorer Keyboard Shortcuts   (continued)

Press	To
Backspace	Navigate to the parent folder of the current folder.
Delete	Delete the selected object.
Ctrl+A	Select all the objects in the current folder.
Shift+Delete	Delete the currently selected objects without sending them to the Recycle Bin.
F2	Rename the selected object.
F3	Display the Find dialog box with the current folder displayed in the Look In list.
F4	Open the Address toolbar's drop-down list.

Internet Explorer Keyboard Shortcuts

Press	To
Alt+Left arrow	Navigate backward to a previously displayed web page.
Alt+Right arrow	Navigate forward to a previously displayed web page.
Ctrl+A	Select the entire web page.
Ctrl+B	Display the Organize Favorites dialog box.
Ctrl+D	Add the current page to the Favorites list.
Esc	Stop downloading the web page.
F4	Open the Address toolbar's drop-down list.
F5	Refresh the web page.
F11	Toggle between full screen mode and the regular window.

Shortcuts That Use the Windows Logo (⊞) Key

Press	To
⊞	Open the Start menu.
⊞+E	Open Windows Explorer.
⊞+F	Find a file or folder.
⊞+M	Minimize all open windows.
⊞+Shift+M	Undo minimize all.
⊞+R	Display the Run dialog box.
⊞+Tab	Display open windows in a 3D stack.

Index

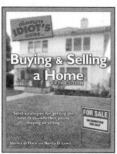
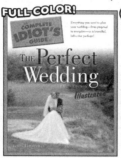

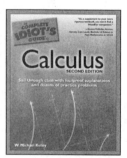